# DANDELION

By

Charlotte Day

1st Edition 2016

© Charlotte Day 2016

## TRUST; A RECENT EVENT

The terror. The trauma. The panic.

I stand at the till. A man approaches me. I have to make the transaction. My body stiff with fear. My heart palpitating. The shock. The thought surrounds me. Can I escape? How? I reach for his money. My hands trembling. I take it like I've had an electric shock. He smiles. I do not notice. I am paying minute detail to the transaction that I am making. He is an imposter. He is an invader. He is an attacker. I am dead.

There are other men in the shop. I look at them, working out if they will pay. How to escape. How to cope with the pressure. The pressure, standing at the till whilst they try to communicate. I try to hide. I try to cope but my hands are trembling so much. I throw their clothes at them. I fumble with the bag. I cannot hide.

I mention to my manager at the charity shop that I cannot do this.

It's not just there. It's at every till. Whether I am a customer or not. The trembling hands, the shot of electric current that runs through my body. The fear. The panic. The anticipation. Getting my money out before I even get into the shop. Going to the cash tills that are served by women. Trying to avoid men. Trying to avoid the panic. Anything to get away.

I saunter out of the shop. I have done it. I have paid. But there are many more to go to before the week is out. I need to eat. I need to buy petrol. Cigarettes I have worked out. There are only women in the shop during the day serving. I am safe there.

I have not worked for five years. I had a manager that flirted with me. I loved him. I longed for closeness, but none came. He was married. I got myself fired. Away from the firing line. Safe. Or so I thought.

Mental health has been a problem. There has been a denial of the facts. A twenty year mental health history because of rape. Rape because of fear. Fear instilled by a psychic therapist. Fear of men. Why? Because she said that Sid was bad for me. He was bad for me. I had been warned against him by the psychic healer. All she said is that he was bad for me. I backed off. I didn't want to increase intimacy with him. Not him. I trusted God.

Now all the fun I have had is trying to get work. I cannot do anything using my hands. Too much performance anxiety. Too much pressure.

Five years of unemployment. No one wants to take me on. I can't use the tills or the computer without shaking. I can't write in front of other people. I can't do anything. I am even fearful of having a cup of tea in front of someone. My hands shake and people notice. Nothing can stop me. I don't know what to do.

Now I can't do anything. I hide. I try. I work hard. I am doing a degree at the Open University. I didn't want to sit in lecture halls with loads of men. I couldn't cope. I am trying. I am trying for a new job. One where I don't have to use my hands. Outside in the garden centre. They are happy there. There is fear. But I will overcome it. I will learn how to use my hands in front of other people. I will learn how to make a cup of tea so that I don't spill it everywhere. I will learn.

I will learn to trust again.

In the 20 years since being raped my life has been destroyed. All that I had was gone. Friends have disappeared. Work has been a meaningless nightmare, since I suffer panic attacks with men and can never be promoted.

I used to be clever, smart, witty, funny, a joy to be around. Now its fear. All the time. All over the place. Any man is a potential arbitrator. Every man is a potential rapist. And I cry. For the loss of the life I used to know where I could flirt and make jokes and be the centre of attention. I cry for the career I never had. For the children I will never know. For the years of parties and holidays that I could have enjoyed with friends. And I ask myself, WHY?

PREFACE; DR R CLARK MBBS MRC Psych

I am a doctor who treats individuals suffering from Bipolar Affective Disorder. In common with Schizophrenia, it is a potentially devastating illness which can strike individuals at very vulnerable times in early adulthood. It can take sufferers many years to come to terms with the implications of the diagnosis of a potentially chronic relapsing and remitting condition. I often use the analogy of a physical diagnosis, Diabetes Mellitus, which can start in early adulthood and has similar implications in terms of long term medication and life style changes, and can take several visits to hospital in Diabetic comas before some kind of acceptance is reached. An acceptance of the diagnosis of Bipolar Affective disorder at a young age can often lead to a grieving process which is distinct from the depressive phase of this illness.

Whilst I have treated many people at differing stages of their illness over the past 11 years, I have not treated any individual for longer than 3 years. The training of psychiatrists is based around 6-12 monthly posts. Consultant psychiatric posts are no longer seen as jobs for life and it is increasingly common for people to see locum doctors. The author and her family have lived with and through her illness for the past 8 years. How best, then to bring together this individual, personal experiential expertise with professional expertise? Bipolar Affective illness, particularly in young adults has always bought up questions of identity. In early adulthood, individuals seek to find their own identity and personality separate from their families and mental illness can exponentially complicate this process. What is a 'normal mood' for this person? It is relatively easier when people are floridly manic but to intervene when someone may be becoming unwell is a more difficult question and requires co-operation, confidence and trust which can only be built up with time. It must be immeasurably frustrating for sufferers and their carers to be faced at critical times in their lives and in the course of their illness (often involving Mental Health assessments) with professionals who no matter how well qualified or experienced, do not know you or nor do you know them. As a professional myself I am always aware of the greater experiential personal expertise of the sufferer and their carers, whilst at the same time giving them the best of my professional expertise.

Bipolar Affective Disorder does not stop life happening to people. Events, life styles and stages of life can precipitate episodes of illness but equally 'normal' affective and behavioural change can be a consequence of such things. Again, part of the stigma of living with mental illness can be that any change in an individual can be labelled as illness. This can apply equally to adolescent rebellion and self-discovery as it can to life changes in later life such as coping with children leaving home.

In terms of treatment for this illness, Lithium is a life saving and changing drug for many people but it is frustrating that a drug discovered in the 1950s has not as yet been bettered. Whilst the new anti-psychotics and anti-depressants have their limited place and do represent improvements in terms of their side-effect profile, the newer mood stabilizers have not yet proven to be better than Lithium as first line treatment. I would hope that newer cleaner mood stabilizers will arrive in the near future.

The author has written a very personal and honest account of her struggle with mental illness and the impact upon her and her family. I am sure that writing her story has been part of a healing process. Psychiatrists can prescribe medication to treat and control symptoms. As a scientist, I would dispute some of the approaches the author has tried, but as a doctor I would recognise that healing is not just about a prescription for medication but is a very personal journey. I wish the author and her family the very best for the future.

'Never underestimate a minority'

Sir Winston Churchill

Manic Depressive and Prime Minister

# INTRODUCTION

I've been trying to put pen to paper for more than five years now, as the story flew through my being, but I could not. All that came out was exasperation and pain, anger burning through the paper, directed from my heart. I have found the time, the patience and at long last, the peace of mind to relate my happenings, so that they might perhaps touch you, and show you what it means to have a mental illness; so little known, and so much assumed.

This is the story of manic depression; the common terminology for what is in effect a chemical imbalance in the brain. A personal account of how I innocently fell foul to this crippling condition, and slowly, but surely clawed my way back over the years to sanity and some sort of social acceptance again. It is a story of destruction, darkness and untold pain, and how I, my family and friends were prey to the exhausting range of mood swings, completely beyond control, that illustrate this illness. It is also a story about how love can see you through and dissipate the bitterness, despair and loneliness, casting the shadows away, to be filled with light and freedom, a future, and most especially, a today.

Who would ask for this terrible illness to come into the life of anyone? Who would realise the torture and social rejection that it brings? The wasted futures of so many and unbearable years spent balancing pills to try and shine a glimmer of light into a never ending darkness and despair. I have been lucky. I have had the love of a family and an unique carer in the form of my mother, who single-handedly looked after me for the best part of my illness, enabling me to re-surface at long last, and re-enter life as most know it, without the never ending, moment by unsuspecting moment, dread of slipping back into the abyss again. The abyss of the mind, that unfathomable, mysterious thing, leaving you no point of reference to cling to, where the waves of insanity throw you onto ever changing shores and everything is circumspect beyond recognition.

Where does one turn in an environment of mental illness? Who knows for sure that it can be labelled as such? In our society I did not fit into the regime, but my increased sensitivity and imagination let me fall between worlds and the boundaries of life and death, joining reality and spirituality to points beyond time and space. Fate has decreed that I walk an unknown path and perform Herculean survival feats in order to find a way out to the sanctuary of the soul. But it has been a bitter pill to swallow, with little recompense beyond what most people consider normal. And the time it has taken to get to this point constitutes for the best part of a decade. Whilst others are out having fun, meeting people and getting married and doing well at work, surpassing the challenges of a conventionally formidable life, I have been locked alone in a bottomless pit of anger and despair, fighting for survival with unknown powers and interminable impracticalities. My will against the strength of an insatiable beast, determined to eat my spirit and spit out the bones, leaving nothing but a bare and brittle carcass. Fated to be marginalised and ostracised beyond repair for my chemical gymnastics and particular perspective, which none but the most enlightened of souls dares enquire into.

The pain is nothing compared to the scandal society projects unceasingly towards the likes of me. I battle vainly with the disrepute I feel seeping through the atmosphere and clogging my lungs, choking me with its disapproving nuances. And yet my problem is totally beyond my control with an independent will of its own. I am merely a puppet and a dupe to the chemical confusion soaring through my anatomy. I am not a mass murderer yet treated like a criminal. It is the ignorance and the fear which people hold dear that really cuts and burns sometimes. I am an innocent victim of a vicious attack, and yet I am sometimes treated like the offender, expected to hide in the dark in remorseful shame. Would you look at someone with a broken leg in the same way? It is just a different part of the anatomy that needs mending. People can be so cruel, heartless and humiliating, hiding their fear of the unknown with razor sharp knives, and pointed jibes.

I often wondered, why me? Well, at this stage I am past caring. I have got my health back and that is all that is important. I have learnt a lot through the illness, and although I would never go there again, I can see the personal benefits that I have reaped in huge measures from this life of living on the edge, precariously balanced between insanity and yet more. Spending ten years either completely with the fairies, down in the very dregs of existence, or drugged up to the eyeballs for a year at a time like a zombie, recovering from the whole affair, teaches you immensely about the value of human life and the bare essentials of its make-up. Standing from the view point I am now, I would not swap it for years of drinking and debauchery, and perhaps even a high-flying career. I would only be glad for what I have learnt, and how on the other side of the pain and suffering lies an oasis of peace and serendipity that will never be lost.

This is a homage to my family, friends and those in the medical profession who suffered beside me, and with their better understanding and infinite care, aided me to the door to a manageable life. How can I thank them enough? They have given me life and only those that have seen it or been there will understand the tears that well up in my eyes, and the quick intake of breath; remnants of a dying pain. They have painstakingly guided me from the bleak midwinter to the sunny spring, and yet the season's cycle was too long to be forgotten in haste, and thrown away at leisure. We have all been scarred for life, and yet no longer hide our lacerations in shame, but hold them high as the great achievements that they are, proud and wonderful for all to see.

This book illustrates the major breakthrough that can be remarked upon only by those who know the difference. The difference, and the knowledge of the depths of the soul, and the lightness and sensitivity of its touch. Understanding of the depths and heights which we all encompass in our humanitarian quests, but which manic depressives soar to such extremes that the results are terrifying, and few dare to feel the proximity of these attacks. Totally beyond control or human sentiment, living with the Gods, or being tossed and turned by the Devil, but never without the shame that miscomprehension surrenders to. It is a testament to the power of humanity, both good and evil, and how we surreptitiously, constantly throw colours over one another and come to rely on each other for our destiny. Sometimes spiralling through ever growing colours and confusion in our desire to be alive and free, and in other's maturity, we have the pale, soft colours of love laid patiently at our feet. And lastly, it is an omen for the future. A future where we cannot disregard the pain and suffering of those around us. An eternal time where caring must be exacerbated, immortalised, and recognised for what it is; a God given gift totally necessary for our survival and happiness. A phone call, a smile, an interest; do you know how priceless these things are?

Who among you knows of the suffering, knows of the bleeding hearted, the numb inside, people oblivious to everything except their own pain? How are you healed? Do you heal others? How do you connect to people, how do you connect to yourself? Do you care? It is a great gift to belong to the tribe of the broken hearted, a special unique entrance to the language of the heart, the real meaning of life. And those callous, ambivalent, ignorant creatures who call themselves human, rushing and frenetic, are wrapped up in their own mentality and consumed by fear. They will learn, one day, and until then, their humanity will be lucky to get a look in. And for all their grace and favour, the hole in their heart will spread like wild fire and eat them and their absurdities alive. I know, because my fear consumed me, until it had had enough and there was nothing left to feed on but an empty carcass and a void in my spirit lasting for what seemed like an eternity.

I hope that this book will enlighten others in the nature of manic depression. It is a highly personal account of my illness, from when I first showed signs of the condition, mistaken at the time for a rather annoyingly long bought of teenage angst, to the present day, as I am on the right balance of medication, and managing the illness successfully; picking up the pieces and seeing what I can do with them. I hope that you will learn from my story the ins and outs of the illness, the colours and the intrigue, and how it is nothing to be feared, but is a condition to be managed with endless help and support available, financial and emotional. And that there is a sustainable and happy future for all who may be living under its terrible, all encompassing shadow. If you suffer from the illness or know someone who does I am sure my experiences will seem frighteningly familiar. And if you are a stranger to the illness and have picked up this book through interest, I hope that I can illustrate honestly what it is to suffer from manic depression, and perhaps in doing so generate increased awareness and compassion for sufferers and the whole issue of mental health.

Everything you have ever had or dreamed for is taken away from you heartlessly, through no fault of your own, and you are left with nothing, but pain and insanity, and precious little human rights. But seeds do grow, and come to fruition, and life, after a long time of careful gardening and endless nurturing, becomes a watery oasis in what was once an arid, bitter and lonely desert. But this is for the survivors. How many countless stories are there behind closed doors, of people still living in turbulence and fear, that may never see the light of day?

PART 1 - BATTLE OF WITS

1.1 - HOW INNOCENT SPENDOUR FELL FOUL TO ANARCHISTICAL OVERTURES

I had been a student at a very academic boarding school since the age of twelve. It was not unlike a touch of Harry Potter intrigue, set in an old convent in the Berkshire hills surrounded by tall and echoey pine trees, in a time warped world of its own. We had a bunch of strangely eclectic teachers, such as an ex-prison officer game teacher who would expect Olympic style performances from us on the freezing cold games pitches. (Our breath vaporised visibly in front of us, as white knuckles clung to vicious lacrosse sticks). Our house mistress was highly staccato for her base tenor frame, and she stuck to the rulebook by the letter, making us practice the 'Art of Conversation' with her at mealtimes. This required a lot of forethought, and a mental itinerary would be drawn up days in advance, usually involving the weather, as she was obviously not impressed by our overtly school girl gossip.

My friends and I were crammed into tiny dormitories; cheek by jowl. The dorms were colourfully decorated with swan and flying pig wallpaper and other such paraphernalia. They were happy years for me. I missed my family and horse, but I loved to learn and every day new doors were opened and showers of understanding and greater sophistication shone forth. I saw it as a great dance of light, literature and learning in which we all danced to a merry tune. Thoughts, concepts, ideas and characters, all with their own rich textures and flavours were placed before us. I loved all the idiosyncrasies, and absorbed everything like a sponge, never feeling tired or bored, just processing this endless stream of information easily and enjoyably. It was an academic breeding ground, thriving on success and results. One girl, aged twelve, was faced with expulsion by the formidable headmistress, in front of the whole aghast classroom, based on the fact that she gained a B average grade in her end of year exams, even though it would be another four years before these qualifications were to be formalised at all. The reign of terror started young, and ambition and dreams were fed heavily so long as they involved an outstanding career.

My family consisted of two lovely brothers, Ben and Will, and wonderful parents. Living in a Georgian farmhouse deep in the countryside we delighted in all that it had to offer; the walks, the waves and all the creature comforts. I loved to ride, for hours at a time, absorbing the beauty of nature and its abounding glory, lost in a sea of splendour spread before my eyes. But the times they were a changing, as the blissful innocence and explorations of youth were uncovering a vastly different world.

Ben had been listening to a lot of punk music, ranting about starving children in Africa and the apparent evil of multi-national corporations. I had pondered and paused over the lyrics. They hit me with their potency, and contrast to my life of indulgent luxury upset me and struck a nerve. It played on my mind; the unfairness of the world, where some had so much, like me, and some had nothing; everyday being a battle for basic survival. These musicians bought alive a world for me that I had never encountered before. A world of real things, a world of life and death. A world where caring mattered. Not the stark rigidity of academia. A world where people came first. Their needs, their feelings, a reality check way beyond a turn of phrase. I bonded with this mentality at a fatal cost to myself unfortunately, or so some might ponder.

I went back to school for the beginning of the Sixth Form. Life was different now in the fact that everyone wore kilts instead of green skirts, and that is about where it stopped. My mind was whirring with a new global conscience I had acquired, unwittingly, over the holidays in the company of so much vinyl; records and their intricate forebodings having offered me tantalising subliminal encouragement over the long summer months. I was approached by a fellow student, named Claire, who has long since gone to live in Ashram in Nepal. My oldest friend, Tasmin, whom I met the first night there, in a teddy fight when I was twelve, joined the merry throng. Soon many spliffs were smoked, many gigs were gone to and minds expanded in all sorts of peculiar directions. Unfortunately I did not realise at that stage that mine was prone to suffer from elastic band syndrome.

It was actually a pair of pink flares that bought Claire and I together. A turquoise mini had run me down, while in London, travelling home from a trip to Ipswich in the school holidays with Tasmin. We had been waitressing; silver service and I had sprayed all the guests with a water pistol whilst serving them. Wham and Bang! I flew and turned in the air, to gasps from a passer by. My face covered with blood, and all the contents of my bag, including a beautiful camera, smashed to smithereens on contact with the hard concrete, so unforgiving. I sat there on the ground, a haze of coloured traffic lights whirring around me in semi-darkness. I put my hands to my face while torrents of abuse where hurled at me liberally by the driver who was also in shock at this colossal happening. Little did I know that I had left a huge dent in the hood of his car, an unmistakable witness to the event. Tasmin ran to me, and cars screeched to a halt, left, right and centre, faces peering anxiously through the mist.

My face was bleeding profusely; my nose streaming blood, and there was a gash to my face that also needed attention. I got the most uncontrollable giggles, and in fact couldn't stop laughing, obviously in shock as there wasn't that much humour in the situation. I got to my feet, only to find that my legs did not support me any more. They completely gave way underneath me. Helpful passers by ran to me, supporting me under my arms. Blankets were found and I was placed safely by the side of the road. Ambulances appeared in the mist from everywhere, (being on the border of three authorities), and I was whisked off to the nearest hospital, with Tasmin in hot pursuit. Tasmin lived just around the corner and her mother was fetched in high alarm.

For some reason, I could not stop giggling; in fact it was Tasmin that had to be put in a wheelchair when she swooned at the sight of all the blood. Hours were spent in St. George's Hospital in Tooting. X-rays were done, and it was finally decided that indeed nothing was broken and all could return to their homes intact, albeit five hours later, and with only a few bandages and a pair of crutches in hand. But nothing could take away the split second thought that I was going to die, and nightmares haunted my sleep for many a long month. It seemed as if the doors of perception had been opened into what would fast become a nightmare. Death had stared me in the face, and it was now a feeling that I had unwittingly become acquainted with. Through these dark thoughts lurking deep in the recesses of my mind daybreak was dawning, and my father came to the rescue, having been alerted by Tasmin's mother on return from the hospital. Gem that he is he drove up to London in the middle of the night, terribly apologetic for the trauma and upset caused. It wasn't until I was safely back home, seventy odd miles away that I felt comfortable enough to break down into floods of tears with my mother at my bedside.

That is where the flares came in. The jeans that I had been wearing were of a dyed pink variety. Huge rips had ensued after the collision, and being of a practical nature, I decided to take the sewing threads out and weave in a splash of green; bottle green corduroy, to give the desired effect. They caused a bit of a stir on return to school, with more than a few raised eyebrows. It was however a cohesive force for Claire, who obviously bonded with such an aesthetic.

The crash culminated the beginning of a new school attitude. Having once been easy going and complacent about life and the people, I subconsciously found I did not want to grow up. I could not envisage a future for myself in this hectic world of high achievement and go-getting finality, and the resultant action was that I became withdrawn and evil. My black moods matched my hair, and I would scowl and growl myself through the days on my ever present crutches, hunched and withdrawn. I took to painting in heavy oils, pictures of snarling dragons and prostitutes.

The fear I felt for the future was resonating from my father's activities. He worked so hard, under such pressure, and I knew too that I would be in that same firing line one day without a doubt. My brain had proved itself so far, and so that escalator would continue. It would be university, a job, the pressure and stress. The days and nights of worry would inevitably follow. The pressure, the pressure. It sank into my heart like a knife. And all the time my mother would give me her heartfelt monologues on how science and technology were wrecking our futures, and what little morals the world had left. All I knew is that I needed to escape. In what capacity could I enter adulthood, to incorporate all these world views which I held so dear. My genes were in denial, they were pulling so hard in opposite directions I felt nothing but utter misery and confusion.

Teachers were no longer enamoured with me, and I began getting into trouble on countless occasions for mere trifles like wearing the school scarf into the dining room, which of course, in its pettiness, did nothing to improve my mood. Teachers who sympathised with my dicky knee, assuming it was a skiing accident were glared at for such elitist notions, and hurriedly backed away. Tasmin, Claire and I bonded to the exclusivity of all others, and we would indulge our suppressed pain and anger at the system in the usual methods.

The life style of sex, drugs and rock and roll rapidly permeated the happy corners of middle England. Hair became dread-locked, clothes became black and then rainbow coloured, all with delightful serendipity. The new age traveller lifestyle was not one that had been intended for us, and many found our tendencies in this direction highly alarming. Tasmin had cunningly purchased a shiny new car, and he was in totality her great pride; a golden Beetle, she named Neville. We would all pile into him, whenever school would allow, namely every weekend and all through the holidays, and off we would set on our little cosmic jaunts. Winding down the windows we would sing along at the tops of our voices to all our favourite tunes, which would be blaring courageously from the radio while hair and tasselled clothes swept along outside with the wind.

One night I went to Club UK wearing my tablecloth dress which I had bought in Next. It had a big chequered pattern on it in blue. What I did not realise was that at the club they had UV lighting which made my white underwear turn iridescent. They had a camera crew there and the camera man loved me, filming me constantly as I danced. A few weeks later we were at a rave in Manchester, which was being held at Cromwell's house. Someone had planted some guns in the ground and the police were everywhere. Eventually it was safe to enter. Later that night as we were watching videos at a friend's house the second video clicked out as it finished and the TV came on. There I was, in my tablecloth dress, at Club UK, on TV, dancing.

There came the time for voting for Prefects. I wanted to be a Prefect and since our year were given two votes I voted for myself and one other. A younger girl came up to me on the games pitch. She asked if I had voted for myself. I said 'yes'. She looked at me and I got the distinct impression that I would never get it. I was too much of a hippy. I wanted to be a Prefect. I wanted the responsibility but knew that I would never get it in this world. I had painted a picture in Art of a snarling dragon. It was hung in the school corridor. Everyone that passed it thought that it had been done by a girl called Merryl. She was very good at art. She also wanted to be President.

Our favourite place was a club in London, run by a Scottish lady, who got all the homeless people to help her decorate it every weekend. Colourful hippy paradise, with swirling colours, enormous balloons, and the wondrous invention of the big, orange parachute that fell on all the clubbers at the end of the evening. Swishing up and down with rainbow light shows from above permeating the cloth to the clubbers huddled beneath who were giving one another massages and generally chilling out. It was a dream world of friendly people, caring attitudes, and acceptance of one another unconditionally. School was at the other end of the universe, where all the girls concentrated on money and exams. Bittersweet comparisons were made and school was duly rejected, with no thought for the future. It did not occur to me to take myself seriously when I was up against a precedent that seemed so hectic and involved relationships that were far out of my gentler range. I just withdrew, into the beauty of nature and my own little private world.

Escapism reared its blissful head, and the outside world seemed so distant, vain and obscure. There was no longer any grip on it; there was no incentive any more to join in the games that people played. I thought that I had discovered the truth of my being and I was loving it. At this stage, I had begun my A Levels, in Maths, Chemistry and Art, and would spend happy hours enveloped in these subjects, all of the abstract nature that I so loved and thrived on. I would go and see bands with Tasmin and Claire. Heavy stuff, fluffy stuff and pure bouncy stuff, enjoying the on-going poignancy of sweat and burst eardrums. The world had become summer for me, but something was not quite right. Was it the location, the girl's boarding school where I could not fly, or laugh with others? I was so wrapped up in myself, defiantly aware that I did not fit in, but hesitantly unsure of what to do about it. Or was it my holidays, where I was meeting all sorts of bohemian people, who were colourfully interesting and intellectual, and had ranges to their personality that I thirsted for survival. Somehow the equation did not relate at all.

Finally the last straw came, well almost the last straw, with a phone call from a tearful Jess, who was my brother Ben's girlfriend.

"All your mother's chickens and ducks have been slaughtered by the fox!" said poor Jess, who had not shut them up properly and was in charge in my parent's absence. I was mortified by her alarm, and tried to pacify her distraction and ever growing tears.

Standing in the school corridor with hordes of students neatly filing by, going into a meeting, whilst listening to her torrents of shame, I was rudely interrupted by a sharp tapping on my shoulder. A full on bollocking ensued from one of the particularly anal teachers who happened to be skulking with intent in the school corridor, for the criminal offence of using the telephone out of hours (exactly one minute early to be precise!) How can you go to paradise and then have to put up with shits like that? OK, he did not hear the conversation, but he was still unfeeling and so dogmatic.

Those were difficult years to put everything into perspective, leading an amazing double life, and not having the heart or internal recognition to bridge the gap in a meaningful way. I was drifting, drifting out at sea, clinging onto an ever-decreasing lifeline of reality, that could drop and snap at any moment, leaving me to drown in eternity. I was not aware of the thought, I was just lying on my back, avoiding the sharks circling around me, soaking up the rays, and thinking how beautiful the clouds looked, admiring their reflection on the water.

It all came to an end, that blissful and blatant year. The tides were indeed turning, and the season to be merry was losing its stronghold to a grey, dull monotony. Mock A Levels were occurring and everyone was studying frantically, to the exclusion of all else, apart from my solitary forebodings in the summer meadow. I went down to the Examination Hall for my first exam, down the flight of wide, circular stone steps that ornamented the lawns, stationary for hundreds of years. There I saw the paper. Sitting behind rows and rows of girls, with my favourite teacher, Mr Peterson, who taught Chemistry, at the front invigilating the stern proceedings. He was an eccentric genius, with the most beautiful expressive hands. He would usually reel off into university level Chemistry because he loved his subject so well, and taught it with a passion. The Career's Guidance teacher wanted to put me forward to do Chemistry with Management at Oxford or Cambridge.

I sat at my wooden desk, in the sparse room. Wooden chair after wooden chair, girl upon girl, all waiting with baited breath. The paper came, the atmosphere was tight. It was indeed Chemistry, and the first questions were pretty basic. My brain whirled and whirred as the pressure of the situation took its hold, atmosphere or internal pressure, I do not know, but the effects were extraordinary. It felt tighter and tighter and it felt as though there was a barbed wire crown sinking straight into my brain. My pain tolerance was overthrown for the first time in my life, and I put up my hand, without question or dilemma. Mr Peterson of course was by my side as quick as a flash, and I asked to be excused. I left nearly two hundred girls with their pens poised and brains working overtime. That was the last time I was to see the majority of them ever again. I walked back up the stone steps, relieved; free, free, free at last, or so I short sightedly imagined.

I went straight to my house mistress as directed, who duly called the doctor and my mother. The doctor allocated stress, and what else I never knew as my mother arrived and I was taken away after a short chat. For how long I did not know, but I was removed from the dream that had turned sour at that time. I was driven back to my mother's nest, to sanity and protection, I thought, but I was horribly wrong. The nightmare, or what was commonly known as a nervous breakdown, was self-inflicted with a druggy lifestyle and dropout fantasies, or was it? There were some ghosts out there who were to haunt me for many a year. Would I ever live to see the day when I could actually be happy and piece together the fragments of my heart, some stolen, some forgotten, many discarded in fury. Put it this way; darkness and negativity ensued fast and furiously. I lost my way, my mind, my reasons for living, and the future was nothing but a black hole.

## 1.2 - THAT ENDLESS VOID

The summer was spent in my bedroom, hiding from the sun, and everybody else in my life. No one ventured in, and my constant companion, my ever-present nightmare, played itself out repetitively to my pained and burning mind. How could I live in this world? I had no routes I cared to go down. Expectations were high, and failure was not an option, at least not to me. I didn't want to spend my life running about as a mad thing, concerned only with money and status. I wanted more than that, I wanted a world that cared, where the price was not always too high, where I could laugh and be free, if I ever managed to understand what that might be. I really could not get my head around this being grown up thing, where all that seemed to happen was a perpetual pressurised panic, and I was no way ready to grow up, so escape it was. How could my sleepy sloth-like attitude ever really compare to this glare projected at me from every turn. How on earth was I to ever do anything in the world that always seemed to want, but was never filled with wonder? When would people ever get enough; shoes, money, cars, houses, that they all longed for with a passion. It seemed that starvation had taken on new percussions that were so warped and twisted in their extremes that they were actually quite sick. Anti-establishment, anti-capitalist, anti-everything I knew. I was just going to have to find my own way through this nightmare of greed and self-indulgence, with precious little other than idealism to go on.

I got to know every inch of my hideaway meticulously, and indeed customised it to make it my own. It was a gorgeous room, overlooking lush green fields, and ponies pottering about in the sunshine. Not that I ever ventured as far as the window. I had a hole in my heart. A hole caused by an excruciatingly painful period of self-doubt and shame. Shame at finding myself in this pit of despair, with no guidelines on how to get out. I hated myself and could bring myself to do no more than commit painful metaphorical lacerations and self-strangling. My soul reaching out for expression, but was barred by myself on every level, and dismissed without reason. I negated my life force so many times that eventually it caved in under immense pressure becoming even more dark and brooding.

I missed all my school friends like crazy. God, I was so lonely, so sad and lost. The phone didn't ring all through those long summer months. I surmised that nobody wanted to know about me, and I didn't think to call them. I had no self-love to perform that simple act. How was I to explain to them what to me was a complete mystery, with my irrational despair, refusal and total inability to leave my black humour behind me. They all seemed so far away, across soul and space, so removed from my concept of gloom and self-denial. I was scared; scared to see the light of day, as I felt I didn't match up. I was impartially obscure to the effect of disinterest, because I had so much unwittingly going on inside me, I could not face being able to relate to myself in any particularly pleasant way. It was impossible to communicate to others. I felt that to succeed in the world one had to be ultra confident and I suppose that the attitudes of subcultures I had picked up along the way had rapidly closed down my notions of a sustainable future.

Life suddenly became an endless void, like the rug had been pulled out from under my feet. I wasn't standing on solid ground anymore, but hovering in outer space with nothing to hold onto and no-one to relate to. I never left my room and ventured out into the summer breeze. I hid in the grey shadowy recesses of my mind and yet I knew I had to find the key, the door into a new and a better life. I could not accept this life of living in the dark gloom of the soul with no understanding and nothing to cling to save my loneliness and despair. I could not face the shame or admit it to myself or anyone else. My life had become a black realisation with no forward momentum of any kind. I lived in a perpetual dead end, where humanity had drawn its last breath, and exhaled its poisoned fumes immeasurably and without compassion.

My parents gave me the space that I desperately needed, as I ventured out of my room occasionally to rattle about the big Georgian farmhouse like loose change in a piggy bank. With me heavy on their minds I was a puzzle they were yet to solve, as they had absolutely no conception of the seeds that were being rampantly sown in my warped and troubled mentality.

I could never sleep, and lay, tossing and turning all night long, drinking endless cups of camomile tea to alleviate the painful exhaustion, which it never managed. I would drag myself around blurry eyed and fractious as a result. I tried everything I could think of, from lettuce leaves to strange massage techniques on the forehead, and then finally hit upon one last option, a cigarette. Knocked out cold by these potent porticos, I immediately seized on them for strength and support, providing restful nights with a twenty a day habit that I have yet to break. Much to my parent's consternation and hidden dismay I drew all over the walls, messages about love, nirvana, the meaning of life, or existence as I called it, and felt it. There were scrawls and doodling, and an outlet for my emotions, my cruel, tortured and troubled mind. In my desperation I had turned to philosophising, drawing ever deeper to conclude answers to the great unknowns that presented themselves so thoroughly to me. Simple questions of meaning, purpose and how to live were causing me such perplexity. I bought endless books, reading avidly, trying to gain some sense of relation in an otherwise devoid world. My parents were in awe of me and unable to comprehend that I had slipped so low, so quickly, and so unrecognisably. Communication for my part was in animal grunts, and my internal struggle clung to my body in a tense, drained chill.

I knew my parents were trying to figure out where to go how, what to do next and what to do with the black cloud that was named Charlotte. I produced endless troubled art work, scrawling frantically for some signs of hope and beauty, staring distantly into space with nothing going on in my heart but sadness and confusion. Their answer came in the shape of a tutorial college, a place to learn and do the final year of A Levels. It was the School for the Gifted, as my father sweetly called it.

I was enrolled, went there, and enjoyed it, because it had character. It comprised of two houses, on a narrow one-way street in Winchester. They were spacious, creaky rooms, light and airy. All sorts of lessons were taking place on a one to one level, so total priority was given to each student. We had to attend for a few hours a day for our lessons, and then we were expected to make the rest up at home. This suited me as I enjoyed the lessons, but changed every syllabus. My art teacher, Dee was lovely and we shared many an hour of talk about how we felt about this and that. She was very holistic, green and friendly and one of the first people I felt I could really connect with.

I was one hundred degrees more relaxed than previously. The social hub and bubbly had gone, replaced by a lot more earthy lifestyle. Thank God, I thought, I'm home. Even so, I had to pull myself through the web of inertia and coldness that encircled my heart. I rarely went out, and when I did I would just sit and stare at the passing traffic, noticing car number plates that proclaimed WAR, while others enjoyed a drink and a jest around me. I forced myself back into humanity by trying to find a tiny spot in my heart that could flourish and grow. I did daily exercises on the way into college each day, looking at the trees and the clouds in the sky and grabbing onto the realisation of their beauty in the hope that it would open the doors of warmth and belief in the goodness of life again.

I found myself a boyfriend, rather haphazardly, during a drunken visit to the pub. Jake worked in the Jolly Farmer, behind the bar, and I used to cycle up to see him, and enjoy a pint or two, and perhaps a game of darts. He sang in a band which played music like the Doors. Very chilled and it all felt so natural and wholesome. We went to bed one night, the Doors music drifting across the room. The bed was low to the ground and we caressed and softly, gently and rhythmically made our own music. I was a happy bunny, sharing myself with him and the gentle night sky as the music permeated our bodies.

The illusion was shattered though. Jake had a friend called Stephen. He played the bass in the band, and looked desperately sad. He was sad about things beyond comprehension, sad about untouchable things, which you could only reach on your darkest nights or your fondest days. His drawn, forlorn looks touched me and made me want to reach for him. One night I did. I took his hands and slowly kissed them, feeling for his pain, and trying to draw it out, alleviate it. Of course Jake saw, and I was overcome with remorse. I felt threatened, guilty and afraid. I dropped Stephen's hand drastically on the table and left.

Later on that week I went up to my bathroom, the yellow bathroom that looked so friendly and exuded painstaking homeliness. I locked the door, and took a pair of scissors in my hands. First the scissors and then the razor. About two hours later my long black locks lay neatly in the waste-paper bin, and scattered liberally around the basin. I went straight to bed, pleased and satisfied with my handiwork, my arms rather exhausted by the exertion. The next morning I shocked my mother appearing in one of my grandmother's old brown hats. Pulling it off I giggled merrily and set off to Winchester leaving her in tears at the sight of my shorn head, covered in little scars. That was a pattern that became all too frequent and too many times for comfort. I would cause her great grief and sadness in my thoughtless and self-centred actions, so swept away in my own self pity to notice or even care that she was suffering too.

I had the run of my parent's home practically all to myself, and I would walk; long, long walks over the South Downs. These beautiful walks involving hills and fields, with amazing views and steep, steep climbs were my life's blood. Exercise is very good for combating depression, and I think I must have been instinctively aware of that. My parents had a beautiful Turkish sheepdog, an Anatolian Carabash, who looked after me protectively, loving me as I loved her. Together we would stare for hours into the distance, philosophising with our psyche, being at one with nature, and allowing the growing of the seasons of the soul to take their course. Thoughts and feelings flowing naturally through our bodies as we watched the birds in flight and the sun settled over the smouldering trees. Sitting on the hillside, staring into the vast horizon, and walking, eating the hours in my determined stride. Even after my traffic accident, I would wake at five in the morning and take out my crutches and walk the harsh inclines. I was a dreamy romantic with a heavy heart, and would take it out often, and calm it with the rustling of the leaves in the trees on an autumn's morn.

I had run away before cutting my hair off. There had been an argument with my mother as she slavishly made her twice-daily journey to come and pick me up from the college consuming two hungry hours from her routine. It had been silly and superfluous, but I had been furious for one irrational reason or another, in a blinding rage reaching decibels of despair. I was usually quite placid, but had nearly broken the door off, and refused to get back into the car. My terrifying anger at the system, previously inverted, was beginning to brew openly, and all that stood in my way were in for a shock. My mother drove the half hour journey back home without me, fed up to the back teeth with her erratic, nonsensical, off the rails daughter and beginning to be quite shocked at my behaviour. Once I'd actually

21

been diagnosed with manic depression how her, and all my family's reserves of support and love flourished daily, sometimes under huge obstacles thrown in by me, and not just for good measure. I was however, always kept away from washing machines and dishwashers in particular, venting my anger on these obsoletes in an infuriatingly efficient manner.

Life returned to normal with the advent of the passing of the driving test. I was independent behind the wheel, the world my oyster, and I found I could indulge in all my longings and passions with no further ado. I had found a pair of dungarees in a disused cottage in Scotland the previous year. The yellowed, mottled newspaper that lay on top of them was dated 1953, and it was with great glee that I resuscitated and customised them, keeping them together, when they ripped dramatically, with hordes of safety pins. I would never take those off, and attracted much attention from the homeless, thinking that I belonged with them.

Exams were taken and I passed fairly smoothly. No great shakes or minor heart attacks. I was in Scotland again, on a family holiday, when my results came through, I took a bicycle to the narrow, wiggly, country tracks, to an old, practically disused phone box on a pine-wooded path, literally in the middle of nowhere, with the Scottish hills looming around me, and put through a tentative phone call to the college. I got good grades for Maths and Chemistry but a dismal E for Art. I had already been accepted by Camberwell College of Art and Design in London which was highly recommended so I was not too bothered and passed the rest of the holidays with little or no worry for the future.

I had been scooped up unwittingly into some sort of life again. My brothers and their friends knocked the corners off my despair, and I found at the college a fair bunch of other people hungry for soul food and ideas. We had all gently lubricated one another surreptitiously, and although my behaviour was still somewhat morose and distracted, my previous pit of deep loneliness and inadequacy had been filled. Life in the countryside had illustrated many things to me about nature and her forces that were deeply relevant to my make-up, the beauty and perfection of which could never be fully explained in words.

## 1.3 - STORMING PING PONGS OF THE MIND

The preparation project for entrance to Camberwell was to build a life-size self portrait, a spire of imaginative revelation, or so the story goes. While in Scotland, in one of the many sunlit, wooded glades, I had found with my brothers, and friend Steph, a deer skeleton, lying lonesome on the ground, decaying and reverberating with the music of nature. I thought about it with glee, envisaging great things and protractions, and proceeded to take the whole thing back to the lodge, dragging it into the boat, and rowing across the dark, secluded loch with everybody holding their noses at the stench, and looking at me in amazement, while I was filled with a fantastical sense of growing delight.

The deer skeleton with all its knobbly bits and flesh, still hanging on, was brought down by car back home. Taking it out of its black bin liner I got to work with the bleach; a tip that I had picked up along the way from someone who knew and obviously did things like this regularly! The skeleton was scrubbed and brushed and of course the dogs loved the rotting flesh that fell off under the bleach's spell, although they were kept severely away from its dangerous overtures. In time it was spotless, pristine and something that babies could play with happily. However, it was only four foot tall, meaning that it was two foot short of life size. The quest continued.

The discovery of the second part of the sculpture came as I was taking one of my innate walks on the Hangers. I was right at the bottom of the hill, which has an incline of nearly 45%, twisting and turning among the natural ululations of the Downs. There was a wooded path, with debris strewn around from the '87 storm. A mish-mash of aesthetic natural charm. One particular such beauty was a large piece of glowing, reddy orange yew. It was nestled on the earth, looking so beautiful and broken, parts of its family scattered liberally around the path. The textures were rough and bark like, and I thought it was ideal, a good contrast to the sublime bone. The fact that both media for my self-portrait were long dead eluded me at the time! Obviously there was a slight logistical problem in that the wood lay at the bottom of a steep incline, and I lived at the top. However, I took my car down, and managed to put a bit of manpower and muscle behind it. Soon the wood was taken from its sunlit serenity and lay beside the deer bones in one of the white outbuildings on the other side of the gravel drive to the house, ready for production and public display.

It looked great the first day at Camberwell, present, there in the room, with all the other life-size sculptures, ranging from huge ceramic objects decorated entirely with the artist's fingerprints, to wiry creations with bits of coloured tissue paper. All the students stood round and their work was examined and discussed, in great detail, the semantics and psychological aspects et al. We all moved around the various options on the foundation course, trying them for size, and seeing what we bonded with. The choice seemed to consist of textiles, fine art, 3D design, photography and ceramics. I chose to do fine art, although I was encourage by the tutors to do textiles. I didn't want to be spending my time in textiles, so fine art it was.

I found Gary to be my tutor, a long greasy haired hippy, who was forging a career for himself in indulging in weird shit. I was to be a critic for much of the course, of which I found it difficult to partake of it. All sense of beauty was thrown to the winds and replaced by inarticulate mental wrangling dressing themselves up as highly inventive imaginings, but to me came across as rather silly and worthless. My love of nature, and attempts to recreate the energy of its essence were met with distraught anxiousness and ridicule by the tutors. The other students quite liked them.

A sufferer from manic depression whom I have met recently informed me that he saw the cause of his illness to derive from a lack of structure in his life. He could completely correlate times when he fell ill to moments when he felt he had no proper purpose or forward momentum to drive him on, leaving him wide open to innocuous suggestions and frippery that he harkened on with his enthusiasm to function. As we are all genetically predisposed to achieve in order to obtain happiness, my confusion and growing blind panic stemmed from Gary's total dismissal of everything I believed in, and his force feeding me of everything that I innately detested. And he kept telling me how crap I was with great vindictiveness. My structure had collapsed once more, and I was left wide open with nowhere to go. Yet again, I would have to fall back on my own resources to create my dream, but I hadn't yet refined or even begun to understand that touch. I felt pretty desperate, worthless, and alone, and I so needed to build up my self esteem, but how?

My now, Sinead O'Connor look was drawing much kudos from my arty surroundings, and respect flowed from all quarters for my emotional dwellings. Everyone had secret inner worlds that were thrown for observation onto the canvases. Happily painting my oil flowers, without a care in the world, and maybe that was part of the problem, I was savagely attacked by Gary. He said that I was crap and tore my work to shreds. Everything I had ever been taught was bought crashing down to the floor, as he attempted to instil in me a notion of the abstract and conceptual, meaning and metaphors. I was highly confused and felt he singled me out personally for vilification because of my public school background. My fears were justified later when I found out that many before had suffered the same treatment. He felt we were only there to pay the bills, and the state educated sector was the honey to by mooned over and enjoyed, while we were to be shunned, and publicly humiliated whenever possible. On the other hand there were some fantastic people there, many mature people, and even a manic depressive who had a penchant for bright swirling colours. It was not for me though, this damning and obscure world of dubious aesthetics, and I went on many a reconnaissance to find my true purpose. One such inspiration was a trip to Cambridge to study politics, in the hope of getting another A Level so that I could study architecture. Politics however is not the subject to be studying if you are young, idealistic and on a quest for truth!

I did make an extensive collection of cigarette butts, collecting them wherever I went. I enjoyed the different ways in which people put them out. The created a whole psychological adventure. A friend of my father congratulated me on my collection, saying that I would end up in the Tate.

I got 'thrown out' of my lodgings, a tiny flat in Chelsea, known among its residents as the Peach Palace. My bedroom became copious and abounding as a result of all my artistic inquiring, until the time came when I had to sleep on the sofa in the sitting room, it being too packed full of leaves, fabric samples and general paraphernalia to use. I moved to Battersea to a friend's house. Battersea, where there are dog turds on the ground, reminding me of home, and I felt much better in this more spacious, family environment. The house was light and airy, with big pine double doors separating a dining room from a sitting room. There were user-friendly people living there too. Jane, who owned big blue doe-eyes that seemed to want and wonder. She was a soft little creature. Delia was maternal, and would organise us all, and make home a home with a heart in it.

I was feeling pretty aimless, and had nothing really to sink my teeth into and gnaw until satisfaction. But I worked myself to the bone on slightly superfluous self-created inspirations. Even late on a Saturday night with the house in full party mode, I would be stapling and cutting, and generally causing a creative and non-productive havoc of unfinished ideas, oblivious to the fun and frolics going on beneath me, desperate to try and find my way on what was fast becoming a rudderless boat again, until I was rescued for a drink.

We used to spend a lot of time in one of the cafes, where Tim with the caterpillar cardigan lived. He wanted to give this cardigan to me; it was nearly full length, made up of soft green and cream stripes. He was a fluffy soul and the bar was always full of autumn leaves on the floor, poetry readings and bands playing. It was tiny, and every inch of it was crafted and designed in a beautiful earthy way. Even the electrical wires would swirl around the ceiling in natural patterns, and that was before we had started drinking! The tables were of stained glass, and decorated like King Arthur's Round Table. Wooden mushrooms, some standing three-foot tall were crafted into the bar. There was an illicit opium den in the flat above, not that I ever ventured that far. Drugs, their stench and their fluffy repercussions fumigated the area. There were all sorts of exotically earthy characters in the woodwork, some became friends, and some of whom made a deliciously deciduous backdrop. I went into sort of overdrive, feeling the frenetic pressures of London, the lack of fresh air, decent walks and animals. I also became a debutante, investigating the high society whirl. My eyes were soon opened from one end of this colourful spectrum to the other.

My mother had been a deb, as her mother before. The whole thing started centuries ago as a court procedure, bringing young ladies into Society. It continues now in rather a dampened form; you are no longer introduced to the Queen for example, but the great joy these days is to curtsey to an enormous birthday cake, baked in memory of the long dead Queen Charlotte. Of course the whole function of the Season, as it is known, is to socialise, have a good time, and meet all the eligible bachelors. The emphasis on getting married has been slightly distorted, as most girls are more serious about their A Levels, and future careers. My days as a Deb began shortly after I cut most of my hair off, and was nearly bald. I was affectionately known as "the hedgehog" among our family friend's small children. I remember standing in a house in London at the first official drinks party of the Season. We were all dressed up the nines; pearls adorning every surface possible, silken suits in a vast array of pastel colours and little hats perched decorously on flaxen locks. We were nervously getting to know one another, being ever so sweet, ever so polite, and talking about school and the likes. I took off the hat that a friend's mother had kindly leant me to cover my semi skinhead look. The gasps and the hush that reverberated around the room when I removed my hat were astounding. Tasmin got more than a few stares too when she came to pick me up in her ripped denim overalls and disarray of dreadlocks, grinning from ear to ear at the irony of the event.

And of course there were the Deb's Delights, otherwise known as men. They had been chosen on the merit of being someone's relative, friend or simply for being loaded or aristocratic. They were invited for us by our parents, and they entered into the spirit of things with every intent of a good time. The free booze, glamorous parties and hordes of deliciously delectable potential dates, offered us an intoxicating affair.

Those were the highlights; costly, expensive and impermanent as highlights often are. The downfalls of the season are that you get a totally warped view of reality and life becomes pretty strange. Can you imagine going out every night and getting totally inebriated for nearly a year, while doing nothing constructive during the day? I found I missed the cups of coffee and cosy chats as life spiralled into hedonism. Actually, I don't think I bothered keep a grip on reality! Delia and I would go to function after function dressed up in our latest creations, night after night. We started to invite homeless people to the parties too, that we met on the tube. I used to go round the markets and pick up dresses, which I would then

26

chop up in various styles, with plunging necklines. I would use the wonderfully frilly curtain trim that I had bought from some specialist shop and deck myself out liberally feeling like the bee's knees! To finish, I made an elegant velvet choker, onto which I had sewn an assortment of pink buttons. I procured all sorts of other specialities, dresses ranging from every colour under the rainbow, and felt incredibly glamorous, dolled up night after night, essential accessories of a drink and a cigarette in hand, and surrounded by my partners in crime.

I thought I looked good, but with a heavy dose of artistic interpretation. I was well removed from the Barbie doll scenario, instead dousing myself fully in an intoxicating mix of far flung genres that huddled together collectively on my being like a Matisse or Picasso. Other girls would go to great lengths to find matching accessories, whilst I would in turn go out of my way to obtain items of dress that clashed and innately did everything possible to stick out like a sore thumb. That, however, was my style, and needless to say, they loved it, apart from a few titillating mothers. Colour co-ordination was my speciality, but as they say, beauty is in the eye of the beholder.

To determine whether manic depression had got its gruesome hold at this point is a difficult task. The seeds were undoubtedly being sown. Drugs are a major key in opening the door to mental illness, but I do hasten to add, that if I hadn't got it now, I think its ugly head would have popped up somewhere down the line. The birth of a child, the death of a parent, moving house, a job, any of these stressful events would issue the passport to insanity. Drugs in their entirety give a very similar experience to manic depression. Acid with its hallucinogenic capabilities, speed with its rushes and ongoing energy, marijuana with its paranoia and sedation levels that can sometimes be likened to depression. The best and easiest way to explain what it is like to have manic depression is to liken it to drugs, and an intoxicating energy trip lasting months, followed by the come down of depression. However, I think that it can also be said, in my case with more than a little shame attached, that this equation can work the other way around too. By opening your mind and your awareness through a drug intake of any kind, you are using parts of your brain, which would otherwise have been dormant. Once these have been stimulated, and especially more than once, it is so very easy for them to activate themselves under different circumstances. Drugs do open the doors of perception, but it is mighty hard to close them again. In the meantime lots of strange and ugly monsters seem to find their way through. In a nutshell, I don't think that I would have ever contracted manic depression if I hadn't been so inebriated, which is a sorry thing to have to tell my carers. On the other hand, I'm sure I would have contracted manic depression later on in life, so it could be seen as a small blessing that I have got it over with now.

Even so, it was there, waiting in the wings, listening for the beckoning call for it to dance with the stars and sail with the winds. I did stand out in this merry crowd, who took my impervious and impenitent absurdity for the laugh that it was intended to be. Twinklings and inklings of mania were slowly seeping through into the pool of calm. I would make up my mind to escape once more before I was discovered, hiding my shame and my ultimate pain. In hindsight, the depression I felt at my art school activities was causing me to soar, just a little something to feel good, anything to hide that total inadequacy which was really haunting my dreams.

Of course, if you're manic at events like these, as I was beginning to be, it goes so unnoticed, as everybody is high as a kite anyway, as a matter of course. Indeed it is rather welcomed and expected in this jubilant atmosphere of merriment and joi de vive. Your natural vivacity, charm and confidence gaining lots of friends and making you the centre of attention in this glittering swirl. I was interviewed by so many magazines, such as Hello, Harpers and Queen and Tatler, eager to have a story on these precious few, who dazzled in their entirety and led lives that seemed worthy of mention as supposed society elite. I was high as a kite, having the time of my life and inebriated beyond recognition before I'd even arrived. But things had not yet noticeably got to a danger level yet. Poisonous obsessions were still in the mixing pot, and for now people were happy to see me so full of life. It never entered any of our minds that I was in fact fast becoming as ill as could be, and that destruction was knocking ever more restlessly on the door.

My lasting memories of being a deb were being very drunk the whole time. We would consume, what seemed like, at least twenty glasses of champagne an evening and there were more than a few occasions when I could be found curled up under my table at art school, still dressed in the fancy outfit from the night before, my guts feeling like they were on a roller coaster, and more than slightly bad tempered in my exhaustion. There were trips all over the country to house parties, where I would inevitably meet some very eccentric characters, tucked away from the bright lights of London. One such man had a passion for ostrich racing, saddles and all. He kept us all spellbound with his tales of in-trepidation. Like attracts like as they say, and it was not until things took a real turn for the worse that I found out the highly negative aspect of that saying.

Queen Charlotte's Ball was advertised as the highlight of the social calendar for us, the culmination of nine months of parties and amazing offerings. We were provided with a whole load of meringue dresses for the occasion. My mother luckily, bless her cotton socks, came up trumps, getting to her sewing machine and producing a beautiful slimming dress within the week. The event was to raise money for Queen Charlotte's Hospital and all the débutantes who chose to enter into the affair, about sixty of us, were to wear white full length dresses and long white gloves and process down some steps in The Great Room in Park Lane, in full view of our awaiting guests, and hordes of photographers. From there we would walk (having been taught how to do that the day before), carrying our bouquet of red roses to the six-foot cake, magnificently designed in honour of the deceased Queen. We were to curtsey to this fine thing, and then waltz, with our Delight (Deb's delight being the male guest). I chose my brother Ben for this glittering occasion. He was very reticent at first, and had to glue his shoes together at the last minute, but soon entered into the spirit of the evening as we all galloped about the dance floor, throwing caution and my bouquet to the winds. The cast from Hair came on to sing and set the scene, and soon we were rocking and rolling until dawn.

The excess energy, because I very rarely slept during the day, and was up most of the night, plus the unnoticed prickling of mania was causing untold exhaustion. I was doing a fair amount of speed on top of this already heady concoction, and would stay up partying all night five out of seven evenings. It was fun, but I had to cold turkey over Christmas from all the vast quantities of alcohol and God knows what else that pumped through our veins and kept us sweet until the early hours. Christmas, usually the booziest time of the year, came as a welcome respite! Depression was imminent, but it is only in hindsight that I can see the psychological threads. At the time, I just wanted a rest from all this rushing, wild parties and I knew in my heart that I couldn't keep up this jamboree lifestyle.

The time for soulful action, solitude and re-energizing, came in the unlikely form of a car auction. I had made up my mind again, alone and dogmatically, and there was no going back to my Deb lifestyle. Sitting on a pew high above an auction pit, my mother and I would watch, car after car, being bought in for sale. You had Porches going for £50, beautifully bright yellow, and they looked alright to me! I was after a van. A van to live in and decorate; my new artistic project. My misadventure and escape from the clutches of London and art school. It was to have a Georgian interior, with burgundy and yellow ochre, stripped wallpaper, with a standing lamp in the same colours softly lighting one of the corners. I didn't get round to thinking how the electrical situation might work, caught up in my own excitement for the adventure. I bought a van. When I drove it for the first time, my mother and the owner were all staring out of the huge windows like a strange breed of goldfish discovering a new habitat. We would look out with wonder, my mother punctuating the conversation with swearing and shock. I was gleeful and excited, getting to know this new mobile that held so much promise and excitement for me. It was my doorway to a new world. At the time I held the notion of independence and freedom close to my heart. I knew I had to escape from the hurly burly of London, but I did not realise that the countryside can hold its own source of poison, reflecting my own inner source, which try as I might I could never escape from.

## 1.4 - ONE WAY ROAD

I got together with Sid shortly after New Year. I knew him through a mutual friend, who thought he was sexy, which of course had ramifications for me in my perception of him. I had jumped, fully clothed, into the shower at midnight of New Year's Eve, and then he and I had sat by the fire with my legs smouldering as the water evaporated off my brown corduroy trousers. He had been tripping at the time, and became highly mesmerised, and the trance for both of us began. I didn't kiss him that night, rather his friend Duncan, who was big, passionate and manly. Sid was upset, and being aware of his sensitivity I got together with him soon afterwards, maybe more in sympathy perhaps, but he did hold some interest for me. We had met previously and talked about killing fish and wearing their bones as earrings in a purely indigenous way. I thought he was so elegant and somewhat delicate, as he moved gracefully around the room.

He became known as 2x4, as I got him to work on the van. He would indulge himself completely with hammers, nails and a saw, and of course 2 x 4 inch wood. Soon the van was fitted out with a bed, and panelling on the walls. I painted the outside, having rust proofed it first. I chose the Aboriginal colours of rust red and yellow ochre, and soon the van, as it became affectionately known, was a beauty. Work on the inside became of frenzy of activity. I made seat covers for the front from a soft turquoise blanket, and painted the dashboard and steering wheel in greens and blues. The effect was very dreamy, sea-like and translucent. The back was bold and shocking, pinks, reds, yellows and oranges. A large orange curtain hung, covering the double doors at the end, and all the insides were painted in beautifully radiant hues. Art boxes, an old Singer sewing machine, and general paraphernalia were hoarded in the back, and we were soon ready for take off! I must say, looking back at it, it was a manic paradise. All the colours under the sun, bought together in resplendent glory. And all for the sake of emotion. Was I feeling crap? Did I need that emotional rescue, that vivacity, that glory, to remind me of what life could be, to fill my exhausted and heavy heart with some of the radiance of life?

One day in London, Tom from Fungus Mungus asked me to drive him and his girlfriend down to Cornwall as there was a rave on. I duly agreed, because I had nothing better to do. Sid came too. On arrival in Cornwall the others went for a walk on the beach. Sid put their rucksacks on a rock and told me to drive back to London, leaving them there – stranded. He felt that they had been using me and they deserved nothing better.

We lived in the van, as I had planned to, eventually settling down just outside Winchester, on some parkland near woods. Acres of beauty were at our fingertips. We would talk for hours, he would tell me his plans, discussing nature, science and art. I would lap up books on Quantum physics and the Chaos Theory for breakfast, and we would discuss the nature of the universe. Night after night, and day after day. The stars were our friends and the moon our mother. We lived freely, with no one to answer to, and no one to care about except ourselves. I felt for the first time in ages that I was a free expression of life, unstructured and unconfined, allowed to roam and wonder as I pleased, wherever the wind took me. I did love Sid for all the traumas and infidelities that he encompassed, and writing about him now, I realise how happy I was, intellectually and physically. I had found someone with a mind like mine, who loved to explore, who would talk and imagine everything. We took no drugs; Sid did not trust himself to take them in company.

I did however, take acid once with him. We were parked up by a mass of grey, blue water. A beautiful lake, big, with bulrushes, and ducks paddling merrily around. In the distance, through the mists of the water was a stately home. Peaceful and settled in the dusk, rooted for hundreds of years. It had been a hot summer's day, peacefully turning into a balmy evening. We dropped some acid, not very much, but enough. This did two things, which drove the wedge between Sid and I. He picked up his guitar and very carefully, painstakingly so, began to pluck out some peaceful melodies, playing and practicing very softly, very gently. It hammered home to me just what I found so excruciatingly irritating about him, the fact that he never got anywhere. I was bored, and fed up, his dreams and great scams always came to nothing, never even getting a millimetre off the ground, and I was exhausted after having thrown the full weight of my support to him time and time again. So I got up and went outside. I banged hard on the outsides of the van, banging a rhythm, a hard loud rhythm; designed to wake Sid from his slumbers. He came outside, and by that time I was on the roof of the van, below the bough of an oak, the birds accompanying me in my ancient melody. He came up to join me, obviously feeling very raw, and scathed in his sensitivities. We sat there for a while and talked earnestly about our differences, mingling argument with fact. He was unhappy too, but only because of my uncertainty. He could be so needy, dressed up in a caring guise. But then, he had only learnt how to hurt, and had cut off all his tenderness and care, and placed it somewhere that it could never be found, or accessed. He had received such blows, that he had removed all form of positivity from his make-up and replaced it only with fear and self-destruction.

Somehow we leapt down off the roof and began playing by the lake, in the long grasses. I gave a run and a high kick and hurt him, getting him across the jaw. This bought me down to earth with a jolt, as I had heard a story of a man killing his girlfriend while on acid, not knowing what he was doing. One primal urge turned to another, and we made love by the lake, oblivious to the path running nearby us.

I don't know what my parents thought of me living in the van with Sid. My mother thought that she would lose me forever if she made a scene. I was pretty unruly and grumpy around the house when I did go back. Low and depressed, I just could not settle. I wanted to talk, to tell of the horrors and the traumas that were facing my soul, the depression, the depths of loneliness and worthlessness, but somehow I just could not find the right words to begin. I felt that I was adrift at sea, with no means of navigation, and was a victim of the tides to see where I would end up. It was not a feeling that I felt comfortable with. I was missing my friends, my security and my reason to go on. I felt I had no future, not in a line I cared to continue with. But I was too tired even to think about suicide. I lived in anger; it was my constant companion, and when I didn't have it, I felt as if I had lost my voice. It is what kept me going.

We drove around London sometimes too. We'd go and pick up Tom from Fungus Mungus and drive through the night into Soho; Frith Street, to pick up some grass. We'd knocked back a bottle of vodka between us, and were feeling pretty good about life. It came as quite a shock, to me, anyway, to suddenly find through my open window a machine gun, and on the end of it a rather stern looking policeman. We were told to remove ourselves from the van immediately and stood shivering in our summer attire on the pavement. We were searched by 2 van-loads of police, all carrying their rudimentary machine guns and holding very enthusiastic Alsatians. They went through the van, looking for God knows what, but finding only sewing machines and paints. I got the giggles with a policewoman, who obviously knew that they were completely off the scent, as she told me that we were an unmarked van in central London, and they were worried about the IRA. The fact that we were reeling on the pavement didn't really seem to make much odds, so we went on our merry way, and decided to give the drugs a miss, all things considered. It might be pushing our luck slightly.

Sid became a heroin addict. He would go from London to Brighton, and deal in all the stuff, liberally helping himself along the way. His next girlfriend, Angela, actually tried to commit suicide. She failed in her attempt an ended up in psychiatric hospital with my good friend Alex, who I was to meet many years later. Angela would never let Sid see me again, which was a testament to the strength of our relationship. I did see him again though, may years later, in a bookshop, but our love had just turned cool, and we were perhaps more than a little self-interested now. We could no longer stretch to the limits we had been surpassing every day in matters of the heart. It was hard work for us both to care about each other, when we had so little reserves of our own, and we were both so desperately needy and full of woe, treading such a precarious path full of nothing but pain and desolation, trying to love from such a lost and lonely point, and never being able to stretch to one another, try as we might.

I got fed up after a while with such a stagnant status quo that went nowhere but round and round in circles in the wheels of our deranged minds. I have a very dynamic father who achieves a lot standing still, so I found Sid and his endless dreams, which never even began to bud, let alone come to fruition, slightly exasperating. I applied to University and also to Operation Raleigh as I needed a quick fix, a breath of liberation, and a reason to go on. Zimbabwe, I thought, here I come. The sun, and nature, all at its most glorious; a complete respite from the gloom and doom that life had become.

My other achievement was to get a place at university. I had received all sorts of little brown envelopes in the post, declining or accepting my personage. My brother Ben had a particularly gorgeous friend, I thought at that time, called Malcolm. He was studying languages at Durham, so when I received a massive brown envelope from this very university I kind of assumed that they were offering me a place, on an economic level. It must have cost them a fortune to provide me with at least two branches of paper. Really, if I had bothered read it I would have realised that it was in fact information for deaf students, not dumb students! However, unknowing and therefore unperturbed, I set off, on a mission, to that beautiful university city that I would call home for the next two years. I was wearing my yellow outfit, one of my many near neon garbs that accompany my illness. Home-made from dyed sheets and a charity bought canary yellow cardigan. I thought I was the cat's pants, but really apparently, on an holistic level, I needed the colour, or so the psychic lady said. I wore it often enough; the same outfit, nearly every day, for two years, until it literally fell off me in a rather embarrassing manner.

I went up on the coach, which took the best part of six hours. Arriving in the beautiful city at six thirty in the morning, with the mist still on the river, I wandered along its banks by the boat houses. The walk was wondrous, and the air was fresh and earthy. The city loomed, mysterious in its medieval splendour. I followed my nose to a roundabout, by the College of St. Hild and Bede's. Malcolm happened to be passing, at exactly the same moment and we joined forces to secure my place. The man in the department of Natural Science took rather a shine to me, as we laughed and giggled flirtatiously, and Malcolm took me on a tour of prospective colleges and showed me round the most beautiful castle. It contained chests over one thousand years old, and other such historic splendour, liberally lining the corridors. I chose to go to St. Cuthburt's Society though, mainly because that is where he was. The whims of youth and flights of fancy – I definitely took a few of those! I had forgotten that he was doing languages and that as a result he would be taking a year out. But anyway, the place was mine, and I left a happy bunny, the cat that got the cream. It was to spill all over me and ruin my fur, and I would be left matted and dripping wet. But thoughts of blissful freedom and romantic intellectual endeavours were all that crossed my mind at that stage.

## 1.5 - WHAT ON EARTH IS HAPPENING?

I had had to go on an entrance weekend at East Grinstead in anticipation of the great Operation Raleigh adventure where we all crawled through mud up to our shoulders; blindfolded, guiding other would-be venturers in a chain, among other such delights. We got no sleep as we were woken every fifteen minutes to go on a trek through the deep and dark night to find some food that was strategically placed miles away and up a tree for us. They liked me and I was in, mainly because I woke up giggling every time, high as a kite and thinking this was the most ridiculous thing in the world!

I managed to finance my trip through my work as a gardener and some fundraising that I did. I bought a rucksack and filled it with plenty of regulation clothes, and my self-imposed earthy uniform of yellow and now a hint of burgundy. My mother dropped me off at Gatwick to save a hefty car-parking fee and I joined the hordes of others all stepping out into the wilderness. We landed in Zimbabwe many hours later and were hit by the heat as soon as the plane door opened. The Operation Raleigh machine run by ex-army, in all its glory, whisked us away to test our swimming skills in a neighbouring pool. This was to come in handy for me later, in crocodile infested waters, although it seemed happily irrelevant at the time, and far removed from the excitements that lay ahead of us.

It was beautifully hot, even though it was wintertime. The light was amazing as the sun would rise at exactly six fifteen, and then go to bed precisely twelve hours later, to the second. Then it would dramatically, in the space of a minute, become freezing cold. It was winter after all, as we soon realised. We would hurriedly put on all the clothes that we possessed, which in our ignorance comprised of a few T-shirts! I dreamt heavily on our first night, and I suffered badly from depression. I was withdrawn and very deeply in my own thoughts not knowing how to communicate on anyone else's rather jubilant level. I found the hordes of people running around on missions, being ultra-happy and bouncy, delighting in water fights and other such trivial humour, very irritating, so I tried to keep myself to myself in self-preservation more than anything else. I didn't want my pain and inadequacies to be exposed to the fresh African air and happy stranger's judgement.

I did find a few people that I could empathise with. These were mainly the YDP's; the Youth Development Program, consisting of people who had had tough lives, involving prison, the social services and scarce little money, unless they had stolen it. Some of them were obviously fantastically well endowed with all the latest technology decorating their accommodation. Nicky, a tiny Geordie girl, was planning on getting pregnant, with the Government offer of her own flat spurring her on. This trip was supposed character building for us all, showing us life outside our usual boundaries. I bonded with these YDP's in their tenacity, and intrigue and plain survival instincts in a different kind of jungle. Some Irish people, unsurprisingly mellow, were chilled out as to be horizontal, providing gentle lubrication and sanctuary to an otherwise bubbling melee of seemingly irrational delight.

We had a program that was three sets of three weeks, rotating people and places from doing an adventure project, conservation project, and then to a community project. I started on the community project first. We were to build pigsties for orphan farmers who lived just down the road. A previous group had already built the houses for them, and it was up to us to provide the pigsties and the farmers a resultant means for their livelihood. There was all sorts of heretic talk that we were taking away the work from the native people, but it was fun; we all learnt a lot, working in a group, with all the dynamics that that encompasses. New skills were being taught and practised such as making drinkable tea and coffee; however, we would usually resort to a very strong mixture of both. We dug ditches for the foundations in the boiling glare and used all sorts of equipment to make sure that they were straight, chewing lavishing on sugar cane for nutrition.

I decided to run away, with two other girls for a few hours before we were herded back into the camp, but we had had enough. There were quite a few politics, and people's vulnerabilities were prone to irritation. A few of them had been sexually abused, and their pent up and well disguised emotions seemed to come tumbling out in the rawness of the Africa after years of shameful denial. Brian had spent five years behind bars for beating up a known paedophile, and felt bitter about what he saw as the twisted lawlessness of the courts. He was older, 26, and very independent. There were fallouts between him and the head of the group, Rick, who did not seem to understand his depths. Brian was very intelligent and idealistic, full of the wonders of the world, with a passion for everybody's personal development; which, helped by a fair bit of acid, sent his anarchical senses into overdrive. I had a very strong sense that something was up, a premonition of the forthcoming disaster. I think it must have been the vastness and beauty of Africa, with its yellow ochre's and clear blue sky. It opened the doors of perception for me too, and I felt very aware, and strangely cleansed. Cleansed to the point where I felt totally at one with nature and its power, and lived under that regulation rather than the enforced laws of Operation Raleigh. The airings of authenticity from the venturers as well as the clarity offered by the magnificence of our surroundings had seeped strongly into my being and anchored me once more. It was beautiful, real, imposing and timelessly strong, and I responded to the call of the wild with peaceful acceptance. Unfortunately we did not all reach a point of calm, as Brian hit Rick, in a noble and chivalrous move and was forcibly removed back into the inferno of London.

We ate round a campfire, with mealy meal, the local dish (powder that you added water to, in various quantities depending on the time of day, making a sort of mashed potato or porridge). It was pretty revolting and I added the regulation mixed herbs by the bucketful to aid digestion, but I don't think anyone noticed because we were treated to other delights. We would sing in the evenings after the sun had gone down. Philip, one of the native venturers, would lead and bring it all together with such gusto and inspiration, his eyes ablaze with invigoration, as we all chorused together. One night we looked around to see a bright red moon, caused by dust coming up from the road tracks. None of us had seen such a wonder before, and the whole camp ran for their cameras to capture this incredulity, much to Philip's dismay!

We moved onto the conservation project, changing people and location, sleeping in big army tents in the middle of a colossal national park. This park boarded on Mozambique, a country at war. As a result of all the incumbent mines, some of the elephants had their trunks blown off, and were not in a good mood, pretty diabolical in fact, leaving the park an even more dangerous place. There had been a heat wave over the last two years and as a result the snakes had died, leaving nothing to eat the mice. Therefore, a mice infestation existed and we had to peg our tents down thoroughly and hang all the food from the ceiling, which did not stop some strange rustling in the night, and a few perspiring brows, especially from some of the more macho men, who screamed and fled at the slightest pip squeak!

At this point, I was sharing a tent with John, another YDP, who had such stories to tell. We would lie in the dark as he told his tales of police-car chases in the middle of the night, him high on acid and helicopters circling in the night sky. I don't know how much of it was hallucinations. He and I got on well, he was a tough nut, and I was deep in the doldrums of depression. I was feeling pretty moody, and had no desire to ingratiate myself with anyone unnecessarily. The feelings I had for my surroundings did not seem to permeate to the company I sadly found I could not enjoy. John and I had an unspoken respect for each other, and we welcomed each other's presence, realising that we shared the same mentality and instincts, relative to our company.

We did a conservation project to find the number of fish populating the rivers. Unfortunately communication was not too good with the native people, and what actually happened was that the lakes were exploded so that the dead fish floated to the surface where they were then counted.

A wasp scientist led our other conservation project. He was a true scientist, in looks and in nature, and he burnt all my careful drawings of African sunsets thinking they were rubbish, for which I was very much exasperated. We would spend hours walking around miniscule parts of the enormous reserve, long metal contraptions in hand to count the figs from the almighty trees. Baobab trees, vast creations that were nearly as wide as they were high. Counting these tiny things perched way above us, mocking us in their majesty. The idea being that wasps fed from the figs, and the number of figs should give an idea of the aforementioned wasp population. Of course we had to be protected at all times by three game wardens who carried AK47's and chided us if we so much strayed a few metres from the path they laid out for us. One night there was a lion that ambled near our camp. I was sound asleep at the time, but it was Philip, the native venture, who was tellingly most upset by this. He ran from his seat near the fire to his tent, praying out loud and trembling in fright at his encounter. Everyone else was rather macho, blasé or excited about the event, and the quiver in the camp reverberated for days, there being a distinctly improved interest in our weaponry and protection as a result. We were living in five army tents in the middle of nowhere, surrounded by wild animals, with nothing but a few old rifles to protect us!

The last phase for me was the Adventure project, which consisted of rowing for five days down the Zambezi River, and then white water rafting down what seemed like the Niagara Falls! There was also a trip to the Chimanimani Mountains, to go trekking for over a week. We did this first, led by a man who was in the SAS. The mountains were gorgeous and we stayed briefly in a place called Heaven Lodge, aptly named as it was set high in the clouds. The lodge was very comfortable; it had beds for goodness sakes! A luxury we had all but forgotten about in the distant mists of time. It was run by a white hippy who lived comfortably enjoying his paying guests, far away from any of the rigmarole of civilisation.

We set off in search of caves and waterfalls and all sorts of natural delights. However, after three long days of climbing at SAS paces, malaria struck Dave, one of the natives, with whom I had a very innocent little fling. We had to rush back to Heaven Lodge, doubling our speed from on the way there. There was an air of great emergency and drama, not least because our leader had also fallen seriously ill. My shoes broke. I had given my high-tech walking boots to a game warden in exchange for his beautiful burgundy mid calf length leather boots, which were seriously to die for, and complimented my colour scheme to perfection. They of course, could not stand wading waist deep through rivers carrying our heavy rucksacks, or the intrepid pace, and split almost immediately! Climbing up the first hillside back to the lodge, after our mammoth do or die trek, I carried little Nicky's rucksack as well as mine. It was nearly the same size as her, and I became totally euphoric on reaching the top such was my exertion. Getting highly overexcited and full of the joys, I thought that the helicopter circling overhead was bringing me some new boots, causing everyone to look at me with a new degree of confusion. It was of course, for Dave, and his suspected case of malaria. Dave got better, from the trek that is. He didn't actually have malaria; it was a totally false alarm. The SAS leader spent the next few days vomiting. We had a welcome break for a few days in our heavenly lodge.

There was one time when we were having a rest from all the walking. Dave and his friend, who apparently was a guerrilla in the civil war, which made him well over the age range for venturers, were chatting on the riverbank opposite me. They were standing on a lovely, grey rock, looking like an advert for shampoo, in all their natural splendour. I had come out of the woods, four hundred yards of refreshing currents between us, and I dived into the river, swimming to them. Only half way across did I remember that I was in Africa, and think of crocodiles, and then swam for my life, terrified that I would be swallowed up at any minute by loud, gnashing fangs, my body being strewn from sides of the river in a bloody mess.

There were lovely times too. I had moments of peace and harmony amongst the tumultuous terrors of people and crocs! Taking a bath in a small pool, with a complete panoramic view of the African plains, families of hippopotamus in the dusty distance. Walking and talking to studious Gareth, and investigating all the insects and strange life forms in the sultry heat. Looking at zebra and elephants cooling themselves in the river as we canoed quietly through the reeds. Being outside in the sun, at one. I did go off in a wave of disillusionment, full of dope and tired of life. I climbed a tree by a herd of hippos and fell asleep, watching them watch me. Havoc reined in the camp, and rumours were rife that passing lions had munched me. However I was found by the leader of the group, whose girlfriend was anorexic, and gently bought down out of the tree to safety, and no reprimand. I think he knew what I was going through and didn't want to add fuel to the fire.

When all was done and dusted, and we had all parted and gone our separate ways, I went to Bulawayo. I had my hair extended and put in braids. I thought of travelling further, and did a little. After changing my flight several times I hopped on the next plane home, along with several other venturers. We actually got to stay in a five star hotel that night as the flight was delayed. After three months of mealy meal and sleeping on the ground, they soon caught on to us ordering room service until four in the morning. What luxury!

On a personal level, this was a time of great solitude, surrounded by masses. The African scenery was so beautiful and vast, still and timeless, and we all felt at one with nature. Even our own nature at times. The relationships I had reflected this, as we were all struck by the mystery and magic that is Africa. All the spoils of everyday life back home were just peeled away as we took our spiritual primal forms. I came back to England with a sense of quiet wonder at the simplicity of life. Life was so free and splendid, and we all felt our own strength and mystery come alive under the African skies. All life had the space to be and to grow, and the majesty and nobility of the creatures was awesome.

It did strike me as rather strange going into some of the shops on my return, and seeing the rows and rows of toxic sweets on sale. I remembered fondly the little shop in the middle of a quiet African village which sold only two sweets, that is not two different kinds of sweets, but two sweets, and one bottle of coke. Everyone recycled car tyres into shoes. It just made me think of what we are lacking in this country, to have to fill it up with so many unnecessary things. Probably a global consciousness and a global responsibility and unreal expectations of what we deserve, often at the cost of other people's quality of life somewhere else on our small planet.

## 1.6 - MADNESS AND MAYHEM IN THE NAME OF LOVE

And so it was that I arrived in Durham, after my year off, slightly deflated but warmed by some of the company that I enjoyed, and with a deeper confidence in my abilities. My hair was still in long braids that I had added coloured felt things and beads too, Africa pulsing through my veins, and still in the habit of eating with just a spoon, which I would do for a good six months yet to come. My two best friends from school had unwittingly managed to put at least half the globe between us, in their trotting and escapades and I felt the slight tremors of being thrown into the great unknown once more. But life was a happy frenzy of activity, filling in forms and joining endless queues for various subject matters, ranging from the bizarre to the extreme. Lots of bright young things jumbled into together making their way about the old medieval city. I was in one of my colourful modes, swathing myself in old curtains, which I manipulated into an assortment of partially finished dresses in yellows, turquoises and oranges, the brightest colours of my mind. Of course I didn't really have much of a grip on things. I would spend hours queuing for the wrong subject, but it was a great way to meet people! One such creature was Jerry, a tall blond hippy, who was incredibly chilled. He used to make fun of me trying to fill in my forms, especially in view of the fact that he had got 5 A's at A Level, which in those days was extremely rare. I would tease him about being an accountant, which stopped him in his tracks, as his father belonged to the said profession.

I was assigned a double room in the Old Bailey, one of the oldest streets in Durham, sharing with another girl called Tamara. We decorated it lavishly with all sorts of colourful paraphernalia and great enormous letters on the walls proclaiming 'THE GREAT END OF ALL KNOWLEDGE IS ACTION'. The cathedral was directly opposite and I would hear its gonging bells every fifteen minutes lending a great deal of charm, and a delightful sense of place. I had some extraordinary friends. Susi was a petite young black girl, who spoke more in high-pitched animal squeaks than anything else. Her kitchen was filled with Marmite pictures of hippopotamus' on the walls. Dirk was a gay German, who took pride in his appearance, donning himself up in cravats and plus-fours, always with the adornment of burgundy socks and anything else that could be that colour. You could always tell when it was his washing on this line! I see him to this day, although the effects of living in London have slightly loosened up his dress code and other matters! He actually used to find being gay in Durham an absolute nightmare. The redundant coalminers would come into town every Friday and Saturday evening to beat up the students, and they had a field day with the gay community. In defiance, Dirk would go to excessive extremes to advertise the fact that he was of that inclination.

We would eat in a long dining room in St Cuthbert's Society. This was also in the Bailey, so three times daily we were to be found traipsing the cobbled streets in order to be fed, with the correct meal ticket in hand. The Bailey led to the river over a small stone bridge. All of this was well over one thousand years old, and it reeked of history and happenings. The river boasted sculptures in wood, and even the lamppost in the Narnia stories. One of the sculptures involved twelve tree trunks. You would sit in one of them, and all the others would align in your view to give a carved picture of a dining room, taken I think from an ancient tale too. So clever, and many a scene of stoned, night time, candlelit vigils, remembering my lost days, friendships ill fared and offerings in awe to a God I thought had forsaken me.

Sitting at the tables of St Cuthbert's Society I would be surrounded by geeks. They were mainly made up of row upon row of bespectacled teenage boys, all rather spotty, and looked as if they had had limited hours of daylight. I would eagerly await for a nerdy conversation about astrophysics, but we spent most of the first week in silence, nervously looking at each other, and concentrating more than deservedly on our food, not yet having mastered the art of conversation. One glorious day, whilst all kitted out in hair extensions, orange dress and smelling somewhat, as I had not yet got back into the habit of bathing, Jerry approached me. Tall and graceful, he reminded me of a figure I had witnessed in my dreams some years previously. I had been about seven years old and dreaming of sticking three pins into a baby. I thought it was something to do with acupuncture or experimenting, but this graceful figure glided up to me and led me away. In the dream we had been standing on ice. He smoothed up again now, and asked me if I wanted to go for a joint with him. I did, not having smoked really for 18 months, but thinking what a nice young man this was, an oasis indeed. I got up, leaving my mangy plate behind me to go cold and congealed, and we began the climb to his house, over the river, and up the hill through the woods, and up that long road they call The Larches, which seemed permanently covered in traffic cones, causing me in future eras to have more than the usual reaction on sight of one.

His bedroom was a marvel, and I would try and recreate it for years afterwards. He had little wooden boxes and lots of posters of a psychedelic nature, bright colours and swirling forms, and a whole library of Carlos Castaneda. He was a total hippy, and a clever one at that. We shared exactly the same eyesight, and I would often go and buy bottles of the drink 20-20 to celebrate that fact. We smoked the joint, me being a little reticent at first, chattering away mindlessly about God knows what. In fact, poor Jerry was straight from school, a babe in every sense of the word! We got into the habit of spending time with one another, smoking dope and talking. I would do most of it, and more often than not he would listen, sharing funny perceptions when the occasion arose, his eyes glazing over

41

sometimes as the conversation became obscurely personal. I would talk endlessly, seamlessly sharing my life for the first time in many years, ranting and raving about all that inspired me, and leaving out the big gaping holes of hapless humanity that I hadn't come to terms with myself. More often than not, he would pass out with the effects of the drugs, leaving me in mid-sentence, talking to myself.

He was the one person in so many destitute years that I longed for and who liberated me. His arm of friendship extended and kept me warm and close in ways that were previously unimaginable. In him I felt safe, secure and so happy. I felt loved. No one had ever made me feel like that before, but then again, there hadn't been anyone in my life to do it. They had all gone. I didn't realise how important that made him to me.

He would always deliver me home, back through the woods and over the river, stopping at the city gates at the head of The Bailey. From there I would pick my way home from the orange starry glow of the street-lights, back through a little door, to the safety of my room, which was fast becoming an eclectic hotch-potch of ambiguous useless accessories to living. I had turned all my tables and chairs upside down, which Jerry considered symbolically correct, but not altogether practical!

I joined the rowing team, which caused huge offence to the other girls, due to the fact I smoked and was not of their tribe. To rectify the situation I would unwittingly turn the four-man boat in circles, while they tried to scramble against my strength but failing irrevocably. I used to spend a good part of my time looking for Narnia characters. This filled me with great interest and delight, as apparently C.S Lewis had based his novels around a lamppost in Durham, to which I would be ever hopeful of finding, donning my rapidly increasing collection of charity shop fake furs to add fuel to the fire. I had not the directional ability to do that, but thoughts of Aslan and his kind overwhelmed me, as did a rather surreptitious stone table by the Cathedral. I was living in quite a few fairy tales.

One day I tripped over a seven-foot branch. I picked it up, not least because it reminded me of the staff in Jerry's picture of Gandalf, but also because I did not want to be conquered by it, in fact I wanted to tame it and make it mine, this heinous creature that had failed me. I set it at the head of my bed, and Jane, Thomasina and I would make little colourful presents to go on it, like a Christmas tree. I had met Jane in St Cuthbert's bar. She lived near me at home, and we started talking through her heavy goth make-up, about philosophy and its rather strange ideas. We were really enjoying the notions of the universe so we went upstairs to smoke yet another joint and really got down to details of our ideas of conceptual chaos. We would both go to Jerry's for tea and hot crumpets with honey, sitting on the floor like little girls and waving our wooden spoon at him, casting spells while he busied himself in the kitchen, like a tall and graceful gazelle, his long flaxen locks flowing in a lion-like mane.

It never occurred to me that Jerry might be shy and insecure with women, I was so wrapped up in my own fears.

I ran out of steam very quickly with academia. It just seemed so rigid and unnaturally turgid. You had to learn about 300 years of thought before you were allowed to be creative. I thought that by the time you got to 50 you might actually be allowed to think for yourself. I was breathing with the wind, and living with my imagination, which aided by C.S Lewis and the like, soared to colossal heights. My great mission was to buy the old Victorian Police Station, which graced the town, even having decorated porcelain loo's. I wanted to fill it with colour and love, and allow it to become an Arts and Crafts extravaganza; every room brimming with curiosities and delights conjured from the hands of those about. The lottery was going to provide for this spectacular, and it would be a place of positivity and beauty. Unfortunately my resolve did not hold on a level unknown to me then, and events would conspire to slightly put a stop to my dream. Like it had done at art school, where I had wanted my project to be decorating children's playgrounds with the children.

I made my mission to test the concept derived by Einstein that imagination is the greatest form of intelligence. I wanted to put this to the test.

I never kissed Jerry. There were occasions when we would curl up together, in each other's arms and fall into a deep dope induced sleep. But there was nothing sexual, not on my part. He had a girlfriend and I had Sid. We were just best friends who did pretty much everything together, even most of the same lectures, always together, from breakfast until bedtime. It never occurred to me that he might like me that way, but then I am a bit slow to catch on sometimes. I was just so comfortable with the situation, and so happy. It felt so good and natural and easy. Jerry didn't have any severe emotional problems, that I could see; he was a nice gentle Yorkshire lad, soft and sweet, perceptive and funny. I think he enjoyed my midnight candlelit vigils by the river, although he did draw the line at my request to make up poetry whilst I busied myself on skip raiding sessions.

Then one day I had a terrible encounter with my Sid. I had at that stage moved into a single room of my own, and bought along my coveted pile of rubbish I had picked up from various skips. I had the Durham Cathedral font water carrier, a big drum that I had converted into a pink table; and a pestle and mortar from the science block, which was probably highly toxic! Next morning, Sid stalked off, in a highly discourteous mood, saying that he would throw himself into the river. I was mortified. I believed him, cast under his traumatic spell once more. I spent the day rushing about asking people frantically if they had seen him. I was in a state of high alarm. Jerry took me to Newcastle to get drunk, which was very sweet of him, very kind. Although I still could not stop worrying myself silly about Sid, until Jerry gave up on his friendly overtures and we went back home. God, I wish I had realised what he was up to. I'm such a bloody flower fairy sometimes.

Jerry turned nineteen, one bright and sunny morning, and there was great rejoicing in the land as he was throwing a party that evening to which everyone was invited. He had been busy in the kitchen all day, or at least delegating some of his female house-mates, who produced deliciously appetizing food, with rather bizarre ingredients. We all tucked in merrily, and got unproductively high. I wanted to include some of the people who had been invited, who all found the food slightly unusual. Unwittingly, I was aware that these guinea pigs were all sitting rather quietly, having been sedated, and on approaching them, Tamara, my old room-mate, keeled over, knocking the lamp and sending us all into total darkness.

All the other guinea pigs rushed about in a state of panic, not realising that this was one of the side effects of the food. Ambulances were called, statements had to be given and you could say the party spirit had been broken. I had started to cry as soon as the evening began, the dope overcoming my normal control, and my emotions letting rip at such a scene of friendship. Jerry, needless to say, was far from overjoyed at what he deemed my destructive behaviour. He was always too stoned to do anything. It was his diet of staple nothingness.

Jim lived in Jerry's house. He was bright, funny and quick. He claimed his mother to be Stella Rimington, the head of MI5, but I think it later emerged that he was a paranoid schizophrenic. One wonders. Jerry and I had arranged to go into Newcastle to see Trans-global Underground play there. Dream of 10,000 Nations. We were to meet somewhere in advance; in all the confusion I can't remember where now. What actually happened is that the phone rang at Durham train station, where I was standing alone in the cold, shivering in the night air waiting for Jerry. It was Jim, totally out of the blue. He told me he was going to commit suicide, mirroring Sid and attention seeking. This slightly held me up, and I did not meet up with Jerry. I got to the concert before him, and was happily chatting on a sofa, pint of cider in hand, to two Scottish men. Jerry marched in and was furious with me. He took me to one side, and before I knew it I was sitting on the ground bawling my eyes out, Jerry being nowhere to be seen.

A very friendly Geordie man with thinly disguised ulterior motives comforted me, and we ended up jumping through an open window where we found the band ready to go on stage. They admired the bright turquoise dressing gown that I was in the habit of wearing and offered me a beer. I had heard that Galileo had been allowed to wear his dressing gown all day at University, as he was widely regarded as a genius, and, in my attempts to be conceptual, I thought that the effects might rub off on me! I went on my way, unstoppable and irrational. I danced and danced with the Geordie man, starting to display obvious manic tendencies, in my desperate infuriation. Jerry and I got the train back together, with Neil and Chris. I went hammer and tongs at Chris, flirting and I suppose trying to make Jerry feel jealous and make myself feel better. Jerry looked furious, and fumed quietly in his Northern way. He and I didn't talk for a week, and I didn't feel any better anyway, taking to eating vast quantities of scrambled eggs in the kitchen, at the round yellow table, unable to punctuate anything, least of all myself.

Chris arrived a few days later in my room, not having seen him since the concert. I'd only met him once before in a pub with Jerry. He took all his clothes off and lay on my bed, fully expecting me to have sex with him. My dialogues with the Deb's Delights was not dissimilar from the one I had had with him, but I had never had that sort of reaction before. On my refusal, and I was pretty fed up with men at this point, he picked up my chest of drawers and began throwing it across the room, leaving hefty dents in the walls. I screamed and screamed and attacked him, leaving his body covered in scratch marks, some of them drawing blood. I was livid. Somehow he managed to get out of the room, with or without his clothes. I don't remember and I don't care. I was safe for a while, but I had still not conceived of any future danger, barely conceiving the atrocities of the moment, which I still considered irrelevant compared to my loss at Jerry's nullification.

Sometimes I wonder whether Jerry actually put him up to it. Sometimes I wonder whether Jerry didn't hate me so much, for apparently rejecting him, although I did not know he even wanted me, that he actually encouraged Chris to do that. Sometimes I wonder that Jerry's pride was so hurt. Me, a Capitalist Southerner, and he a Northerner, and God, did we all have to listen to that. It did make a difference then, and I wonder that his pride was hurt so much that he intentionally encouraged Chris to do that and then just walked away and left me to the most scarring moments of my life, which took me 15 years to recover from in part, but not yet in full. He did it on purpose, and that is what I have been denying all these years. I had no one in my life to support me at all, and no one back home. The fact that the one person I had left in my life, the one person I trusted and loved, turned his back on me and left me to be attacked.

Jerry couldn't be bothered to do anything about it; he just sat in a stoned heap and evaded the whole issue. He closed the door on me literally as I lay utterly confused. Chris came back again. This time with a friend of his, who actually had the audacity to draw a huge picture of an angel on one of the walls, complete with an erect penis. This made me very angry, not least because of the relationship that I had just been in. I covered the self same walls with oils, liberally put on and energetically felt. What happened next was the beginning of a nightmare. People would come into my room, and add to the painting. Just like that, willy-nilly. I think they must have thought it was a community art project or something; maybe Jerry was behind that too as I certainly didn't invite them.

I had Jim painting a tree laden with fruit, Rachel painting a woman on fire, and Chris of course, had to add his touch; an ancient symbol for medicine. Maybe these were strange prophecies of what was to come. Of course, there was one day when one of the staff members came in, having heard vile rumours rife from the mouths of the cleaners. Luckily it was Davina Longhorn from Student Support, who was to provide a great deal of commitment, but bare little success to my cause. I was holding an incense stick, and was probably stoned. I spent the whole day stoned, and couldn't get out of bed with or without my rudimentary joint. Of course, she was visibly concerned, for the room and for me, but terribly kind in her method of management. To save a bill of £400 I decided to repaint the room myself. It took six coats in some places, due to exclusive store of damaging paints I had concurred. Davina and I discussed the problem of Chris, and whether I would like to press charges for his violent behaviour, but I, in my naivety and misplaced compassion assured her that he had already suffered enough; he had had cancer, and so no further action, on that count, prevailed.

Jim, very sweetly, came to my aid, breaking into a spider infested broom cupboard and duly putting me up for two weeks on a soggy mattress on the floor, with nothing to look at save rusty nails and knee deep dust. The last scrap of humanity disappeared, as I had to be kept a secret from the cleaner, who would be fired if the authorities caught a whiff that I was living there. I resorted to wearing my thick furs to stave off the chill, and reading Enid Blyton books to restore my humour. I couldn't read any of them however, as my concentration span had diminished to about five seconds, but the pictures were nice.

I had short black hair and glasses at the time. I had an exact Harry Potter scar on my forehead from the car accident. I sometimes wonder whether or not JK Rowling actually saw me in the broom cupboard when she was on the train, inventing her story of Harry Potter, which came to her in a vision. It would be in keeping with what was to come.

Jerry kept away from me at this time, probably thinking I had lost the plot, and running like a scared rabbit into the safety of his lair, too aware of his own discrepancies to risk the authoritarian limelight, with little or no thought for me. He did walk in on me, when I was in the arms of another man, and ran off, annoyed. I told the man to leave immediately, and ran after him. But it did no good.

I moved on to BG's, another Cuthbert's House, where Chris was squatting. Some boys broke into a room for me to dwell in, and I would spend the days painting crazy nonsense, listening to my music, which blared into the corridors shaking the foundations of the building, and smoking a constant supply of dope. It did not occur to me that I was failing on yet another count by not paying any rent, although I was harshly reminded of such by the Head of the College. I was duly ejected, and the room boarded up, and it was probably on that count that I crept into Chris's room one day, just down the corridor, probably also looking for some form of inebriation to get me out of this inertia, back to that happy land that lurks somewhere in the mind, coming out on occasions to grace the day, namely when Jerry was about. The association of dope had sunk too deep. But Jerry did not want to get involved with a sinking ship, and he in his immaturity had all but dissolved our friendship when he said that I was obviously spiralling into disaster. The taunts and jibes that he hurled my way when I did summon the emotional strength to go and visit him totally negated our relationship, leaving me desperately alone, in a very precarious state of mind. My only real girlfriend there had taken flight on a mad drug induced panic. I had introduced her to one of Chris's friends, who happened to be the spitting image of her worst fear; Bob, in Twin Peaks. The fact that he shared the same name didn't help, and she made her escape, away from the evil hedonism and hectic life of living above the bar, back home to the safety of her mother's nest.

Chris welcomed me in, and gave me a joint, and that really was that, the pattern was sealed. I did not really want to be there, but my lack of alternatives had diminished beyond existence. My ever decreasing awareness led to my life being lived out within the four walls of Chris's room. A tiny box, which I wouldn't leave for the next two and a half months, save to use the bathroom. All spirit died in me, I couldn't remember my name, the day, the month, the year; I had no idea of anything. The only thing I did was read a book Sid had given me about a girl, whose father was a professor in the university, and who had been captured by the barbarians. The only thing that kept me going, which stopped me wandering off the edge entirely was thoughts of Jerry and how I might possibly see him, or at least be near him physically. That is the only reason I stayed, as the relationship I had had with him was the only nurture I had had for years. But otherwise I gave up, trading my proximity to Jerry to constant abuse by Chris. He took it as his God given rite, with no appreciation of my perspective, that he could use my body for his own ends, night after night, day after day. The lights went out in my head as I was continually pumped full of poison and hatred. He kept me on a string, a tight rope of compliance, as he knew my weakness, and by feeding me an endless supply of dope he had me right where he wanted. Unable to fight, struggle, to think or even get up and walk out the door, I was his sex slave, to do with as he pleased, and he made the most of it. Bastard.

I felt so alone, alone in the world. A nervous breakdown at school had severed all emotional ties, and the ones that I had picked up since were merely transitory. I did not see my friends at home enough to trust them with how I felt. Jerry had been the one good thing in my life; my safe haven of love and laughter. But he too had rejected me. I blamed myself, and had no-where else to go. I was tired, exhausted by my fruitless search for meaning, and endless travels. I missed him, I screamed to myself daily. He had become my mantra. He was my life and he had thrown it in my face. I felt desperately alone, too exhausted to go on, and totally shocked at how life could be so cruel.

Chris and I never talked. He used my shell, and burnt my heart to smouldering ashes. This was the man who would later go on to gang rape, and beat lovers senseless, so much so that one committed suicide, leaving behind two young daughters. This man saw no sense or reason in the female temperament, only wanton hussies to be used and abused. I was not scared; just very, very tired. He would be too stoned to be violent, although if the inebriation did wear off the effects were disastrous. Emotionally drained from the outset, and devoid of any nutrition and care, I knew this man could fly off the handle at the slightest remark. I had already seen what he was capable of, so kept my head down and dwelt in a private world that had dwindled to a nightmare of massive proportions. He wanted sex, and I let him use me, I didn't feel I had any choice. I was not there. And I wanted to be near Jerry. In my misery I had evacuated and my spirit was sobbing uncontrollably, undeniably distraught, lost in a bitter arid hemisphere, where no one could reach me. I would not let them; I could not let them see my shame. I just pretended it was not happening, no one could see, no one knew. I could not face the burden of discovery, the worried looks, the aghast expressions. No, the shame was too much. How could I put into words what my mind refused to acknowledge. I had no friends I could trust with this atrocity. Lost in the mists of marijuana I was incapable of stringing a thought together, let alone hatching a plan of escape.

Deeply depressed, I felt my life spirit vaporise. The sense of loss that overwhelmed me laid barren any survival instincts. I had come to the end of the line. A long and arduous road of misery and despair, culminating in the most degrading thing of all. But I put up with it, because there was that little glimmer of hope that twinkled ever so slightly on a bright day, ever so often in my breast, and it was the one thing I had left to go on.

I could not bear the thought of losing Jerry, when he had made me so happy and complete. I could not let go of what was in reality a memory, as I had no other strings to cling to. Everybody in my life had gone, and our journeys were incompatible and incomparable. I clung to was Jerry, and hoped against hope, that we might be friends once more. One or two friends from Downe House were at Durham but they barely acknowledged me when we had passed on the street.

Molly of indigenous descent, who lived next door, would give me stones; meaning to be like the Philosopher's Stone. I managed conversations with her that were so bizarre I floundered for a context. Chris kept his silent stronghold over me, willing me into total servitude, whilst my diminishing power bound me ever more fervently to my secret dream.

Jerry did come round once, in those long months of coldness and nullity, lending a spark of hope to my proximity. He came for lunch. There was a group of us, the first social occasion that I had been involved in since the abuse began. No one said a word throughout the whole meal, fixated as they were by intellectual snobbery, and not having their words dissolved and dissected like rats, exposing their internal systems to the harsh light of comparison. There was not a lot of trust.

After this delightful affair we played a game in the meadow with a purple Frisbee, and I found a golden ball lying nestled in the grasses. I ran to Jerry and showed him the ball, wanting to play with it. But he just looked at me in disgust, seeing only hippy madness and crazy symbolism, outlandish beyond his extreme, and threw his weight back into the road, hurrying off, not undeservedly into a healthier sphere of recompense. I felt such loss at Jerry. Loss and dismissal, as if I wasn't good enough for him anymore, and he had discarded me beyond retrieval. He came only once after that, and that was to play a round of cards, which again dissolved into a mental competition that few were interested in apart from Chris. He probably thought that I was there by choice, never bothering to find out for sure. But I had been in such a bad way, and had already suffered things of which he knew nothing about. This was to put such a massive rift between us that has caused me such grief. I would sit huddled in silent horror, a cold numbing taking over my body, disabling me of the ability to do anything or think anything. My life spark had died and all that remained was total disinterest, and a hollow soul, functioning only when my body bellowed at me of its requirements.

I felt so let down by everyone who I had been close too, and it would take me years before I could trust people again. I would howl in absolute honest-to-God pain and misery if I felt my mother was being less than 100% caring to me. I was totally abandoned and unloved, and I had absolutely no one in the world to turn to.

If I had really thought about it, i.e. if I wasn't so stoned and deeply depressed, and could form a plan, I would have gone home. I did eventually, but not before I had really had my insides ripped out, and my confidence and all the other emotions that go with it burnt and frazzled nearly beyond repair. The other pain of course was that I felt Jerry had totally rejected me, which in reality he had. This was something more that I could bear, and carried the pain of his dismissal for years. I had no friends with whom to talk with, they were all new. I needed my old and trusted friends, like Steph. I could talk for hours to Steph if I wished, about every topic, no matter how sensitive, under the sun. In fact the more sensitive the better. It helped her too, to hear of such stories. It helped her come to terms with her own experiences and to heal a little more.

This abuse that I was subjected to on a daily basis for two and a half months was something I kept as a closely guarded secret from everybody that cared about me. The shame and emotional pain was far too great to see it aired and scrutinised. All I really wanted to do was hide the embarrassment and shame that welled up uncontrollably in my heart whenever a man would get too close, or a girl talk about her lover. I wanted to hide, forever, and never let anyone see my indescribable grief. I did not tell anyone of the abuse for years. It only came out through atmospheric pressure when watching TV years later, and the built up repression and dejection would soar through the roof. I would find myself violently carried on a sea of hatred and fury, seeing similar stories that burnt a hole in my heart, making it impossible for my sea of calm and deadening lies to continue any further.

It was not until later that I learnt that it had, in fact, been rape after all. It is not a prerequisite of rape that violence is used, and although I never voiced my rejection, overcome by drugs and depression, I more than hinted at it in a thousand other ways. The fact that Chris had been violent with me previously would have swayed public opinion further in my direction, but of course, unless you are raped either violently or by a stranger, the whole area is such a grey one, that it is an area that needs to be reassessed by the law to protect women and men, who inevitably have their lives shattered as a result.

However, it gave the whole affair clarity, and a resonance that I felt it deserved in my breast. The continual waves of heartache, and the dreadful repercussions that made even the slightest contact with the male species nigh high impossible, has rendered my life a lonely, barren desert for many a year, and it is only been through intense will power and constant vigilance that I have been able to get a grip on the situation, and slowly steer it to brighter waters. But this has been a long time coming and the end is still not in sight. I have never been able to do more than kiss a man since the rape, and it is now nearly eight years on. The days have been tricky, the nights even harder. Many have been the moments of uncontrollable sobbing into my pillow, hysterical and violent, barbaric reactions to those bittersweet ten weeks of utter misery.

Working for a man has proved incredibly difficult, straining every ounce of emotion and determination to make it succeed, and more often than not, not being able to produce the necessary goods. I have never stayed in a job more than nine months, and really struggled in all those that involved working with men. I just feel so scared sometimes around men, whether they be user-friendly or not. The whole time I am under constant vigilance for signs of attack, and would be constantly mentally calculating methods of escape. If I had known one iota of the scaring that would accompany those ten weeks, I would have got up and walked away from the situation without a moment's hesitation, but when you are caught in the thick of things, your survival instinct relates only to the present, and not to future repercussions.

Help came in the form of a phone call from home. It was my father's birthday in early April, and I had, on an off chance rung home a few days previously. My mother suggested that I come home for his birthday, probably rubbing her hands together in glee, because she no doubt was worried at the shape of things in Durham, coming down the telephone as a massive 'HELP'. I didn't really need another reminder, so I hopped in the car and off I set, leaving behind the misery that would take years to distil from my heart. I didn't say goodbye to Chris, or Jerry, or anyone. I climbed out of the window, leaving all my possessions behind me, desperate not to be noticed. I could have just vanished into this air for all they knew, or been abducted by aliens. All that I cared about at that time, is that I had my passport out, my passport home, to people who loved me, and people who cared. I didn't need another reminder.

I got home, albeit rather late at night. Once home I don't know what state I was in. I remember longing to get hold of some dope. It is addictive, no matter what anyone says. I did some work, and last but not least, I missed Jerry. I thought of him a lot; constantly to be precise. I thought that I had lost him forever. I was terrified that I would never see him again, caught up in the grief for whom I thought was my best friend. My only friend. He was everything to me, the light that shone so strongly throughout all my years of misery. He was the warmth that I had been craving for, longing for with all my heart, when I hadn't even really known why. He was that one kind soul, who had so fleetingly seemed to care, for me, for the world, and for humanity given a shot, and I needed him, when all I perceived in my world was ice, despair and darkness. I was desolate. I was like a little dog that had lost its master and was totally alone in the world once more and didn't have a clue what to do, but pine. Someone had once offered me their love and I hadn't even realised, but then rebuked it at the last moment just when it really mattered. It seemed too cruel to be real;

no one could operate on that plane. Was he being kind? Did he care? To me it meant everything, and to him apparently nothing. These thoughts tortured me during those long summer months and they were the reasons that shaped my decision to go back there for another try.

I must have been a major encumbrance to him, with all his carefully weighed flights of fancy that didn't really seem to fit my kamikaze tendencies. While he would quite happily indulge his passions for kaleidoscopic psychedelia, expanding his mind in whichever direction it chose to go in response to his vast illicit intake, he must have despaired of me wreaking havoc, as he would painstakingly clean every nook and cranny. How he liked to surround himself with the artistic and emotive, when all along his mind was as pure and logical as could be. What drove him and I together, when in retrospect we were as different as night from day; his refined, well kept heart to my belittled offering of mud and grime, his immaculate clothes to my dishevelled attire, his brilliant mind to my anarchic mess, his hard won success to my bitter, angry and destructive trauma. I think the life he entered in Durham was too hot for him to handle. He thought it looked like a tantalising temptation, but the people he surrounded himself with would in time become too much for him to bear, and he would retreat to the zones of safe and clinical starchiness where he could disinfect himself from all his youthful pondering, and start to get down to the serious business of life, without pain or much emotion at all. I was the first to be dismissed.

I met a man in the local market, back home, who drew the pictures that decorated Jerry's walls. He had a beautiful one of a girl in a garden, called Creation. It was better that the one I had, of God creating Adam, with his outstretched hand. I listened to a song on the radio that reminded me of him, and how his love was free. That made me cry, as I had been caught in a state of indecision about how expensive emotionally such a relationship would be. After my previous relationship I was terrified of going into another, something I could never explain to Jerry, such was the pain. It was something he never understood, and I suppose that was why he was so angry with me, because he thought that I was rejecting him, but in truth, I was terrified of intimacy. I could not see past my own fear to understand where Jerry was coming from, and in truth, he was very naive.

Everything paled in comparison to Jerry, and this is slightly ridiculous, but that is how I loved him, even though that love proved impossible and the situation escalated into obsession. All my former friends dissipated into near nothingness. I just could not see their value, and suffered total lack of interest in anything. Really I could not talk to them of Jerry, because it would mean having to discuss my sexual abuse, which I was fiercely ashamed of, not wanting to be hurt. I wanted him, and yet my scars meant that I could never have him, without being honest. Since I could barely recognise my own feelings, I had no way of communicating them to another.

So I got more and more isolated, and pinned all my hopes on Jerry's love returning. I completely withdrew, withdrew into my secret world of love and loss. So strong were the feelings resonating through my being that I didn't even have time to acknowledge the rape that had occurred. My heart was torn into shreds, and I didn't want anyone to come anywhere near it. It hurt so much that I felt nothing at all, just a strange compulsion to listen to the wind. Any sign of Jerry through the atmospheric waves would be noted and embellished with sorrow. I waited all summer for news, but no return. I took a week's holiday to be with a friend in Italy, and as we walked through the splendour of Rome and Florence, all I could think of was that he might be there. What would be the chances of Jerry being at the airport? Would I see him? My relationship with my friend, which had once been extremely close, began to dwindle into nothing. I could have willed Jerry into existence such was the power of my thought. He seemed to me to be the key. He seemed to be the answer to everything I had been through, throughout eternity to this point. I loved that man with a passion and conviction that will hopefully never be equalled in it all consuming and completely exhausting power. He held for me the promise of a good life, catching the subtleties and complexities of everyday living that just made everything seem so divine. His outlook and perceptions could never be captured, bagged and transported onto my own mentality so it would have to be him and that cheery, witty warmth so deficient in intensity and excitement that made me long for him in his sublime simplicity. Even to this day, sometimes when I smile, I feel his smile coming through my own, and I know that he is smiling with me. I feel the lasting impression that he has left on me, and I smile back at him. There is a part of his essence that I will keep with me forever. He did have the sweetest sense of humour, which I still enjoy!

But all through that summer I gave in to my feelings, and did nothing all summer but look out of the window waiting for him, to no avail.

He did live about 400 miles away, although he told me that he had come down South that summer, and seemed very upset not to have seen me. I had told him that I lived in Winchester, although I lived in the middle of the countryside, as I did not think that he would have heard of my village. He was quite pissed off, because he thought that I had lied to him about where I lived.

I think my mother was fairly shocked by all these happenings. She had prepared me for a contented life, not necessarily on the well-beaten path, but she had always placed a great emphasis on being happy. She would listen to me for hours as we sat around the kitchen table, night turning into day, compassion and understanding flowing naturally in a tidal wave of love. All my stories and troubles came pouring out for wise dissection, scrutiny and endless nurturing. Of course, at that time, I withheld certain things, but her emotional strength, and sensitive intuition guided me, even when I was blind to her and her pure, true motives.

My mother's home of healing devices; the garden, the dogs, the walks, all beckoned with the promise that she had so lovingly instilled in them, and the peace that radiated from her every activity began to ground me and let my heart settle, soothed and calm. She gave herself an unannounced purpose of constantly lapping up the melancholy from my heart and washing away the gloom in such a sweet and subtle ways, being endlessly caring, endlessly forgiving, even when there was nothing to offer but an all-important ear to listen. And how I very slowly began to realise the precious beauty and texture of the gifts she gave. She was going through difficult decisions herself, as my parents were soon to separate. I don't think she knew anything was wrong with me. Well I suppose she did, mother's do, but had no inkling of the enormity of the scarring, and I was a closed book to her of my real heartache and loss, as well as everybody else in my bitter world of desire.

I went back to Durham after about seven months off because I didn't want to go to art school as had been suggested, and I wanted to see Jerry again. I would have probably seen him anyway if I had not gone back, but I did not have faith in my convictions. Jerry was literally my salvation, my healer and friend, and I continued to see him dangerously in that light for a long time. I had also been told by the faith healer that University would be good for me. I was angry with her, as her advice had led me to have sexual problems after being bullied by Sid. If it had not been for that I would have gone out with Jerry without a moment's glance. The faith healer's advice led to me being raped, and I was angry with her. I wanted to test her, and see if what she was prescribing was true. I had begun my test of true love, basing it on Jerry but also testing faith. Jerry always used to tell me that everything was relative. What he did not realise, as events unfolded, is that he became the absolute.

I don't doubt my parents would have had extremely strong reservations of me returning to Durham if they knew what I had been through with Chris. I just kept it all in, and as I say, I found it incredibly difficult to talk to with anyone. My inner world was so much more important than my outer one, against my wishes, and I guarded it bitterly from attack, continuing in that vein for many a year until finally the poison had been vanquished. But I longed for Jerry, who was quite unlike anyone I knew. He was the coolest and the best thing in my world and the fruit of my labour. I thought he was a shining valiant angel, there to set me free. How wrong I was to immortalise him beyond compare.

## 1.7 - LEARNING THROUGH PAIN

I saw it in a book once, a great dusty delight of knowledge, lurking deep within the library walls. Mania, it informed me pertly, well, let me see. Symptoms of happiness (much greater than usual, and I breathed a sigh of relief at this point), energy untapped, total inability to sleep, and yet never feeling zapped. Also on the menu were hearing things that popular perception negates as untrue, and a creeping irritation with these uncouth arbitrators of treason who disbelieve your wild fantasises of reason.

This looks like a box of tricks, indeed, I thought. Perhaps one to save for a rainy day, my last resort. Little did I know that my partial preferences were to be proved true, because ringing in the back of my mind, and in yet another dusty hard back volume that I had failed to complete, were perhaps the cause to the effect which would bring the human genome scientists running and scrambling for a closer look. The words stood stark and bold from the page 'research has shown that manic depression does seem to run in families, and that it seems to have more to do with genes than upbringing'. I would have thanked the Royal College of Psychiatrists for this toxic titbit and fallen feint to the floor. However in later years my mother would have scooped me up, and sat me comfortably down, attending as always to my needs, which were to scream the roof tops down in my struggle for sanity in later years.

The Department of Health in the UK added to my dilemma by informing me succinctly that mental health problems can result from adversities that are related to social exclusion including; unemployment, low income, victims of abuse or domestic violence, people with drug or alcohol problems, the homeless, minority ethnic groups, the prison population and those with a physical illness.

My mother, as if in a vision - a voice in my head saying in her wise and weathered way, although oblivious as me was she to the reality of events unfolding. 'This illness, Charlotte, which seems destined to appear, affects about 5 people in every 1000 of the population; similar numbers in both men and women.'

'What will happen, what will it involve?' I asked tentatively, clinging on to the side of my chair, my bare white knuckles beginning to shine. The answer was clear.

'Manic depression is a psychotic illness, which in the manic phase you will believe that you are famous, or gifted with supernatural powers, indulging in reckless extravagance and with a total lack of social inhibitions.'

My fate seemed certain, and looming ever closer. I chewed the cud faintly as she went on.

'You will feel on top of the world, probably a little better besides. You will deny vehemently on your life that anything is wrong. You will cause great distress to your family and friends, and destroy most, if not all, of your personal relationships. You may have to be sectioned under the Mental Health Act, and I tell you now, you will become closely acquainted with hospital.'

My visionary mother looked up from her prophesies, taking a long hard look at my jubilant mood, which had become crestfallen with despair.

'All is not lost my dear. After you have lost everything, and everyone you hold dear, you must work to build your life up from scratch. But let me tell you this, to save you from utter despair, the gift of creativity which clings to this dark and dangerous brew has saved others in their time; poets, writers, actresses, comedians, even the odd statesmen here and there, have all found their recompense through their illness, in their art.'

'Will I ever get better?' I whispered hesitantly, with a parched mouth and dying breath.

'Oh, you will in time', she harkened, eager to catch my fading, dissolute attention. The theory in practice is that parts of the brain, which control your moods, are not functioning properly. In time, and with the right medication, this can be resolved. However, stressful experiences of any kind, whether it be in a job, lack of support or even physical illness will bring manic depression crashing in tenfold. You must remember that,' she added kindly to my despondent mood.

'You will not know anything is wrong the first time manic depression creeps up on you. You will feel wonderful, and if anybody tries to say different you will think them a fascist. You will totally lose touch with reality, and only once you have been bought crashing down to earth will you realise fully the shame and miscomprehension of your actions.'

With this my mythical mother picked up her bag. She kissed me lightly on the cheek, and headed purposefully to the door. Turning back to look at my shivering countenance, the dream dissolved into the smoke filled air that it had come from.

'Remember Charlotte. I am your mother.'

And she was gone.

## 1.8 - HAUNTING TERROR THAT HELD ME IN ITS GRASP

The first person I saw back in Durham, for the retake of my first year, was Jerry, joy of all joys. I was in the phone box, wearing my comparatively muted pink gingham trousers, trying to get our phone connected and having a giggly, girly chat with my friend Trudy, from home, who was getting to grips with student life as a first year. He ambled up to me with a smile on his face, delighted to see me, and we were friends once more, quick as a flash, all notions and disappointments put behind me, or so I surreptitiously imagined. But for now we made the perfect fairytale. I had moved into a house in Wellingborough Street. Mick and I had joined up to share with two others, Ginny and Percy. Mick and Jerry soon became firm friends, through accident or design I would never know. He would be at my house in the sitting room every day, smoking dope and drinking tea with Mick, listening to music that lifted people off the street outside in its volume and intensity.

Mick and I had been on Operation Raleigh together. He very much got himself settled in, claiming his chair, draping it with African fabric, and putting his stereo system and pictures all around the room. A very earthy feel permeated as a result, and it was not beyond Mick to fill the place with plants and flowers, with only microscopic details of the original space left to spy. Ginny was upstairs, with a bigger bedroom, enough to fit a sofa in as well as her desk. She was to eat baby food for at least two months, mainly so she would not have to wash up. She and I would have a lot of fun together at the Jazz Cafe and the few nightspots we frequented in Durham, dancing around like stags on the warpath, practically with blood dripping from our cheeks, causing waves of appreciation and nervousness in the bystanders. Although Ginny and I lived in such close proximity, we never did an awful lot together as such, meeting instead at four in the morning for a period of fuzzy logic, punctuated by hysterical giggling.

Percy was downstairs. He was doing a PhD in electrical engineering, and was very quiet, studious and gentle, a grounding force amongst us. His room was also big enough for his friends to all file into, and then a few hours later, all file out of, having watched Star Trek. I didn't really spend much time with Percy, he being as quiet and studious as I was not, but his caring face was often seen in the kitchen distilling our toxic brews.

I keeled over the first fifteen minutes of being with my new house mates, the strain was so much. I had just spent the last seven months in quiet solitude, getting over my experiences, and all this frenetic activity and joyousness was overwhelming. Mick was a great host and soon the house was full of people, drinking endless cups of tea and getting gently inebriated. He would do personality tests on us all by getting us to draw pictures of people, houses and trees, that kind of thing. They were usually pretty accurate. Mine was highly trippy, with psychedelic swirls with a rainbow young thing dancing merrily through the magic, with no barriers or protective devices to my name, as all the others had. They were all whisked away by an artist when he saw them for his personal pleasure.

I was doing Maths and Philosophy again, but this time with Ancient Medieval Literature. This was the stuff of heroes, and something that I really loved, particularly being in a medieval town with so many saints and heroes historically attached. St Cuthbert's Society was for mature students and attracted all sorts of weird and wonderful characters, many of whom looked as if they could have come straight out of the pages of the Middle Ages. That was actually my favourite subject, where I could let my creative juices flow back through the ages into the times of Chivalry, full of sacred symbolism. I loved the lessons and often would fall asleep during them, exhausted by many a manic episode, able to relax for the first time, and grinning as I drifted off into dreams full of knights on white horses and pretty ladies giving their favours. I would sometimes fall asleep on the shoulder of a fellow student, who happened to be a re-enactor at the weekends!

With Jerry I was less than romantic. I launched into him full scale, yabbering my little mouth off as if my life depended on it. I would try and impress him with my quick wit and turn of phrase, and vast knowledge of all things scientific. But he was too stoned to give a damn, and thought the whole thing quite funny, much to my consternation.

My entire sense of loss of everything came launching out at him, and he represented to me a make or break situation. It was either loss and betrayal of everything, or a complete rebuilding of trust of everything.

And he failed me so badly. He didn't even bloody know.

All he must have seen was a girl desperate to connect, while he wanted to sit back and relax. He did not know that this situation was so loaded for me, and for every time he teased me, I took it as a personal knife through the heart. And I went back for more. Please love me, please like me. Please help me, please pay me some attention. I need you. Except that I wrapped it up in things that I thought would impress him, but they didn't, because all he wanted to do was sit and get stoned and it was in sitting and getting stoned the previous year that he had abandoned me to my fate. And God I was beginning to hate him. God I loved him.

He was there, every day without fail. Did he not have anywhere else to go? He grew crueller, the more desperate I felt. I hated him. I loved him. I began to blame him. He had left me to die, and now he was laughing at me. I hated him. I loved him. Did he not understand that? I wanted to hurt him so badly. I wanted him to know what he had done to me by leaving me.

I wanted him to feel the pain. I wanted him to take some responsibility for the friendship that we did have. I wanted friendship to mean something, like it had not to anyone else. I had been so badly let down. Destroyed by friendship. Destroyed by having to play a game in order to belong, and if you don't want to play the exact same rules of that game, if you want to play a slightly different game, then you don't belong, but then you don't belong to the other game either, because all the games, the socio-political, cultural games........except that this had long ago stopped being a game. It was death. And I knew it. This was my death.

And he was the only person who could have saved me. He was the last symbol of friendship, and if he failed me, he had proved the failure of all the others.

I was fighting for my life. I was fighting for hope. And it was Mick that gave it to me.

Energy was my essence, and I talked in wavelengths and stratospheres. As my relationships with humans lost their potency, so I found a fruitful intercourse with the universe giving me their reckoning.

I would see bright colours and auras around the lecturers, flashing lights swirling around the lecture theatres as they spoke. The energy of knowledge dancing a pretty path into the minds of a chosen few, and becoming intensely inspired by minute details of their learning, seeing worldly ramifications beyond belief. I would feel the vibes of the ancient town and felt totally full of goodness, entranced by sunsets and the beautiful surrounding countryside. I would spend hours wondering and wandering, sitting in the market square meditating as a band played and people danced, or watching the cars swirl, making me dizzy and confused. I was highly sensitive to others and the environment, and living in a hostile home, which I think more than participated in sending me off the edge. I was going to make this work, and never fall prey to the barbaric velocity of the previous year, and in my quest for perfection, and lack of stability, I became totally uncontrollable, full of zest, and nothing and no one could get me down. I would paint incessantly, all through the night, and stick all sorts of funny quotations up all over the house found in the lyrics of my favourite songs. The desperation of my sinking ideology was sending shock waves around the town. I felt on a mission to educate everyone, and share some of the joys that I felt. I couldn't understand how anyone could be so uninspired and boring and grey. I was fighting death. I just wanted to fly, and reach for the moon, see the stars and glitter until eternity. But my untamed chemical profusion had reached a point where my brain would constantly explode with myriads of perceptions and reality fireworks, all twisting and convoluted in their fight for recognition, banging on the door of my sanity.

Jerry did not know how high I had raised the stakes as a response to his total disinterest and damn right rudeness. He hadn't got a clue what had hit him as he watched me fly by at the speed of knots from one colourful encounter to the next. But when I continued knocking on his door in genuine friendship, he hurled me traumatically on my back, before dousing me in flames and slamming the door in my face. Well, traitor, who left me to be sexually abused while you got off your face on drugs?

Jerry did however suggest that I become and MP as in his eyes I was so interested in people, diversity and in what made them tick. I had a vast array of friends and acquaintances from all walks of life which is something Jerry, in his nerdiness, found rather astonishing.

I just did not want to be hurt again, which I suppose was the unconscious, self-protecting point. So I lifted myself very thoroughly out of everyone's reach. While still desperate to join in, I would never let myself; the wounds were too raw.

I spent months in complicated arithmetic and juggling equations with the facts and slippery figures hurled at me constantly by my subconscious. Sometimes I felt like I was doing such complicated balancing acts and investigations that I would have thousands of inter-related ideas all bubbling around, sniping for attention and conclusion to another matter. The television, books and radio all seemed intent on giving me deliciously personal messages, and people blared Truth to me that they had no idea they were passing on. I lived with the zest for adventure that comes with such discoveries, but also with the heavy weight of responsibility. I felt I had caused tragedies that I had heard on the news. Hundreds and thousands of people starving half way across the world, and I carried that as a personal burden on my shoulders, feeling directly responsible by my actions for the affair. And sometimes it would be such a small action, like moving a piece of paper, or not answering the door. My perceptions can probably never be scientifically proved, but it seemed real to me, the Chaos Theory taking a gruesome hold, and I would be full of a painful remorse, and desperately try to make things better and causing incessant worry over my behaviour.

My sensitivity led to me becoming a complete control freak, overtly worried about the side effects of every innocent thought, action or perceived symbolism. I lived in total fear of myself and the weighty burdens presented to me on a daily basis. Maybe it was my lack of control in the previous year that led me to balance the books so furiously, but whatever it was, it was absolutely exhausting, and I was fast running low on energy reserves. I was high as a kite; my heart seemed to be beating at 30,000 BPM, and my brain was whirring at double that speed, totally powerless and heading for self-destruction. I had left sanity behind a long time ago, and was clasping at the bottomless pit of complete collapse. My notions of reality were becoming ever more precarious and socially unacceptable, living in a world of self-derived, sensational symbolism that others could not appreciate, and cast aside as madness. All shared points of reference with people had gone, and they began to view me and my actions with the fear and distrust that accompany such misunderstanding. The clock of public opinion was ticking (for which I would be eternally grateful).

Nicky from Operation Raleigh came to stay for a few days. A friend from school came to stay too. She had been teaching in India. Jerry could not believe how well I got on with Nicky. He just didn't seem to understand. His small minded bigotry was so damaging, and all he read in my pain was his own story and not what was going on for me. He was judging me according to his own truth, which in all due respect to him, was somewhat limited, as he had only just come straight from school and not done much else. He had never met anyone like me before and had very, very fixed ideas of what I should be like. If he felt rejected by me in anyway, and he did have an interest in me sexually, he would get very annoyed and bitter. He didn't understand that I had been sexually abused. I wanted him to understand, and he wanted me to be his girlfriend. He punished me if he felt like I was rejecting him. He began to assume that I was being a snob by not going out with him. I had absolutely no control over the situation because my body would convulse in fear if I ever got close to him. I was in absolutely no position to have a boyfriend, due to the rape, but I would have loved to have been with him and the sanctuary that he so tenuously offered. That is what made the situation so incredibly painful and so difficult to get over.

He was a bastard, and used to dominate my house all the time. I had no refuge, I had no sanctuary, just some dictatorial, self-satisfied git who thought he could control me, and know what was going on for me, when in fact his actions, or lack of them, had been the cause of the problem in the first place. And it wasn't just a problem; this was going to take nearly twenty years of isolation and suffering to sort out. I had been raped in the most awful possible way. The situation was so loaded because I was furious with him. Furious for being let down, again, just when it mattered. I wanted to give him hell, but I would never tell him what had happened to me.

If he actually just looked at the facts, it wouldn't have been hard to guess.

Chris tried to hit me again. Jerry had had the bright idea of moving in with him. Jerry had asked me in for a cup of tea, after finding me trailing around in a destitute fashion outside, loitering around his house like a bad smell, flashing colours and furry fabrics decorating the streets. He left me with Chris, who hurled a few fists at me after I had thrown the pint of milk at him for losing his temper, fed up as I was with his personage. I screamed and screamed, and nearly blew the flat down. This was a flat with at least six locks on the door, being a drug den. My wails shock Chris out of his black humour, and I was relieved. He luckily couldn't wait to see the back of me, although Jerry seemed to find the whole matter remarkably funny at my expense.

Jerry and I did actually nearly manage to get it together. Apparently he was extremely happy about this.

Mick rang my mother a few times and helped me home.

This time things were looked into more carefully, having heard mountainous noises from the North East, and doctors were called for, post-haste. I was diagnosed as having manic depression and sent to hospital. A doctor called Dr Greenside came to the house. He looked at my bedroom, full of stuff in the weirdest orders, every last millimetre filled with cosmic and symbolic connections, a manic haze of misadventure, at finding the path to Jerry's heart and my other worldly missions that I had acquired. I was sent to hospital, believing myself to being going on holiday to the New Forest. That was the guise that I happily accepted, taking with me atlases, globes and other incredibly important paraphernalia to continue my studies. I wore an enormous floppy hat with yellow daffodils sticking out of it and a great big badge, proclaiming the fact that I was 65, having degenerated all sense of time. But this new abode was deeply removed from the frenetic overtures of university. It was a place of instilling peaceful reflection and was deeply sensitive. There were people there with lacerations and cuts all over their body; every centimetre. Everyone was highly traumatised, and in great emotional pain. And there was me, I couldn't believe I belonged there. There must have been some mistake. I got put on shed loads of drugs, all designed to keep me quiet, to stabilize me. That was the plan. I did run away on more than one occasion, and had a powerful horse needle injected into my behind to sedate me. I was to be drugged up to the eyeballs, and then slowly have my dosage bought down, until I could return to normal. Whatever that was?

This whole process was to take about a year, and I don't think I ever returned to a so called wondrous state of normal, having totally lost my confidence and being a shadow of my former self. But maybe that was a good thing. Maybe I became like everybody else, and actually felt things like fear, and self-loathing sometimes, instead of negating everything bad, and riding high on a mania that made you believe you could do anything filled with the courage of your own convictions. Maybe it was about time that I faced my emotions, fears and failures head on, honestly, and with no turning back and knocked them on the head.

## 1.9 - DABBLING WITH PIRANHAS

I got over this first recognised attack in the fullness of time, and was put on the rudimentary, first port of call, Lithium to keep me in balance. Time had passed. It was now September, that was a full six months out of my life, taken up by being a zombie, lifesaving drugs and ambiguous doctor's reports, even though I had only spent a month in hospital. Condemned to half a year of staring in front of you, dribbling; focusing on nothing in particular, save the deep rooted void filling your being to expansion, and showing no sign of life whatsoever. A friend would come and see me every week for lunch, her bright blue hair lifting my spirits. But I showed total confusion at her laughter and vivacity, falling asleep at the strain of it all, and being so woolly. I began to be a little annoyed with myself for this state of being, but there was nothing I could do. I was forcibly on these pills, apparently for my own safety, and I just had to play the game. I was a mouse caught in a very intricate trap, with no form of escape, and no hope of imminent death, just a very long torturous process, which might eventually lead to escape, and renewal, not that I had any contemplation of what normal life might involve. Notions of time had departed leaving shell-less days, punctuated briefly by a meal or two, of which I tasted nothing anyway. I was like a baby, totally dependent and unable to do anything for myself. I felt a terrible sense of loss, as if my whole world had caved in, although I had no notion of why and what to do about it. No form of counselling was offered, no nurses came to my door, as I had been on private healthcare, (which does not provide for CPNs), and my once jam-packed busy lifestyle had flown. My nest was empty and the truth seemed unexplainable.

I suppose this was preferable to flying around at the rate of knots in an acid like trance with ideas popping out of your head faster than you could say Jack Robinson, getting mixed up and convoluted, producing babies and incestuous relationships themselves in their dance for freedom and expression. It was a time of reflection and healing, but not very sophisticated at that. The food for thought that I had collected was distilled and refined and what came out? Well, as you might have guessed, it was thoughts of Jerry. My bedroom had turned from a jungle of colours and concepts, to a calm sea of tranquillity, but yet it was still Jerry that I turned to for inspiration. And turn definitely I did.

I was picking through all our encounters, mesmerizing them for detail and meaning. The one thought that kept popping out at me, springing me with surprise was Jerry's obviously benevolent idea that I should go home and get to know local people. This was rather an unusual adaptation to my life, having gone to boarding school, and subsequently all my friends had been littered around the country, and the ones I knew from home were working in London. However, I gave it a go, and headed off to the local art school.

To tell you the truth I was doomed. Doomed as I had been before. I pandered to their requirements and did the clever thing of concepts and portrayed all my emotions on the page, as I had painstakingly learned previously, but I was not a drug addict, nor did I live in a bed sit, and to their knowledge did not suffer from any kind of trauma whatsoever.

All they were aware of was my posh accent and tutors' minds became set. Set against the fact that there were people who lived in different ways to them. Set against the fact that being a heroin addict is not necessarily a prerequisite for being a great artist, which seemed to be the case. Set against the fact that anyone other than the financially hard up might be sensitive enough to produce anything of lasting aesthetic value, or perhaps even suffered, however minutely to them, in their own way. I had entered an ecosystem that was stagnant and rotten for me, with little room to flourish and grow, except in the direction of the Exit.

1:10 - INTERVIEW WITH MY MOTHER

'Begin, baby boy, to recognise your mother with a smile.'

Virgil. Ecologues no. 4, 1.60

'When you first went to hospital I,

a) Didn't know anything about manic depression, and thought that you'd be cured after your aftercare, and

b) I suppose as a carer one didn't see the signs at the very beginning as one does now.'

'How did you feel about me before I was diagnosed? You must have thought me an utter nightmare.'

'And the answer to that is yes. Emphatically. You were a teenager, rebellious, and therefore it was difficult to separate the two. Because one didn't know that you were ill, and to think five years ago you were on drugs.'

'And how did you take the news of my manic depression.'

'It was quite a shock, a totally new area that one had never been in. I don't think people know about it. When you started manic you were fun and bubbly and slightly over the top, and therefore you might have been drinking. You were always good with people, right at the beginning. It was only until you went to Durham that your mind started racing.'

'As a carer what support do you have?'

'There was no CPN (community psychiatric nurse), until you came out of hospital. I was rung by the GP to have a meeting with the psychiatrist, but you wouldn't see the psychiatrist.

I had no life of my own. I couldn't ask people to the house, because I didn't know how you were going to behave. You were on so many drugs that I had to pay attention, and you couldn't be left alone. The CPN was a lifeline; I was very lucky with Bill. I could have rung up about anything and they would come over anytime. They came, by appointment about once a week.

It was very tiring; you were shaking (from the medication), and accident prone as a result. I never knew what was going to happen next. You would be up at three in the morning with the wireless blaring, painting in the kitchen wildly. It was a twenty-four hour thing, but I had to get my sleep too.

It took you five years to accept your illness, and I was isolated from leading a normal life. It was immensely tiring and draining, and there is a certain amount of stigma attached. When the Robinson's rang up to say that Will had broken his leg, I couldn't leave you in the house on your own. I had to ring my sister and get her to drive the three hours over. You couldn't be left for a second. You behaved oddly out shopping, which was very hard to take. You had a passion for yellow, and got really aggressive with the shop assistant for not having it. I never knew how your moods were going to swing.

You made so many things up as your mind would race. I didn't think you were raped or abused, because of all the other things you had said. There were so many stories, and you didn't say that you had been raped at the very beginning. You appeared as a person I didn't know as Charlotte. There was so much screaming and yelling, and I felt like a piece of chewed string afterwards. I went into zombie mode; auto pilot, living day by day. I could laugh and joke, as that was my safety net.

When you were sectioned that was the most painful thing, so horrendous. It makes me want to cry just thinking about it; so horrendous. There was an irritating social worker, and you were calling him a fucking bastard. You knew you were being trapped, and I couldn't get through to you that if you took your pills you wouldn't have to go. But you just let rip. He said that he wasn't going to be treated like that.

After half an hour of swearing at the man you stalked out of the room, upstairs, knowing that you were going (into hospital). When you're manic you like to have baths and order things obsessively. You could have been cutting your throat. But you had a bath, and packed my mother's suitcase, ready to go, and went down calmly. It's such a Jekyll and Hyde. At 11.00pm the ambulance came round. I went with you and the ambulance man. Laughing was the only way to keep me sane. You kept standing up looking at the view, it was a twenty minute journey and you could have flipped again.

We got to hospital and I had to leave. I had to go back with the social worker. He said that I could cry now. And I was buggered if I was going to cry. He took me back home, and I asked him about sailing. I was really irritated, fucking man; he'd just sectioned my daughter. I drank half a bottle of whiskey, having had to go back to the house I'd just left through divorce. I was in floods of tears and shaking like an aspirin leaf. It really took the stuffing out of me. There was my baby going off in a straight jacket. There was enormous tension in getting you to see the doctors in the first place. Don't you see that you did have to be sectioned?

It was painful; you were in hospital for a month. I went every day. You decided you didn't want to see me. It was painful to see you drugged up. You tried to kiss one of the patients, and I rang up to say. They kept a more watchful eye on the two of you.

I moved house, with a new doctor, and you came home. It was difficult because you were so drugged up. You shaved your legs, but took half your shin off. It didn't hurt because you were so drugged up. You burnt your hand with boiling water. Things like that happened the whole time, and I always had to be watching you.

Because you were drugged up the whole time, but awake, you had to be amused, as your concentration was zilch. A normal patient convalescing would read, watch TV, but you couldn't watch TV because it spooked you, you couldn't read and that's why your painting was like it was. And that's why I did papier-mâché things, and I ended up making it all. Everything you did had to be childlike. You could not face anything with horrors of life, like the News.

The whole day was basically being a zombie. You got through sheets of paper, painting, but with no concentration. You have only just started reading in the last year. When you walked, you walked like a marathon runner. I got black toes. At Ben's party you decided to leave, and raced for the tube. I couldn't keep up and half my toes are black now. The doctor said you shouldn't have gone to London, and he was right.

I had to take you in a taxi to see the psychiatrist in Harley Street. And you attacked me verbally the whole way. Difficult as it was, it was me who had to take you to see the doctor. And you kept trying to get out of the door of the taxi. I did feel sorry for the driver. You pinned me into a corner, blamed me for being injected the first time in hospital, do you remember, when you ran away; and you really pinned me.

After having seen the doctor you were cowering in the waiting room between a chest and a chair. I'm amazed they didn't help me more. Walking down Wimpole Street every time I tried to talk to you, and for some unknown reason it was quite busy at the time, you threw yourself in doorways. One had to laugh really, in this yellow duster skirt. Rather pretty doorways, railings and steps. You screamed, 'don't touch me,' and cowered as if I was going to hit you. Wimpole Street was the longest street I've ever had to walk down, and you threw yourself into every doorway.

We were meant to be going to the very smart chemist with those lovely pots, Webb and something. At the traffic lights we had to wait there and there were a lot of well dressed, pinstriped suited men, waiting to cross, and you screamed if I went anywhere near you. Oh God, it was dreadful. You then stalked off. I had to go to the chemist and get your pills. Having thrown yourself in doorways you then disappeared. And the sooner I got one of these pills in you it would calm you down, so I had to get the pills.

I got the pills, and went home, hoping that you'd get back there. I was actually in quite a state, because I was seriously worried about you. And I rang up your father. I was a dithering wreck, because if you didn't take the pill they were going to come and section you. You came back, screamed and yelled, threw yourself at doorways. It's actually quite scary because you can't help, and you've got someone who is uncontrollable. And my job, the only thing I had to do was get you to take that pill, but you were fighting, and that fighting is seriously powerful fighting. Mentally, physically, it's really scary. I don't mean this unkindly, but with a sane person you can discuss and reason, talk to them, and they'll know what you're trying to say.

There is always one last thing, which I'm always very grateful for, there is something with you, when you're at your worst that always listens to me. There is a little core in you, after hours of fighting. Throwing yourself at doors, screaming, and you are hysterical, which makes it very difficult to get through to you.

They would have come and sectioned you if you hadn't taken the pill by six o'clock. You eventually took your pill, which immediately (15 minutes later) calmed you down. They are amazing those pills how they do work really (Haloperidol). Anyway we then got in the car and drove home. At the end of that you do feel like a wet rag, a bit of chewed string. It totally takes the stuffing out of you. You can't lead a life.

A lot of friends have said that they don't know how I've managed because they could not have taken the mental and verbal abuse. I haven't really done anything for the last five years. I suppose it's because you're tired and drained. You're always working on overdrive.

You lost your confidence, every time you became ill, and it might not be so much confidence, but the fact that you had to pick yourself up, and get a job. You're actually a very gutsy, plucky person, and if you think how debilitated you were when you came out of hospital, on drugs, shaking, dribbling, that you actually got yourself that job in the shop. I mean from your point of view it's a major achievement. It's quite difficult as a carer to have to listen to your anger at what you think you've lost, but you've gained other things. Being the plucky little soul that you are, you solider on.

You and I have actually got on terribly well, we've always had fun, and this is a Mother talking, rather than a carer. And it's quite painful sometimes to see how much you've hated me. And I suppose because we've been thrown together there's a lot of resentment on your part, which is quite understandable, but still quite painful. It's not just me, although I've had it for five years. But when, I was thinking of how it affects the boys. I suppose it's like, when you're on a low, if you're pulled down; you like to pull us all down with you. It totally throws them. This is going back more to the illness, that when you're manic, you're actually playing power games, which is quite difficult to cope with.

You started off by being manic in the spring, and in the autumn you became depressed, and then you started getting manic and depressed at the same time.

I was very upset that I didn't get the support from the doctors and CPN. When one rang them up for help, they would relate it back to you first before they did anything, which made you as an ill patient extremely angry and resent me. But then having said that they were covering their backs as you were over the age of consent. One did get their support, but it was second to you. As a carer I was alone to look after you.

Bill did say; 'I'm meant to be getting all the shit not you,' but unless he was there all day every day it was me that had to do the looking after. I said to the doctors, 'I'm meant to be looking after Charlotte as a carer, and I need to be able to talk to you without Charlotte necessarily knowing about her condition.' They then, I think, understood where I was coming from.

You did get deeply resentful, but having said that you would never ring the doctor, you always wanted me to ring the doctors and nurses. It's only recently that you've started ringing them yourself.

'I suppose it's because I didn't accept my illness, which was mainly due to the stigma I felt I was getting.'

'I think that's exactly it.'

'And God shall wipe away all tears from their eyes;

And there shall be no more death, neither sorrow,

69

Nor crying, neither shall there be any more pain:

For the former things are passed away.

And he that sat upon the throne said, Behold, I made

All things new.  And he said unto me,

Write:  for these words are true and faithful.'


Bible

Revelations ch.21, v.4

## PART 2 - BRAVE SQUAW

I was sitting in my mother's beautiful garden. It was the same one she had for all the other seasons too, except summer was tops. Bumble bees, butterflies, you name it; it was there, including some very strange insects no-one had ever seen before.

We were visited by some strange people too. Strange but true, and they heralded a dawning and a death for me, and Mummy. Pink corduroys that were falling from my hips due to weight loss and low funds and a delicious pasta salad beckoned. As did two men with stories that spanned the emotional spectrum. Two of the loveliest men to grace her table and the reason was not clear. Ideally, some might say that the fine psychic abilities of one were there to help the other, but from where I stood different ramifications were playing themselves out.

Reading the psychic mind I deftly slipped out of a dangerous liaison with the other and was quickly projected to noticing the unbelievable attachment I had formed with my mother.

Eight years of caring, against unbelievable odds had formed a bond of iron and steel that was hard to break unless you had the magician's key. He had it in his mind, and he gave it to me. So strong was our attachment that we were beginning to erode. The seeds of time had begun to take their toil and a new cycle was born. These men heralded an evolution of consciousness.

I moved to London soon afterwards. The eight years of misery of mental illness left behind on the hearth. Olly had moved to London too. All I needed was a friend to confide in; someone who saw the emotional drawstrings of a wounded heart.

My mother waited for me for two years; bless her. Life handed her her golden watch. She deserved every chime.

Olly and I shared a few moments, here and there, in London. His flat, cafes in the King's Road, punctuated heavily by the blowy, autumnal walks across Battersea Park that joined our two domains. Leaves rose high into the air to be buffeted by the stormy winds as we aired our inner turmoil. True to form, he did most of the talking. I had no words. I could only piece together my story from the words of another. And he talked. The pain etched across his face was visible, laudable, laughable in its absurdity, but still we strode on, determined in our cause.

I had procured a job. I had literally been blown in with the gusts of Chelsea, energetically driven through the doors of the French interiors shop and straight under the eagle eye of

Emily, who was ever so busy, as per usual, setting up shop. I sometimes wonder the games she used to play as a little girl. Emily gave me a cursory glance and on hearing my posh voice echoing with questions, smiled from ear to ear and decided immediately that I was exactly the sort of girl she was after.

The stability that job offered me was quite extraordinary. I felt safe for the first time in years. I was in London of all places, working in the middle of Chelsea and surrounded by beautiful things. It seemed as though my life has taken a turn for the better. I enjoyed a peaceful walk through the streets of Pimlico, past the heavily laden antique shops of Pimlico Green and up through the bustle of cafes at Sloane Square. And I had my independence. Gone were the days when I longed to save the world, instead I was saving myself and enjoying every minute of it.

I cleaned the silver and the glass with precision every morning, and enjoyed a hot Panini at Starbucks every lunchtime. This was only for three days a week at present as I had over the last year completed an aromatherapy diploma and was busy trying to set up a business.

So the shop became central to my life. Emily turned out to be something of a teacher. She had a raging temper and frequently had us all reeling. What could have been a wonderful learning ground for us all in the delights of language instead became a sullen, silent place, and we all colluded in our turns to stand near the window and away from her roving eye.

My head became full of memories and dreams in this silent world. Looking out onto the streets for inspiration for a better life and always wishing for the future. I spotted a taxi with the words emblazoned; 'Sicily is too big for the girl'. It got my mind moving in the direction of leaving London. It got my mind foraging for answers to questions unknown. It took me to strange places that did not yet have words or colours or meaning. It got me projecting.

At about this time my brother Will and I were about to embark on a move to my stepmother's house to join the rest of the family. My Dad had recently re-married and they were living in a large, roomy house in Fulham. Estate agents had been showing around potential buyers over the last few months and Will and I had been diligently modelling the computer, the sink and all aspects of living to interested passers by. I was sad to leave Pimlico. I had such memories of there. The streets were littered with an easy country charm. Labrador's and wellington boots were a frequent occurrence and I loved the place for its terrific absurdity and juxtaposition to the decadence of neighbouring Chelsea and sombreness of Westminster. Our haven in the heart of London surrounded by wonderful people and friends. But we packed our bags and left.

On arrival at my stepmother's house I made myself at home and enjoyed the delicious nightly feasts of Jamie Oliver that she made for us. Tom, my youngest stepbrother, having just left university kept slightly different hours to the rest of us. I was on my way to bed one night, wearing woolly socks and wrapped up in a secure dressing gown, feeling slightly weary after standing on my feet for eight hours a day and enjoying the snowy round trip of a few hours to work. This physical activity, needless to say, had a wonderful grounding effect on my mentality. The TV had been left on and was starring fuzzily to me. I leant down to find the remote but as I did so the room turned to chill and a voice came out of the ether, proclaiming loudly; 'The Importance of the World to find a Bride'.

I froze on the spot for a moment, recognising this supposed psychic event, as the hairs on my arm had all stood on end and there was certainly no-one about in the room issuing such a communication. The volume on the TV was not on, and it still maintained its fuzzy illusion so could not be the culprit. I switched it off and plodded up the stairs to bed, mulling this thought over in my head, slightly at a deeper level, full of glee to be back in the saddle again.

I thought about it all day at work, and the next before deciding on a plan. The plan seemed so ludicrous that I enlisted Will's advice and it took me a long time to pluck up courage to do anything, but Will urged me on, if not to close doors more than anything else.

What I eventually did, and feeling extremely absurd about it, was to drive down in the darkness to an address I had for Jerry. He was first on the list of people that I wanted to marry. In fact there was no other. So off I headed, and it was with shaking hands that I knocked on his door. To no avail, he had moved house several months ago, although I did manage to squeeze an address out of the new owner, with my hands shaking merrily as I wrote it down.

Again with a push from Will, I launched into action and began my second plan of attack. I located his new house, many miles from London. A neighbour asked who I was looking for and pointed me in the right direction. One cursory glance in the car parked outside told me all that I needed to know. It was abounding in toys. He had children. That was that. I did not even know that he was married.

So my hunt was over. There were no more doors to knock on. I thought to myself. 'I have done my bit. If you want me to get married God, well then I shall await new direction'. I did not have to wait long.

I did not notice it at first as the big boxes from Paris came pouring in. I didn't notice as the items were all carefully unwrapped and logged in. I didn't notice as we placed them all meticulously around the shop.

When I did notice it hit me as hard as a brick wall with its certainty. It gazed at me and sung a strange, long forgotten lullaby of peace and tranquillity. It announced to me so smoothly, so intently and leaving me no room for question. The bowl that sat before me had two words painted on it, which were 'Just Married'.

To anyone else it may have seemed like a generous offering, a gift of celebration. To my eye and my eye alone this bowl dictated to me a choice that was beyond reason, and reason that was beyond question. For every time I looked at the bowl I read the unforgettable words; 'Just Marry Sid'. I thought of Sid Edwin, a man I had once loved dearly.

God, those words filled me with peace. A deep ancient lullaby soothed me as I gazed at those infinite words. They seemed so tender, so loving, so full of promise and yet so distant and so far away. The bowl hypnotised me. It held me softly in its spell. It wove a weave of enchantment around me that I gently allowed myself to enter. The dark storm clouds of the night that I had dwelt in for over a decade were beginning to shift. I could feel them dissipate in my mind, and in their place came a rhapsody.

The images and feelings that sang to me took me back to when I was 18 and he 21. We had lived in a van; my van, decorated beautifully so that it was decked out like a rainbow. And we had parked by the side of a nature reserve. So sublime were the hues and textures of nature, guiding us through that spring and early summer. So bright and round was the moon gazing at us benignly from the clear, warm sky. The stars sang and danced for us. Words were not spoken; none were needed. We were young innocents with heavy hearts and ideal minds. How we loved and cherished the other. How we made our worlds around each other.

But it had come to a crashing halt. I had become ever-increasingly depressed with my lack of direction, lack of certainty and he had been mortally wounded by my blow. I had chosen to up-sticks and leave, first to Zimbabwe on Operation Raleigh and next to Durham University to study Maths and Philosophy.

Of course, we both floundered. In each other we had found the support that we were looking for. We shared a passion that spilled from the bedroom into our bones, and our common unity was a bond that no-one could break. There was no question.

Except I did break it; I did question. I was asked by a book; 'What would you do if you and the one you loved most were in two adjoining rooms of which there was no way out. You would both die in ten seconds. If either pressed the buzzer in their room they would save themselves, but the other would die.' I had mulled that question over for some months before I met Sid and had never found the answer. That was the puzzle that I had been trying so desperately, through the dissolution, to solve.

I did not realise it at the time, but Sid became a heroin addict shortly after I left him. He carved up my van with a chain saw. I asked him to come and live with me in Durham but he refused and told me that he was going to commit suicide. We both died that day.

I continued this relationship against the express wishes of a shamanic healer who had declared without question; 'Sid is bad for you'.

How could she know the drawstrings of my heart? How could she sense my isolation and loneliness and still yet dare to declare such a fact. The fact unwittingly became a factor that ultimately led to our downfall, and perhaps if she had not presupposed we would have done our business then, all those years ago. And perhaps we would have not, and life may have shown yet more audacity in mind. Who knows?

As I looked at the bowl all the memories came flooding back. I thought of the time Sid had said to me that if I was still listening to Simon and Garfunkel when I was 28 he would marry me. I was 28. I let the bowl speak to me some more. I let the thunder and pain of the past disappear and as spring rose around us I felt my heart come into bud once more for the first time in ten years. The darkness was gone. There was new life, the shadowy spell had been lifted and all I felt was hope for the future. The bowl had never lost its certainty. Never lost its message of expectation; its tidings of the path being laid out so brilliantly before me.

A few weeks before I turned 29 I rang Sid's mother.

Sid's mother spoke with a tone that told a story of what I was not sure. So did her quickness to get my number and let Sid ring me back. He did, and I delighted in listening to the intonations of his voice on my answerphone again and again until I plucked up the courage to ring him.

Sid had just appeared from the pub when I rang him. He sounded tickled pink to hear from me and we laughed and giggled like old friends. He gave me some dates to come down and see him. I chose the nearer of the two weekends because the second date was my birthday.

So off I toddled, filled with glee and in-trepidation. I drove through Black Friars and turned left onto the A15 down to Henton. I turned off at the junction indicated and wended my merry way through the villages and lanes that greeted me. As I came to the gates of the enormous stud farm where Sid worked I typed in the aforementioned code and drew nearer his cottage.

He came out to greet me with a ready smile and a helpful hug. I was drawn into his cottage whereupon he and a colleague had to literally disappear for a few hours on a vet's call. I was left in the kitchen with another lady who was also new to the game.

Sid re-appeared with apologies and a delicious lunch of smoked salmon. We got talking about jewellery, a penchant of his. I had collected together all my broken gems and bought a few more besides in the hope that he would repair them and redesign them. Unwittingly he was to do this in more ways than one.

All was going swimmingly. Sid began talking about the benefits of marriage, to which I retorted rather defensively that the only benefits of marriage were tax benefits. He laughed. However ugliness appeared in the form of his question as to whether I would like to lie on his bed and read a book. I suffered major panic at the thought of such an idea and had to make a speedy escape back to London.

My dealings with men over the last ten years amounted to one or two married friends of mine. I did not expect a hot-blooded young male eager for my flesh, and he was certainly not going to have it. I racked my brains on the journey home and decided to follow my brother Ben's advice, whether or not it was appropriate in this case. I rang Sid and told him how I felt. Sid listened gently to my overtures, but did he really understand the depth of my despair?

How could he ever begin to recognise the emotional spectrum I had gained since our last friendship? The sexuality which had played such a prevalent part in days gone by had died a tragic death and was only just beginning to re-surface in an incredibly fragile ecosystem.

It had been ten years since I had been sexually abused at university. Ten years, which had taken me so far down the path of mental illness that I had to claw at the cage for survival. I had it now, after years of torture, but I had felt so hard the blows of stigma and rejection that I never wanted to let go of the thought processes that had so deftly flooded my mind. Part of the scientist in me still remained. Enough to want to take up the reins of discovery and explore this world of meaning I had been so expertly handed.

My friend Alexandra would ring me up constantly and complain laudably that I had totally missed the point, but I wanted to be special, I wanted to have a Divine Purpose. I wanted this to be real, so I ignored her protestations that thoroughly encompassed my own and kept on hurtling.

The root cause came out one day when I was feeding round the paddocks with Sid. I had left my cigarettes back at his house and was becoming rather tetchy. I got in the pick-up truck and said to him adamantly; 'I am absolutely determined to have a full and happy sex life'. He giggled at this, and it was only later when we were back at his cottage on his bed, he leaned over to kiss me and I froze. The tears came pouring down my cheeks, as I accessed part of me that had remained forbidden for ten years, and as he leant round to hug me I had an enormous panic attack in his arms. He held me close, he held me tight. He did not let me go. He did not let me fall. I felt safe now that he knew my secret, had seen my fear. He was my accomplice now. He had made the decision to be near.

I longed to be loved. I remember a holiday in Dorset with my family. I had glanced on a newspaper headline about a woman who could not have a sexual relationship, even twenty-five years after she had been abused. I remember breaking down in tears at this, full of frustration and hatred for my circumstances. My father could not stop the tears flowing either, because it tore his insides out at my predicament. How we both cried in that sunny Dorset garden, and how we both felt so very vulnerable and powerless.

Sid talked about marriage again the next time I met him, sitting huddled in a busy cafe in Henton. He pressed his point and only let it slip away when the neighbouring table started pricking up their ears at my defensive overtures.

Sid, for his part had had a hell of a ride. Eight years of heroin addiction, throughout which he had continually worked, with racehorses in the main. This had culminated in thirteen months of therapy at the Tale Centre based in Howe; a residential rehab where he had received a torment of verbal abuse in the form of group therapy. Social Services had stopped the practice of residents having to dig their own graves and girls and boys alike having their hair shaved off. The place reverberated like an army boot camp and Sid carried the scars of his battering deep in his heart. But he held his head high; too high for my liking, and with too many people. It spoke of a pain and a shame that wore hard.

Sid isolates. When I met him for the first time he had two or three sexual partners, both male and female. He found his intimacy and love in sexual pleasures. He did not know how to talk. I do not really know what he had been through but I know how I found him.

Free from addiction but deeply scarred, and living on a schizoid's paradise at the stud with an iron barred gate or two to protect him from the real world.

I suggested to him very quickly that he study psychology, and put his abilities to good use. He leapt at this like a man who had not eaten for years. He consumed books, ordered courses, made phone calls in precious minutes off until he had information at his fingertips and he chose. Within weeks he was on a foundation course in psychodynamic counselling at a very good college in London.

I told him of my marriage bowl, sitting in his local pub one day. We took over our usual leather sofa and feasted on the most delicious food. Sid was treating me on the handout of a Sheik who kept his horses at the yard. I told him of the bowl. I omitted the voice from the clouds. His heart leapt. I carried on talking, bringing another's metaphors swiftly into the equation, to protect myself because I was unsure on what ground I stood.

My trips to Henton increased in frequency and soon it came to the end of my six-month tenancy on my flat in London. My choice was made simpler still as in my Jungian way I would walk into a card shop for example, and the first card I would pick out happened to have inscribed on it, 'Leaving London party'. My mind was so there with Sid. It had been in the last five months I stood staring at that bowl. My desire had already carved its path; my desire to do God's Will. I did not really question my own will too much on this occasion. I was seduced by the beautiful Hentonshire countryside and my escape from the endless streets of London. I was desperate to find the answers to my mental illness and gain some understanding. Luckily for me Sid did not need that much persuading. How could he after all he had been through. I was probably the answer to his prayers. At that point at least.

My brother Will had found me a room through his connections from his days in Henton. It was large, although somewhat dark and only had a single bed. I lived there for four months in what felt like to me, in those cold winter days, my dark dungeon, stemming largely from the fact that my social connections in Henton, bar Sid, were nil. Sid would complain about having to come on the long trip to visit me in the evenings and I was in truth very lonely. It was a far cry from the evenings I used to spend with friends at Cafe Rouge in Knightsbridge, laughing and talking and re-working conversations we had had a million times before. It was a far cry from the colour and sounds of London where I had felt, although imperceptibly at the time, at home.

I had bought the bowl with me. The 'Just Marry Sid' bowl. It seemed to have lost its appeal since I had plucked it so certainly off the busy shop shelves. It still held its logic, although it seemed miserably misplaced in this other setting. I tried to explain this to Sid one night after he had run away and had an affair with another girl. He had taken her up to Scotland and I was devastated. My bitter-sweet world of meaning seemed rapidly to be falling apart, but I still clung to this way of thinking that had brandished me mad in the hope of one day finding my way out of the maze of metaphors that clouded my mind. I used to sing to the Gods sweet laments, pleading for help and certainty. They only offered three words of consolation, of meaning. 'Just Marry Sid' was the answer to my prayers. These words reverberated round my being finding little sanctuary in which to rest easy.

I wondered if this was really what I wanted at all. I was doing it for the love of God, not for the love of Sid. In truth, what did I really feel about him anyway? Tenderness is a word that springs to mind, as it did twelve years ago. Tenderness, mixed with fear. Fear that I could not achieve the mission that had been handed to me so unmistakably. Fear that Sid, for all his beauty, honesty, and goodness was not the right man to help me evaporate the uncertainty that still remained after being sexually abused all those years ago. I really needed an incredibly steady, grounded man and for all Sid's constancy, of which I was more than certain, there remained a large abyss in my emotional life of which I was acutely aware.

He wanted to chase, he wanted to play. He wanted life to be full of all the joys he had known since he had discarded his burden of addiction. But my burden still wore hard. It was not obvious to see. I hid it well, so scared was I of its all-encompassing terrors. He did not understand my reticence, my uncertainty and just wanted to jump in pure delight of being alive, and being with me. How he loved me. His nostalgia was purely divine, but deathly terrifying.

Our sexual escapades hadn't really got off the ground. Ever since he abducted another female I felt under undue pressure to perform. I had stipulated rather stupidly that I didn't mind him having other sexual encounters while I was getting my feet off the ground and I suppose that trail blazed low self-esteem all over the horizon. However, when push came to shove I was totally distraught. He didn't want to take my phone calls and when he did there was a high-pitched giggle accompanying them. I suppose I felt very alone. I unwrapped my marriage bowl; wondering its purpose. There were so many ulterior motives playing themselves out, so many other outcomes of this journey that heralded peace and love and yet went under the cover of this more sinister guise.

Fortune came beckoning in the form of Social and Health Care. I worked for a really wonderful lady who took me under her wing and embraced my illness with a heartfelt smile, knowing full well what I was going through as she had been a social worker for many a year.

We worked hard, and the work itself was fascinating. I would prepare all the documents and take the minutes of the weekly meeting on children's issues, where doctors, lawyers, social workers and staff would discuss the rights and their permutations of children being considered for care. Most of the children came from homes rife in mental illness or drug abuse and it was a crash course in empathy and ramifications intended.

Melissa, who had taken me under her wing, wanted me to take the permanent job and train as a social worker. I had told her about my background and that of Sid's and she was more than a guardian angel to me, encouraging me in so many ways. I loved every last minute of my time there, but unfortunately did not realise my good fortune until too late.

I don't know how much Sid still fed into my illusions of marriage, but he was certainly helping himself to a veritable feast of psychodynamic counselling. He delved into his new subject with an insatiable appetite and used to amuse himself with mind maps, which would send even the clearest of heads slightly round the bend. He was happy and had found his dream. He had found a language and a context, which suited every aspect of his being, and if it did not, it only presented a new sumptuous puzzle of permutations to unravel with great joy, and the compassion in his heart could understand what words would never explain. I saw that time and time again, and grew to love him.

His work at the stud was arduous and hard. Long hours, temperamental weather conditions and reckless horses all beckoned a difficult time and moments of relaxation were found in a long, hot bath at the end of the day and the depths of a glass of red wine. He would eat for England and yet it all fell off him as he did another round of feeding in the paddocks and mucked out yet another multitude of stables. He was happy there.

The colts and fillies were kept separately, and he would be up at six every morning, enormous food sacks on his back. He'd park the pick-up truck around several paddocks and venture into these fields filled with a dozen or so horses at a time. They'd all charge at him, trying to take bits out of his flesh, which more often than not they did. They'd turn their backs on him and let out a great big kick before fighting for their place in the pecking order. He'd duly fill up all the buckets, check their legs for injury and carry on to the next field. Quite a way to start the day, particularly as his alarm would only go off moments before, and he'd just pull on his clothes and be out of the door. At about eight he'd be allowed back in for a cup of coffee and breakfast.

Sid did have to protect himself from these untouched thoroughbreds. He'd tell me how the colts could put up with a whack across the nose, and take it in their stride. He said, however, that the fillies could not. Once hit, a filly would remember it for the rest of her life.

80

Sid and I had begun to sleep together. Ever since he procured another girlfriend and promptly whisked her off to Scotland for a week I felt destitute. I sat in my room contemplating my fate. I did not have much to do, or be concerned about. I just had to marry this man. So I enticed him to my mum's house for his birthday and showered him with presents. My mother plied us full of wine and spirits and we took off to bed, where I had sex for the first time in ten years, and we both smiled. He felt so nice, warm and smelly. My own feelings about sexuality spiralled out of control as I tried to get closer to Sid, as I thought it was God's Will.

It was all grins at breakfast the following morning. All grins and scrambled eggs and we set off back to Henton with a spring in our steps, happy that we had at last ventured into the next phase of our relationship. And I was happy to meet this man once more where we had left off all those years ago. I loved him, I cherished him, and I would have given him my heart forever had I thought he had the skills to care for it. He did now. So off we toddled.

New Year bought welcome relief in a change of residence. A friend of a friend had a cottage near Heningham down a little country lane. The house itself was so remote it was not recorded on the postcode register, and I took up residence in the middle of January dancing around the room in my bed-sheets with glee.

Both my parents had recently moved house, as had my brother, so I found myself kitted out with all a girl could want. Curtains, pictures, washing machines and hovers all wended their merry way through my doors and made themselves, and me, very much at home.

How happy I was! I even had a small terrace garden and a whole host of plants. I bought some deliciously Cornish blue planters and filled them with aromatic herbs. I dithered over a mellow red rose, only to invite it into the already overflowing garden. I enjoyed many a lazy summer afternoon playing around with watering cans and my outside tap, which I held in high esteem. I had many a dreamy evening, glass of wine in hand, watching hedgehogs run across the lawn.

I was now a mere ten minutes drive away from Sid on the stud, and a deeply furrowed path was created between his house and mine. We used to share most evenings together, consuming a bottle of wine and taking to bed.

Sid was working hard on the stud, as it was foaling season, and he was on call a few nights a week and often had to appear blurry eyed at all hours of the morning to pull a young foal from its mother. They tried to get them all born this side of New Year as all thoroughbreds have their birthday on January 1$^{st}$ and it would not do the foal's racing potential any good to be up against colts or fillies 360 days older.

The foals were removed from their mothers at some point, which had to be done only two in one day, such was the consternation of the galloping, grieving mares. Sid's house was right next door to the yearling yard. He would go and check them out each night, feeding them and making sure any rugs were okay. I'd go with him more often than not, taking time to have a chin wag with some of the cuter ones. The separation anxiety they faced when they were first boxed, having spent all of their previous life in a herd in the paddock, was huge, and the sweating and weight loss would go on for days.

All this time my work life had become more interesting and varied. The cogs of Social and Health Care were becoming more finely oiled and life had increased in speed and value. My office consisted of two other temps, namely Tim and Alexia. Tim was quiet and bookish, on course to study publishing at Henton University, and used to punctuate our high velocity conversation with manly humour and philosophical temperament. Alexia was a unique case of incongruity with her surroundings. Whilst all the middle aged ladies who frequented the Council were worried about the social ills of the world, Alexia would relay in great delight and exquisite detail as to the choice of champagne she drank with her husband the previous evening and spend hours searching the website so that we could all admire the cabin of her 47$^{th}$ luxury cruise. We all loved her for it. Social and Health Care was the sort of place where even the birds were looked after zealously. Out of the window every day could be spied one of the ladies filling numerous bird feeders with a feast fit for a king.

In fact the whole of Henton was like that. There was a distinct do-good vibe that permeated the entire town and I had not got as far as Elrig yet, which abounded in earth mothers and news of meditation and yoga courses. Up in my previous abode of north Henton, which was reserved for the more middle class of mind, politeness and kindness permeated the atmosphere like a warmly fitting glove. Mothers and fathers alike would cycle the streets on strange contraptions that encompassed not only one but two children among it and they had a distinct air of summer breeze about them. I had entered a city of cultural charm that wended its way through all the inhabitants and held them close.

Sid and I had embarked upon a strange territorial space. I had no inner dialogue other than drawing up my charts in which the epicentre way always Sid. He was driving a machine to distraction, which involved the nuts and bolts of his psychology and derived a faintly healing tune. He had procured work doing sessions at the Tale Centre on a voluntary basis; stage five and six, the final two stages. There he listened to problems, reasoned and empathised and always came home with the firm footing of purpose.

The groups at the Tale Centre opened the door to an afternoon of relief work at a drug rehabilitation centre in Henton. Sid's progress through therapy was still punctuated by a sixty-hour working week with the horses and many sleepless nights with the foaling. He would be working from six in the morning to past ten at night with only a few hours break in order to eat. And still he had time for me.

His years as an addict and at the Tale Centre had given him a keen sense of survival. Gone was the man I used to know with long, flowing locks and an ability to romanticise under the stars and instead was a workhorse intent on survival. Sid is lean and angular, with the chiselled features of David Beckham, and every ounce of his body, every muscle on his face, the very core of his being lay on high alert pretty much all of the time.

I was becoming more and more stressed by my work at Social and Health Care. There was always a slight discrepancy as to the cause of my stress, and really if I was being honest, which I was not, Sid lay pretty firmly at the root of it. And yet it was not his fault because I was deluding myself into thinking that I was alright, when in reality I was fast losing my grip.

In the end, a week before I was going to be made permanent, a position we had all worked hard for, I gave in my resignation. My manager cried when I told her. But I was set. For my send-off she gave me a wonderful present of a gentian plant, with its vivid blue flowers. This bought tears to my eyes as Sid had set me the task of finding a gentian flower on a recent trip to Austria. I had searched high and low on the mountainside and bought home two; one for him and one for me. We had placed them in the same book. It felt, after nine months of listening to horrific stories of abuse and emotional turmoil that I was getting somewhere nearer his heart.

Sid was becoming increasingly concerned about my own state of high alarm. Poor man, could not have done more, could not have been kinder. He was always there with an empathetic ear, listening, reasoning and understanding. I was being driven to distraction by the goal that I had set myself. And Sid was there with me on that goal too. I could just not do it. And I don't know why. Except that deep in my heart it did not feel right, for all the love we shared. Even though I would have done anything for Sid and we both quite often did, our partnership did not sit comfortably. I was being torn apart by my mixed metaphors and meanings.

But apart from this strong need to nurture Sid; none of my needs were being met. I had no-one to talk to, I had lost my job and Sid did not have the time to love me as I needed him to. I had turned from being a happy, relaxed Londoner to a highly wrought girl living by the skin of her emotional teeth.

The equation never did weigh up. The equation that tore both our hearts as it tossed us this way and that, locked as we were on its unsung melody. We were never meant to be. I should have seen it then. I should have known it amidst the magnificent beatings of my heart. This man, who I had lost my soul to all those years ago, who I shared a love that clung to reality in such a shared expression of misery and reflection, he was probably not for me. I wanted to do 'God's Will' so strongly, so desperate was I for a reality that was secure and my heart longed for Sid in a way that was supernaturally attuned. I felt his thoughts, his whims, his reason. I could read his mind as if it was my own. Better than my own. It seemed his heart was beating with mine and our thought were one. I remember the line from the song; 'Sometimes when we touch, the honesty's too much'. But it never was for us. We thrived on that honesty, that healing heart that we shared and cherished together. We relished the moments we spent together giving each other the freedom that we had both been craving for, for so long. Ours were both listening hearts, and at long last we had found someone who could hear.

But physically I could not be with him. One of us needed to be the caretaker in our relationship. Both our bodies were so deeply scarred and the wounds lay open and bleeding. They were very hard to ignore, and even harder to heal, as neither one of us had managed it for ourselves yet. During sex I would freeze up. My body became stiff and I was unable to move. Sid would simply flip me over and carry on having sex with me, which is technically abuse.

Sid was on tender hooks as the time approached when he was to find out whether or not he'd been accepted on his MA course. The man that walked down my steps to greet me that evening was a man who'd been practising alchemy for many years and had finally discovered the gold in his soul that was always there, always wanting and waiting. It was now revealed. He'd got his place. He'd pulled himself up by the boots, out of heroin addiction, where the success rate of his rehab at 75% was considered the highest in the country. He would now be seeing his own clients and was fast on track, and this was a mere, short two years after leaving rehab. His smile of overwhelming gratitude resonated from his very core. I felt so proud of him.

I met some of his peers at the Tale Centre and found a peaceful pleasure in their open-hearted communication. These men who were so brave, so solid, so grounded and so absolutely kind, embraced me as one of their own and suddenly my all-consuming world of illusion became real as for the first time in years I could actually speak without fear of stigma. Their emotional repertoires were so rich and varied that support came from all angles and suddenly I wanted to shine.

It was with great joy and some in-trepidation that Sid and I started house-hunting and came upon a cottage set two miles down a farm track, liberally in the middle of nowhere. We were delighted, or rather more to the point, he was delighted and I was delighted that he was delighted. So we raced into Howe as fast as the speed limit would allow and sat ourselves down in the estate agent and filled out forms. I put the house in my name and Sid showed a keen interest in buying a beautiful country home in the Wealds.

We were invited to a Bonfire party by our landlady who owned the farm. It was to be held two miles down the farm track that ran outside our door. We duly dressed up warmly to combat the cold November air and headed off to the sound of fireworks and seeping smell of gunpowder. Sid was wearing his head torch and our Wellington boots were doing a manageable job in the thick and slippery mud. We were greeted by the happy site of a blazing fire, reaching for the heavens and adding to their light. There was an ample marquee stacked with hay bales to sit on and a much needed barbecue and bar. The atmosphere was jolly and the tent full of folk intent on having a good time.

Sid helped himself to a beer with cheery good humour to a girl who took it upon herself to flirt with him. He made a valiant attempt to save my feelings, but I removed myself from the spectacle in my entirety and took to the bonfire, which I stared at in my vanity. My feelings of security were so scant. My modes of expression were so far removed from sanctuary, and I could not bear to face the reality which I already knew.

Sid, bless him, stood by my side. Stood by my side with such a gentle quietness and care that after a while I could no longer stare at the bonfire with such hatred and glee. I could no longer gloat at my misfortune, because the truth lay bare. This man really cared about me, enough to forgive me for being such an arse. Enough to let me come round in a way in which I did not lose my pride, enough to go on and have a really good evening, getting pissed, having a laugh, and at long last letting our hair down. We sat on the bales until the early hours, laughing and chatting with others. If there is anyone who had the calling, the empathy, the sensitivity, the love and the respect to be a psychoanalyst, that man is Sid.

Home was a fine old affair. Our lovely house was freezing cold and we would have to huddle round Sid's heater that he'd bought down from the Highlands of Scotland for warmth. He used to patrol the hills with his sheepdog, Milly, calling for her in the wilds and winds and gathering his flock. It was beautiful and everything we'd ever dreamed of, our cottage amidst the fields. We'd suddenly become grown-ups and I took to cooking zealously, taking great pride in my trips to the supermarket, stocking up on vegetables I'd never heard of and devouring recipe books for new ideas. Every night would be a home cooked feast, bottle of wine and welcoming bed.

Except that for all intents and purposes I still did not know how to communicate. I was hard up against a bed of nails, and each one that pierced me bore the name of my abuser a decade back; the torments, the atrocities. Sid, for his part, bless him, peeled away my insecurity the best he could, but he could not understand the deeply entrenched maze of emotions that lay beneath the surface of the girl, he had once known so well, and who became correspondingly ever so willing to please. And in the next breath would be lying, terrified, gasping for air, unable to breath, as the torment played havoc with her emotions and her body ricocheted out of control in a full blown panic attack.

How he held me close, and how I inwardly cried, for him and for me. And how he stood by me, again and again. I would never cry. I did not know how to. The tears would escape in a shudder, as if someone had just kicked me hard in the stomach. The emotions wanted to vent their fury, their fear. The endless cycle of repetitive violence my body took me through night after night left me exhausted, but a cold observer. Sid's hand on mine gave me reassurance as did the tender warmth that came seeping through his veins. But we were alone in this nightmare of my making. None of us saw a means of escape and so tried to hide the audacity from our eyes. Sid longed for me to be better. He cherished me so. He would have done anything for me. He hid his pain to save mine. How I loved him, and yet what could I do. I didn't know what on earth was going on. This man was making me face up to what I had spent a decade trying to heal. I had healed the subsequent manic depression, or at least I thought that I had. Leaks were beginning to appear. But the devastating effects of sexual abuse were so evident. So all-consuming, and so bloody celibate.

It was after one particularly savage panic attack that Sid faced me the next evening. I was building a fire that we shared in the sitting room, where Sid had sat me down to watch countless films incorporating themes on sexual abuse in an effort to heal me. They had not even touched my heart. I had watched them with a cold certainty and knowledge and not even an inkling of emotion. I knew what he was going to say. I had felt it in the winds.

'I have rung the therapist today', I informed him, and I felt terrified at the soberness of the path and the extent of my problem. The days that passed were sombre, as was my drive to Henton for my consultation.

I had to fight so hard in the consultation room. I did not understand the meaning of the therapeutic relationship. I thought that talking therapy meant just that, and how I talked. I told the listening therapist of all my knowledge, my desires, my need for approval and how to get it, my methods of making decisions. I swiftly saved some dodgy counter transference, which Sid laughed at later when I told him, and I thought that I was doing really well at illustrating my internal anatomy until the therapist came down at me with a crashing halt.

'You are not suitable for therapy', she said.

Sid was at absolute pains, because to him this was the end of a dream he had been carrying in his heart for over a decade. He saw me going to seed, coming back to him full of nonsense and flippancy. He knew with such deep sorrow we would be parting because he could not, after all the hard work he had done since his addiction and starting his MA; he could not be my carer. It was a role he absolutely forbade himself to play, and rightly so.

His work at the stud continued, as did his other groups and he was distant, always somewhere in his head. He never actually stopped working. Even on the weekends when he would take a break from his studies he would be silent on our short perfunctory walks, thinking of the mind and its many maps. My attempts at conversation were always somewhat crushed.

Sid was terribly worried about the effects of my medication and became convinced that it was not working properly. He wanted me to go to the doctor to ask if it wore off, and should I be taking it at a different time of day, as I always seemed to be argumentative in the evening. Little did he realise that there was another root cause. He had absolutely no idea of the Pandora's box that we had opened, and to be fair, nor did I. I think, if I did, I would never have moved down to Henton. I would never have put him through this.

All through the summer, all through those long, balmy and idyllic days at the stud I'd been miserable. I used to eat my sandwich on a mound near the Naffy at the MOD, pleading with the gods for direction. I wanted to leave, I wanted out. I wanted to go home, back to the life where people cared about me, where I could be flippant, laugh and giggle. I kept repeating in my head the mantra; 'I want to go home, I want to go home'. It rose unchecked from my being, with such force and integrity. All I got in response was this voice, screaming back to my mind from my mind in double velocity and strength. 'Just Marry Sid' it repeated in tones so strong that I gave up to its force and command.

And now all that was being put in jeopardy, and with good reason. The isolation of the cottage had ricocheted my emotions, spiralling them out of control. The panic attacks I suffered in bed with Sid had become so severe that my whole body would convulse violently for the best part of an hour. I could not breathe, I could not cry. The emotions that wanted to escape from my being could come out as violent pulsations that I had absolutely no control over. I felt nothing, could see nothing. I just felt a great dark abyss fill my being, leaving me no room for referral.

We slept in separate bedrooms for a while. I had wanted him to leave in January but he refused to go. The next two months were miserable for me as the man I loved and had been programmed to marry sauntered past me on his daily chores. He was always sweet and thoughtful apart from when I tried to seduce him. But it broke my heart.

It was a really difficult decision to make, but eventually in March I asked him to go. It was a painstaking journey down to Devon where I saw ghosts and visions. Ultimately it was the same survival decision I had faced twelve years ago, and after hours of debating and changing my mind, and keeping Sid fully informed throughout, all of which he completely ignored, I asked him to leave.

He moved out the weekend I was away, taking his things to Coombe to sleep on a friend's sofa. There had been a room available in that house in January and he had not taken it. Everybody, including me thought that he was being very stupid, but ultimately Sid was after a new start. He would answer my phone calls saying 'Hello Home'. God, it broke my heart.

There was one evening in those troubled times when I arrived back from work to find the key in the door. It was under the mat as my mother had been staying and I had left it there, encouraging Sid to come and go and use the computer, but he was in London that night. I walked around the house, implements in hand, ready to defend myself as I was deeply concerned that someone was there. Finding no-one, I relaxed somewhat and went to put the kettle on. When I found out the kettle was still hot, and I had not been in the house since seven that morning, I squeaked and ran out of the house, informing my landlady and alerting my lovely neighbours, who came running and searched all the nooks and crannies.

Sarah and Nick from next door were wonderful neighbours. She seemed to have a penchant for rescuing kittens and he played the guitar on those summer evenings so that it wafted over the hills and far away, cooling in its temperament.

The following evening I returned home and quickly looked around the house. On reaching the upstairs bedroom, which looked out onto all the lovely cornfields, I became very anxious to notice the door to the attic was ajar. My imagination ran away with me and I could not bear to be in the house alone. I felt the energy was pushing me violently out of the door, scathing me in sorrow. I called the police, and my dad, who said that he would come and stay the night if necessary. After spending over an hour in the local pub I went home and bumped into Sarah, coming home from work. She asked Nick, who rather dolefully told me he hadn't put the cover back on properly the previous night. The event was sealed, but it said quite a lot about how strung out I was and prone to the slightest deviation. Things settled down a bit after that. I had got rid of my psychic energy, and Sarah, Nick and I settled down to a warm cup of tea and lots of adjacent giggling.

It was revealed to me later that it had been my landlady's deceased husband who was behind the encounter, wanting me to move on, as I had done my work there.

Now that Sid was gone I had a fairly clear head-space and could begin to move on, if not yet emotionally then in other areas. I had begun to look for properties in Henton. My father had been extremely generous and given me a very substantial amount of money to get set up. I was exceedingly grateful for this, but was on top of the world when I saw in real terms what it meant. Having done a lot of research two years previously I came upon the idea of Elrig in Henton. I booked in to see two houses. One, two beds, and the second, three beds.

The first house was lovely, but I did not get the right feel from it, so the estate agent and I walked round the corner to the second. This was the house of my dreams. Not only did it have three double bedrooms, but also it had a wonderful conservatory that could have been made into a dining room. This opened up to a beautiful secluded garden with a deep fish-pond and a wonderfully scented magnolia tree. There was also a room at the front to use for aromatherapy. This was perfect. So perfect in fact that I felt as though I was walking on air. The estate agent did all the sums for me and said that with two lodgers I could afford it. I was ecstatic and walked away in a smiley haze.

And so I had a long, blissful four months on my own. No one really came to see me, apart from a few smatterings of friends from London, which highlighted my summer days. I went off into the recesses of my mind and found the longed for peace and serenity that I was silently craving. I would often walk at night. Off on my own for hours at a time as dusk settled on the patchwork landscape. I saw snowy owls carrying their prey, deer silhouetted against a glowing moon, snakes and muscular badgers. I entered their territory and they entered mine. How I loved those months, and yet how I longed to move into my new home and enjoy company once more.

I was desperate to try and find the truth to my mind. I had been sectioned, hospitalised, pinned down and injected with horse needles by over-zealous psychiatrists, put on shed loads of pills and still my mind remained unaltered. My emotional life had balanced over the last seven years. But I was so keen to find out the truth.

What really bothered me was the ferocity of the call; the bloody mindedness of it infect. God's Call to marry Sid. The total certainty, and the pain; this was the most painful path I had ever had to travel, and it had yet to be unravelled. I had been acting in faith for a very long time and it had pulled me up to the grips of sanity and I was not going to let mere details such as panic attacks, a broken heart and total isolation stop me now. There was healing in this somehow, for both of us. For all the waves of emotion that Sid and I had shared, for all the bottles of wine that displayed our inner truths, which so perfectly mirrored the other. For all the healing we had derived in the comfort and the certainty that we gave to each other, I was glad. But it seemed as though the voice, which had been shouting at me for two years had gone. The call to 'Just Marry Sid', which had been so deafening in my ears had been cut short and my constant internal dialogue had been replaced by a calm still, in which I was grappling to find meaning. The bottom really had fallen out of my world.

I had had an enormous urge, whilst sitting in our broom cupboard that served as a computer room, to buy a book on Jungian psychology. The urge grew stronger and stronger over the months until eventually I made the two hour round trip into Henton and bought 'Aspects of the Feminine'. It all seemed like double-Dutch at the time, but the urges would return, as would the understanding that would grow with every passage that I read. Here was a man who was telling me that it was perfectly alright to commune with your subconscious and listen to your dreams. Here was a man who was beginning to give me the answers I needed to that long and twisting road that I had taken. So I dived in head-first and felt the full force and richness of my imagination unleashed, and only grew tired by the maze of metaphors and lack of timescale.

I had professed since my days of mania at university where I was catching tails and illustrating fantasises, that there was only one mind. I could not distinguish between my mind and that of another. Which were the boundaries of the most tangible but intangible of substances; that of thought? I had no story. I lay open to the winds and whims of suggestion.

I listened into conversations a million miles away. I felt the pain and the happiness of those I loved whilst I travelled though the cool night air in my car. I saw their emotional landscapes etched into the fabric of the world around me. I felt the gusts of intuition telling me with peaceful certainty of the fates, futures and feelings of all those I held dear. Direction and meaning meant nothing more to me than the call of the wild, the sniff of Spring. The wind carried all the answers to my heart.

My saving grace was the house. It gave me such strong focus. The final evening in the cottage I took a glass of wine and sat in one of the fields overlooking paradise. This was my last evening living in the countryside, which had proven to give me comfort for so long. I was to head to the city on uncertain terms to a home, which I could at last call my own. My eyes filled with tears as the sky surrendered the day with a warm, pink glow that melted my heart. As I lay in bed that night there was a colossal thunderstorm right overhead, the walls reverberating with precision and lightening blinding my eyes; a rightful goodbye.

The next day two removals men appeared, in various states of wakefulness, and helped me move my things to my new home. I had had many offers of help but chose to do it on my own as I felt that I could unpack faster. By the end of the day I had unpacked every box and cut the hedge on a stepladder. Not bad, although I was uncertain of city etiquette of hedge cuttings falling on the next-door garden.

I busied myself with the job of painting the conservatory a gallery white and filling it with a long, cherry wood table, complete with leather chairs. The two girls' bedrooms were a task in that one was bright pink and the other orange with a blue ceiling. These became yellow with white woodwork in a Cornish vein. All the doors, skirting, windows and ceiling were done too. My bedroom in the attic I left with its soft violet hues. The sitting room also presented a problem. I had to strip very 1960's wallpaper and was remarking rather dolefully, whilst painting, and chatting on the telephone to a friend late one Friday night, about the large holes left in it. He wonderfully announced he used to be a plasterer and got to work soon after. After that it was just the aromatherapy room, which had to be stripped of wallpaper and repainted in a beautiful antique yellow. I had a pot of paint from Farrow and Ball despatched to me poste haste, which arrived the next day.

I was in seventh heaven overdrive. My mum, bless her, came up from Devon with curtains, which fitted perfectly in the two girls rooms, and endless drills and bits of amazingly vital machinery.

I advertised on the local website and soon had non-smoking females appearing from every corner. I was very nervous with the first one, but soon got into the swing of it. After about ten days I'd got the house fixed up with two extremely nice people and the show could go on.

Sid, throughout all this time, had entered into a realm of which I knew nothing. Whilst I regaled him with escapades with paint and electricians he was submerged by difficulties involving his work with drug rehabilitation. Having propelled himself from his solitary days at the stud, putting up yards of fencing he was now surrounded by crack cocaine addicts and serious governmental politics. It was more than a small leap for man, and I knew the isolation of his room would not be doing the world of good for him. He was torn between two spheres, and no amount of will in the world can help someone who had closed the emotional door.

Fortune played her cards to me in the shape of an old school friend. I was walking down the road warming up for my nightly run. A bicycle stopped in front of me and a familiar face said with a smile; 'Hello Charlotte, would you like to come for a cup of tea?'

I went with her with glee. It was Jane, who I had not seen for years. She had been a good friend to me in the past and we had shared many a happy day. We sat down in her garden and discussed life. She asked me if I would like a ready-made social life as she had been living in Henton for twelve years. I smiled and thanked my lucky stars.

And so I began to settle into Henton life, doing some temping work, making some friends. Sid was never far from my mind, but so distant in personage. He seemed totally removed. I longed for him, but was slowly coming round to the fact that I had lost him, although it broke my heart. Even though he lived just a one minute walk away from my house, and I felt his vicinity so strongly; it could never be.

My mind reached out to him with its usual velocity and courage. I found a theatre show of the Happy Prince, which struck me with its certainty. The Happy Prince; a statue which looms up into the sky, and who cries for the suffering of the city even though his heart is made of lead. A little swallow agrees to help the Prince with the suffering of the city before she flies off to a warm Egyptian paradise. Apparently, in actual fact, the little swallow dies, because she is so busy helping with the suffering of the city that she misses her flight to Egypt and dies in the cruel night air. The Happy Prince also has to be destroyed, as the town mayor does not like him anymore now that the little sparrow has taken his gems to feed and clothe the poor. I did not know this at the time, but was so struck by the story and the subsequent vans, which seemed to appear outside Sid's house saying, 'Join Us', that I really took note.

I sat for hours in the churches of Henton, surrounded by all the mystique and learning of centuries old. I wondered if I would ever find mine. I settled in the wings of a church, mulling over the suffering of the city and what it would mean to me. My heart hit the floor. I willed it to survive, but it wanted to sit in gloom and misery. There was still a part of me that needed to converse, needed to help, needed to heal. And so I decided, as I sat smoking in the non-smoking graveyard, I would help Sid with the suffering of the city so that my heart too could sing.

And so life went on some more. I was beginning to be invited to parties. Starting to have some real fun, and yet all the time trapped by my mentality regarding Sid. But I was nearly ready to let go. I was being torn limb from limb with a heart that rang true but could just not be heard. And he too.

Several torturous months later, whilst out walking one day I rang Sid up and complained to him that he never spent more than about ten minutes with me whenever he did actually rarely come to see me. He listened, but ended the conversation gently as he had a friend there. I knew he was beginning to be ready for a new relationship and several other factors all just added up to make me want to eject. My internal programming had totally short-circuited. I was busy joining conservation clubs on the advice that 'volunteers were needed'. Of course my frazzled mind, lack of my own story and exemplary sensory tuning to Sid led me to read 'Ne Sid Sid'. That was one occurrence amongst a daily overload. I was being tossed and turned by my inner vocabulary, pushed and pulled so violently that I froze on the spot. I tried to dial my mother on my mobile but instead got Matthew, the past life healer.

'Hi Matthew', I squeaked, and began the verbal diarrhoea of my story. He listened and told me that he could feel the strength of the affection between Sid and myself. He said that Sid and I had had three past lives together, two of which had been traumatic. In one of them, which is the one I was healing now, Sid had been my son and he had died. It had not been my fault but I had felt terribly guilty. Matthew said that I was picking up Sid's energy in that he was creating the wish to get married. I was merely responding to the thoughts that Sid himself was generating. I had been reading his mind when I picked up the marriage bowl. I first saw it at exactly the same time he left the rehab and according to his friends, he had never stopped talking about me at the rehab. Matthew said that the voice from the clouds that I had heard telling me of 'The Importance of the World to find a Bride' was a reflection of my subconscious wish. He also said that although there was a lot of affection between Sid and I it would never work.

I had been reading Sid's mind all along, and I thought it was God. So transparent was I in my wishes – all I wanted to do was God's Will, that I had stumbled across a new stream of consciousness. This was different. I was able to tap into other people's minds, and it was a good thing that I realised this as I had been breaking my back trying to marry this man and no good was coming of it. I wondered how much more I did not know about the subconscious mind and the connections we have between us. For now I was too frazzled by my recent encounter to take the matter further. It was enough just to survive.

All those days in London, nearly three years ago to the day, Sid had been on the stud working with the horses. I had caught his dream as it came wending its way towards me in the shape of the bowl; 'Just Marry Sid'. So I had answered his prayers and he mine. I had left London and had a relationship for the first time in years with the only man I have ever really felt comfortable enough to go out with. The only man I trusted in the depth of his experience and compassion. And his dream was not to be in its entirety, because he could not alter my free will, but he came away with a prize that lay within him, waiting for expression. He came away with a career that will carry him in his entirety. And the love we shared built us both up from the burnt, singed creatures we had become. We lifted our hearts and minds to each other and to God. The powerful resonance of love that spilled through our beings changed the very make up of my DNA and I know it did for him too. Sid was more than a good object for me. He is a very good friend, and I feel so very blessed and proud to have had him in my life.

This book is published with Sid's permission.

Love is patient and kind; it is never jealous; love is never boastful or conceited; it is never rude or selfish; it does not take offence, and is not resentful.

Love takes no pleasure in other people's sins but delights in the truth; it is always ready to excuse, to trust, to hope and to endure whatever comes.

In short, there are three things that last; faith, hope and love; and the greatest of these is Love.

Corinthians 13

PART 3 - COCKTAILS AT DAWN

She walked into the garden centre one day, her long, black hair flashing in the wind. She'd taken her dog, Snoopy, on an eighteen mile round trip on the tow path to Cowfield the day before in the baking sun and her flexed biceps and bronzed skin reflected her attitude and desire. For two months now she'd been off sick from work, tired of the endless office routine, tired of life and eager for a change.

After having decorated the entirety of her house and done all the chores she could possibly think of she happened on an evening with old friends, who took the matter into their own hands, and re-iterated her mother's advice.

She'd left their house equipped with a suitable list of employers, ranging from stud farms to the boat houses that littered the banks of the Birchester in Henton, and with glee the following morning she set about her task.

Leafing through the brightly coloured phone book she chanced upon the section for garden centres and began to try her luck. Engaged sounds accompanied her every call, until about the third or fourth time when a cheery voice beckoned her closer.

On asking about possible job vacancies, the reply was positive and she hot-footed her way into oblivion. A piece of paper was presented and on filling it in with her particulars and duly returning it she was greeted by the regional manager who just happened to be passing, and was invited to sit down for an interview.

Charlotte sat in front of this bronzed Greek god who admired her courage and fortitude and total lack of suitable qualifications. He smiled lackadaisically announcing that the horticultural manager was leaving at the weekend and would she like to start tomorrow. Charlotte grinned and replied that she would.

She was greeted the following morning with a rather nice attire of green polo shirt and trousers that were far too big. Her Thermos and sandwiches were ushered into a shed by a welcoming creature called Sarah, where she was introduced to the kettle and above all Adam who was to show her the ropes for the following two days before he left for greener pastures; namely to hybridize plants with an old associate.

In the next two days, which by chance happened to be the May Day bank holiday weekend, the garden centre was a flurry of activity. Adam, in all his glory, had vastly overbooked a huge array of bedding plants in a valiant attempt to end his career there on a high point, and they pulled an army of trolleys, laden high with bidens and hollyhocks, and dumped it in a highly eclectic array of colour in the covered area, arranged for the bedding plants at that time of year.

Adam was justifiably pleased with his achievement. Charlotte was gagging at the bit for some more activity, but slightly concerned about the hundreds of different types of plants that had appeared, most of which she had never heard of before. Adam took some photographs, and promptly left, leaving her in charge of these very small babies, areas of trees, shrubs, perennials and a huge stack of compost, to name a few.

Charlotte was delighted, and in the forthcoming weeks took it upon herself to move every plant in the garden centre, usually in a howling blizzard or gale, as the summer was not altogether too promising. She enjoyed the physical activity and exertion and the fact that she did not have to think.

The other staff of the garden centre consisted of Abigail, Sarah, Pete and Simon, and some weekend teenagers, but no-one really got in her way much, apart from the odd managerial inquisition where staff visited and told Charlotte that she was doing it all wrong, only to be told differently the following week by another delegate.

The garden centre was deficit in three managers. No-one was running the show. Tom came in occasionally to keep an eye on things, and they all managed to struggle through to the beginning of June until a new face arrived on the scene.

As soon as he walked in the door Charlotte knew that he was going to be dangerous. He had such charisma, such confidence, and such a beautiful smile. His dark hair and flashing eyes said it all, and his jaunty good humour was too much to bear. Charlotte turned on her heel and strode off in the opposite direction, not even bothering to communicate.

She'd obviously communicated effectively enough. On arriving at the shed, which was trumped up in stature by being called the staff room; Tom and this enigma were sitting having a coffee. She raced in, put the kettle on and again turned on her heel to use the bathroom. This one single gesture bought jeers from the two boys who seemed intent on pinning her down. She was in truth scared. On returning for her coffee she was told that the dark and dangerous man, named Sam, would be working with her, outside, for the rest of the summer. She did not like the sound of this, but was strangely intrigued. Tom reminded her that she had been asking for help, so she nodded and got on with her tasks.

She had been driving to work two weeks previously, her birthday enjoyed and behind her. She had just finished a major piece of work and being of spiritual intent raised her eyes to the heavens as she travelled around the roundabout and asked; "What next God?"

A flash of vision came before her, accompanied by the words; "a TV program". She saw herself scooting about dynamically, pulling the trolleys that littered the garden centre. Hiding amongst the lavateria later that day, she constructed in her mind a gardening TV program in which the subject would be social and health care, with the theme tune; "I'd like to teach the world to sing". Content with her vision, although it was not altogether complete, she carried on with her work.

Charlotte had been leafing through the theatre brochures whilst meandering her way through the cafe at work. She'd picked one up announcing, "The Sacred and the Profane". She'd made a big thing of it whilst first meeting Tom, the Acting Manager. Being deficit of managers, he'd been brought in to run the show and Charlotte had proffered this word in defence, although not defiance. His authoritarian gesture belied his need for personal space and she gave it to him, having bandied about this word, which she now understood to mean "devilish".

It was not surprising that she got the shock of her life when Sam walked in. All through May, working outside on her own, and having high velocity jokes and comradeship with her colleagues inside, she'd been praying for an adventure. She wanted a man to walk into the garden centre and ask to take her out to dinner. She'd been praying so hard for an adventure that it fell on deaf ears when it did eventually arrive, beautifully packaged and eager to be undone.

She was in truth bored. She had little stimulus to keep her going, apart from a vague dream she'd had months before, in which she had sat at the end of a very long table full of guests, enjoying a dinner party. The man at the other end of the table, tall and well built, and in high spirits, had toasted her merrily; "Happy birthday to my beautiful wife", he had said. She had never remembered feeling so incredibly happy, even more so when she saw her happiness reflected back at her. She had not recognised many of the faces at the table, but her ex-boyfriend had stood up and continued the toast. She had reckoned she was about forty in the dream.

This dream had kept her going all those long, winter months as she fought for her place in the world. Endless temping jobs seemed to dissipate to the winds and the house that she owned seemed devoid of meaning or logic as she searched for stability and strength. The constant stream of lodgers reflected her growing disquiet. But she had trust and faith in this man who warmed her soul. She'd questioned God as to who it might be, and was told either a Jungian therapist or the name of a psychic healer that she knew of old. She'd pondered on this a very long time; she did not have much else to occupy her thoughts. She was new to Henton and had been carrying a broken heart with her a very long time.

97

Charlotte had dropped subtle hints to the psychic healer, Matthew, over the months. She'd informed him over a text message that she was just back from Devon and doing some interior designing. He'd been furious with her ample overtures over the cosmic frequency and a loud argument had ensued about her intentions and why the hell didn't she leave him alone. They'd argued for an hour, telepathically. Charlotte had felt the force of his fury, but had been determined not to back down. She'd eventually shown him the picture of the dream in her mind, to which he retorted, exasperated; "Well, do some fucking reiki".

Charlotte had caught his dream years previously when Matthew had come to teach her reiki. She'd told him of a recurring dream in which she went into a three hundred acre summer meadow. The earth was placed on a plinth in the middle of the field. She placed her hands on it and healing energy was transferred between the two. She'd felt his vibe, his question, before, but had barred it at the connotation of the word; "Master", that followed reiki, that followed him, and turned him down with a foul stare. Now it was she who must do the running. She held onto him so tight for security, for peace, for an ending to this eternal nightmare of solitude and transfiguration.

Charlotte had lost her previous boyfriend because she'd chosen not to buy a heart-painted set of tea cups, or at least that was the decision that turned the tide. She'd been treading water for too long.

Sam's arrival at the garden centre at least bought an end to the monotony that was fast consuming her soul. The following day he marched out to greet her in the warm, spring air. Pete had already arrived. He was tall, with dark, curly hair; an incredibly intelligent entrepreneurial spirit, who seemed determined to flunk school, but equally become a millionaire. Pete watched in blank amazement as Sam and Charlotte began battling in conversation with each other, loosely disguised as flirting, but really in a quest for dominance.

Sam had worked for the company for ten years. He'd been the shop manager, and almost all the staff treated him as their buddy. Tom, the acting manager, and he, were old friends, and as rumour held, had consumed many a bottle of wine late into the night as they went over figures.

Charlotte, on the other hand, had absolutely no horticultural experience, but had worked her butt off for a month with totally contradictory messages coming from all sides, and she was going to be stuffed if she was going to be told what to do.

They battled over the bedding plants for a good half an hour, moving plants back and forth as it if were a tactical analysis that actually bore fruit. Pete, bless him, looked completely confused and didn't know whose side to join. Sam's venom won the day and Charlotte threw up her hands and walked off in a sulk. They had known each other for less than an hour. Things were not looking good, especially as Charlotte was still on her probation period.

She made herself a cup of coffee in the staff room, muttered a few oaths, a took a long drag of her roll-up cigarette, before realising that she was at work, and pulling herself back out onto the shop floor.

Sam looked suitably embarrassed and Pete was regarding them both rather goofily, as if they were both completely bonkers. He sided with Charlotte and probably Sam as well. They went back to the bedding plants in a rather more lackadaisical fashion. Each gave each other slightly more space, decisions became slightly more joint, and the atmosphere lifted slightly. The day ended on a good note.

They tootled on after that, each getting to know the other, enjoying the warmth and charisma that flowed through their beings. On going into the shed in the following few days and finding Sam sipping tea gently from his "Siemens" mug that he held with a smile, Charlotte was stuck by the thought that he was her husband in a past life. She was rather disconnected by this idea, not totally convinced if she believed in past lives anyway. The husband bit appeared very strongly in her mind, it was only the "in a past life" that seemed a hushed addition.

She was even more alarmed to find that she was growing very used to the idea. A song on the radio was talking about marriage, "Maybe you'll get married, maybe you won't". She was rather alarmed at the force of her transparent greeting to Sam, who was once again sitting drinking his tea and enjoying every minute of the encounter.

God how she ran, how she inwardly ran in fright as their conversations grew in the June sunshine. They worked steadily away together, chatting away merrily. He said his ambition was to own his own garden centre and he wanted to have his own television program there. God, what a reality check Charlotte was having. This was total information overload. All her sensory perceptions were on high alert and singing the most delicious tune. But something was wrong. It was not just the dream; it was something her friend Marcus had said, who was an engineer at the Strone laboratories just outside Henton. He had told her of a girl he had met a tango classes previously. She had been wearing a red dress and knocked him dead with a feather. It was only after she had had him followed for a year by a private detective and they had sat together in transactional analysis classes that he realised that often the people who hit you like a brick are there to teach you something. They are not necessarily going to bring you peace, love and unity; perhaps by default. That thought lurked in the corners of Charlotte's mind, washing away the cobwebs and preparing her for battle.

She did not have to wait too long. Sam and she had spent the entire morning reducing the prices of the wallflowers. Now, with the sale price and her staff discount she could get them for seventy pence each. She covered ten such plants, in exotic shades of yellow, copper and orange into her bags and stood grinning ear to ear by the door of the garden centre, swinging her bags in glee. Sam, taking stock; let slip, with a smile, the utterance from his lips; "beautiful". On hearing these words Charlotte just turned on her heel and ran from the shop, overcome by emotion.

She ventured back in the next day, her heart on a roller coaster. She managed to get to the end of the week, the unspoken attraction causing her much grief and he increased sensitivity. Both parties were doing extremely well, until two elderly men, obviously regulars and good friends of Sam, made their way into the garden centre. After much jesting, they happened upon a rose. Charlotte was passing, dumping a set of tools in yet another shed. She commented on the rose and was told that she was in full bloom. She grinned at this, and meandered into the hut to get rid of the broom. She was still smiling on exit when she heard one of the men telling Sam that he ought to be paying her more compliments. He stood grinning, ear from ear, in his full power and retorted; "Compliments are not part of our job description," heavily emphasising; "Are they Charlotte?"

Charlotte stood there, grinning inanely, working out the job description, and doing a quick calculation realised that she was standing on unsteady ground. She turned, as quick as a flash and ran, only turning her head momentarily, remembering her manners, to wish Sam and his friends a good weekend. Sam smiled with joy as he watched her go.

"Sod this", thought Charlotte as she got back to her house. Her nerves were frayed. Her heart was skipping beats. She was so overcome. The next day, which she had off, she took in her little puppy. She'd wrapped him up, so he wore a scarf around his neck, and looked very Parisian. On entering the garden centre she informed everyone that he was a sophisticated Parisian, re-iterating this fact to Sam, who had taken it upon himself to shadow her. She came upon Jim, who gave her the information she hastily construed about a cistus. Satisfied, she made her way out, only to be stopped by Sarah who wanted to adore Snoopy for a moment. Ever eager to have Snoopy adored, she proffered him to Sarah's oodling arms in such a gesture of proud motherhood, that Sam's, who was standing from afar, heart leapt a beat, joining the moment of adoration, but with Charlotte as the object of affection.

You could have hit her down with a feather. The force of love that struck her with such certainty from across the room had an instantaneous reaction. She grabbed Snoopy back from Sarah's welcoming arms and ran out of the shop. Sam followed her, only to hear Simon stop Charlotte to tell her that her dog was a rat, and not a proper dog, and she should walk him on the roads more often, as his nails were too long. As Snoopy was placed back in the car to beat a hasty retreat he gave his owner a look of disgust that said everything.

This was all becoming far too much. Charlotte's kettle was bubbling over and whistling a long forgotten tune that had her cringing in uncertainty. Her hormones, and especially her adrenal's were having a party that she had difficulty keeping up with, let alone understand.

Charlotte got it into her head that she had to make something. She wasn't quite sure what it was. She wanted to know what everyone was allergic too and then revved up the volume and speed, throwing caution and ideas to the wind. Happening on an extremely complicated sun lounger later that day, in full view of all the watching staff, she hurled herself about in it to and fro, only stopping to tell all innocent bystanders that it didn't work. Sam had shown her how to work it only moments previously, with a gentle tapping of the foot, but she was having none of it. She re-enacted her sexual abuse in front of all, and then declared to a wary Sam that he was to have a good weekend, feeling her way into his fantasies.

They were all a little more cautious of her when she came in the next day. She ignored them all and got on with her job.

It didn't take long for Charlotte to have a good clearing out of her broom cupboard. She hadn't had a male friend since she was nineteen; that was a good thirteen years. She'd only been out a handful of times in the last year, and as she was fond of telling Sam, she had spent the entire year talking to fairies. He thought her very sad, but continued to be pleasant and kind.

Charlotte was feeding into a force of another kind and her protective instinct that told her to disregard the male sex took strange forms of expression. She asked male members of staff to come and play with her whilst dead-heading the roses, and rocking to and fro suggestively on one of the trolleys, asked Sam to take her for a ride. Of course she was being naive, but they could not believe how so. She topped it all by discussing the television program that they were going to have in the garden centre and how she and her male lodger thought that it should be a porn film.

The emotions became too much from that day forth. Pete got cross with her for occupying a dangerous position in his mind. Sam's imagination was caught, so much so, that as Charlotte walked around the garden centre doing her daily chores she began to feel as if she was in a porn film, and secretly she loved it.

He on the other hand, had other plans, and began making rather suggestive comments about mutual masturbation. This had been fuelled in part by Charlotte's previous declaration that she wanted to train as a psychic and that he should too. Charlotte was anxious. Sid had told her when he left her that he could feel men's sexual fantasises about him. Charlotte had also had a dream that Sid and she were cooking in the kitchen 500 years into the future. She didn't know what to think. Charlotte had got into the habit of sticking her head through hanging baskets full of purple petunias, and other such activities, in an attempt to look attractive. It had obviously worked, as Sam continued his suggestive comments about his nocturnal activities.

Unfortunately for all, it did not have the desired effect. There was an element of Charlotte's brain that was extremely sensitive and Sam's imagination was feeding straight into hers, but not in the way that he intended.

For the following two months Charlotte did not go to bed until two o'clock in the morning. She downed a bottle of wine every night, having taken her dog Snoopy out for a two hour walk, and completely ignored not only her two lodgers, but everybody in her life.

Sam, on the other hand, was having the time of his life, enjoying his nightly rituals to such an extent that he would tell Charlotte the result of them, perhaps assuming that she was interested.

Charlotte kicked out at him with a daily load of intense sexuality in an attempt to scare him off, but it did nothing but fuel his flames.

It was sitting in the shed one day, as Charlotte was going through her enormous, blue, flowery bag, that she had bought on the inspiration of her sports massage teacher, who had got similar swimming trunks to help alleviate his mood. Sam made the comment about all the dirty things she had in her bag. Charlotte looked at him, and said; "I have got something so dirty in here, but it's too disgusting to tell". She had been well trained, but perhaps badly advised, in the art of keeping her negativity in. It was bound to seep out in some capacity. She didn't realise how jazzed up Sam was and how intrigued he was.

It was only the next week, when Sam seemed adamantly determined to come and help her fix her computer that she began to wonder. Her house-mates, bless them, had all taken it upon themselves to play love songs very loudly, and all get heinously drunk, apart from Sam, who sat wearing a baseball cap and long coat looking decidedly uncomfortable. After about three hours of fiddling about and making endless telephone calls, he decided that it was a great shame he could not get her firewall off and came to join her on the sofa.

As the ten o'clock news blared loudly from the corner, with Zoe avidly watching, Sam let slip that he had been gang raped at the weekend, by three men.

This degree of empathy was something she had not expected, and her heart went out to him. She offered to walk him home and told him of her similar tales. She held him, but he refused to let her in, so she told him tales of trust, covertly sneaking a glance to his face. He was looking at her with such love that her heart skipped a beat with excitement and she danced out of the door, zooming down the wrong street in her elation, only to be corrected by his smiling face.

But this was more about her than him. His wanton stories of disrepute had ceased to be replaced by a more sinister fear. Slugs, snails; every metaphor under the sun was bought in to explain the size of his willy. Charlotte thought this was rather odd, as she liked him so much that it was like saying, well you can't possibly go out with me because I've got muscled calves, which she did have. But he was building a barrier, and she couldn't get round it, because she was scared of his willy too, for her own reasons, lack of experience and complete ineptitude as to know what to do with it.

So they were both scared of his willy. It was a very dividing force among them. It played havoc with both their mentalities as Charlotte, having now got to bed on time, was beginning to experience some of the strangest sensations in the middle of the night.

But concrete ground had not yet been reached. Sam's decided attitude to go full on into paranoia allowed Charlotte to do the same. She found herself drawn uninvited to his front door, bottle of wine and Snoopy in hand, and allowed herself full therapeutic rites, boring Sam rigid about the state of affairs and enjoying a heartfelt hug. He thought he had got rid of her, but she cunningly curled up sweetly on his sofa next to him, and judging from the look of love that greeted her, decided that it was imperative and proper that she therefore stay the night. Standing in his sitting room whilst he looked on with folded arms and turned head, she screamed at him for a full twenty minutes; "Please can I stay. I just want you to hold me. I don't want to have sex with you", in full regression, eyes and jugular popping out alarmingly. She eventually got the hint and was politely pushed out of the door.

Things were getting tight at work too. Both of them had raised their game as their sexual excitement increased and the level of activity outside in the garden centre was extraordinary. The flower stands that they set up in the middle of the covered area were becoming brighter and bolder as they communicated their sexual desires to each other.

Sam had told Charlotte in the previous months that she was not allowed to think. Charlotte charitably later thought that perhaps he was protecting her insecure framework, but in real terms she was being bossed about, told exactly what to do, and made to do all the heavy work. She had politely referred to her colleague as being disabled in a recent job interview with Stockton College in Henton, before she excused herself. In truth, she could not bear to be apart from Sam, a fact that had torn her apart as she went into the interview, even though it was paid much better money. Sam was disabled; disabled by his need to succeed in a family atmosphere of contempt for his choice, and a growing disquiet at the nature of his surroundings.

It was not until the regional manager appeared and proclaimed that the garden centre looked better when Charlotte was doing it that she saw her chance to strike. She walked into the office and asked Tom whether Sam had any authority over her at all, to which the answer was negative. She then asked Tom to tell Sam off. Being the best of friends, this did not exactly happen, but Charlotte kept her cool whilst she mimicked kicking Tom up the arse to his turned back, much to Sam's amusement.

This was war. Tom had joined Sam in his taunting and telling of sexual dimensions. Charlotte had quite simply had enough. She hadn't slept for months, instead been lucid dreaming on the sofa. She had to fight every corner.

Sam was lauded for being ever so artistic having made a pair of trousers made of stamps. Charlotte had retorted to Tom that she was going to make a dress of AMEX cards. Tom wanted to know where she got them from, to which she just growled at him. Enough was enough. She would have to revise. She would bring down this stronghold which was quite simply suffocating her, treating her like a useless sex object, and yes she had issues. She had a lifetime of fucking issues, and this was the end of the line. She went home to brood.

Brooding very quickly took her to Borders, the bookshop in Henton that stayed open until ten. She found the book that wanted her; "How to think like a CEO", and took it home justifiably pleased.

She settled down to read it that night. She had a rare three days off in a row. The following Monday the garden centre was being inundated by seventeen members of staff from other centres in preparation for the arrival of the CEO and all the major shareholders on Tuesday. There was a state of great excitement about the future of the garden centre, particularly from Sam who had visions of buying it up for himself.

Charlotte had gone for a walk earlier that evening by the river, her head searching the clouds. She had bumped into Michael, with whom she had struck a friendship. He was a big, kindly man, with a history in the merchant navy, a passion for drink and an extraordinary ability to create a community amongst those who travelled the tow path. Charlotte was one such whom he had taken under his wing, and she loved the stories he told with panache and verve.

Tonight was one such occasion as he was feeding the swans with his friend. He engaged Charlotte's attention very quickly and pointed out with dogged determination the formation they were making as they swam home for the night.

"Do you see?! Do you see?! The female is the leader. Then follow the signets, and the male brings up the rear to protect the brood", he exclaimed excitedly, pointing. At that moment the male swan delightfully illustrated his point by flaring up his wings at a passing boat full of rowers.

They watched together, Michael re-iterating his point animatedly, as the swans left the Birchester and took a turn up a canal, out of sight, and home to bed.

Charlotte thanked Michael for his story, couldn't believe his accuracy, and carried on her way.

As she got home that night, and settled down to read her book, she was astounded by the similarities that "thinking like a CEO" had to those who had gone through recovery programs for drug or alcohol abuse. The only point that she found really worth noting was thinking before you spoke. She put the book down. Zoe and Paddy were having a boozy Friday night.

Charlotte was exhausted. She'd completely cut contact with her two lodgers. She'd race through the house after work and sit in the garden staring into space with a cup of tea for half an hour, before setting off on a brisk two hour walk with Snoopy by the river. She'd finish the evening with a bottle of wine and dinner on her own.

Zoe had been so good to her. She was a feisty, Scottish lass who'd fought her way gracefully through life, working with the homeless, mentally ill and drug addicts. It was she who had suggested to Charlotte that she go on benefits in March when life had become a little too much. She was entitled to, and all Charlotte's voluntary work with a mental health charity, had taught her was that stigma was such she would never be offered employment there, even though they had praised her thoroughly before learning her guilty secret i.e. that she had suffered from mental health problems herself.

Charlotte had stood outside with Zoe, telling her of this most amazing parallel life in which she was really happy, and how absolutely determined she was to find it. She was having to look quite hard. The man at the dinner party was still haunting her dreams.

Paddy had recently arrived in the house. For some reason Charlotte had trusted him implicitly and had given him the house keys without a deposit. He was a beautiful, blue-eyed, sensitive soul, and it did not surprise Charlotte in the slightest to hear that he had been a heroin addict for eleven years, since he was seventeen. He was three months out of rehab and trying very hard. She loved his presence as he was a country boy, and brought the smell of cut grass and bird song with him. He had his struggles and Charlotte's lack of connection did not help his mood.

But for now she resigned herself to the fact that it was kinder for everyone to isolate. She twisted and turned in her mentality but at last realised there was no way out.

A trip to the river on Sunday recognised that fact. She met Michael again, who was in high spirits and had something very important to say to her. She could have sworn that man was an angel.

He told her of the story of Snoopy and the Red Baron. "Snoopy", he said, pointing to her tiny, scruffy little terrier, which made her laugh, and he enjoy the story all the more; "Snoopy was the British plane that bought down the Red Baron in World War I"

The tale of Snoopy versus the Red Baron came pouring out. The song was sung, during which Michael's eyes were full of tears.

Snoopy was the little fighter plane with two wings, that had taken on the mighty Red Baron, a German plane with four wings, that had destroyed most of the British air force.

Michael went to great pains to explain how Snoopy had hidden underneath a cloud and got the Red Baron from behind as he came out from below the cloud. She thought of Sam and Tom. Snoopy had been injured in the battle and had gone to live in a museum. She thought of her mother. In her village in Devon there was a social and healthcare garden, in which her friend had always promised she could get Charlotte a job if she wanted one. She thought she would travel a bit further first, but the thought was beginning to become appealing. She thought she'd see what further injuries she incurred before making her decision.

And so it was these thoughts that were swarming around her head as she strode into battle on Monday morning, hair pinned tightly up in a pony-tail and decorated with a big, blue flower. She arrived bang on nine and the till area was full of staff, none of whom she recognised apart from Jim. Tom smiled warmly at her, and she noticed Sam paying rapt attention, but not wanting to connect. Charlotte was a bit disconnected as she was standing by the exit door, which had an alarming habit of opening and closing behind her. She decided to move into a more comfortable position by the till, and glared at Tom, not standing up straight as her book had told her to.

Tom, in his charming blue-eyed boy way, reeled out loads of information and gave everybody jobs to do. Charlotte started the day slowly, dusting with Helen, but then decided to rev things up. She just went mad, in a sort of seventh heaven overdrive, team-building to the extreme, egging everyone on, bantering and bullying in a disconcertingly feminine way until everyone was doing exactly what she wanted them to. She gleaned stories from passers-by, shared information only if she wanted to and kept a very close eye on Sam who was quite whitewashed by all this activity, and hiding behind male company, quite charmed but extraordinarily pleased at this display of affection, which he had never seen before. It was a way of communicating in which they were both familiar.

Charlotte had decided to take the entire matter into her own hands, even though there were some highly experienced horticultural managers there, who did not really want to play ball, but stood on street corners discussing politics. So instead she used another feminine trump card, which came into play as a sacrificial lamb decided to drop a pot on his foot. Barking orders in the staff room, watched by an amazed Sam and Jim and finding ice-packs in the fridge which she told to stay; like you would a small dog, she managed to show Sam how completely controlled she was under pressure, even though the pressure cooker had melted in the heat and she was shaking like a leaf throughout. Sam was rather perplexed by this show of affection. He thought she'd at last gone stark raving mad, bonkers in the extreme. He did not understand what the hell she was up to until she surreptitiously asked Jim to go for a drink when next down in Devon, in such a contemporary way that he needed some prompting from Sam, who at last was beginning to see through the madness and understand her methods, even though they were totally outdated, extreme and rather dangerous, but quite funny all the same.

Charlotte at last felt she was beginning to make some headway when she was picking over the clematis with a girl who was giving her ample information about her boyfriend who had asked her to marry him on their first date. Sam came along and threw something in her trug with such a balls eye and smile that she felt her mission was at last being vindicated. She had been told to get married by God, after all.

The day ended on a high note. Lots of positive team building had been done. Jim was beginning to understand and respond to her methods. She'd been able to make a derogatory comment to Sam about obviously not understanding business in front of Jim, so that the nature of her discrepancy was aired, and yet all the time knowing full well she was talking bullshit. To end, she thought she'd ask Sam to go out with her, to which he'd replied, "Never!" with such force and venom, causing Abigail to smile and Tom to look worried, and then she just sauntered out of the shop.

The next day was spent waiting, and waiting, for the majestic CEO to arrive. Regional managers huddled nervously smoking, whilst the staff dragged their heels, thinking of suitable jobs that would get them out of the line of fire.

Charlotte and Kurt went to top dress the clematis right at the top of the garden centre. Charlotte liked Kurt. He was a very softly spoken, gentle boy who wanted to become a consultant psychiatrist. Charlotte had had numerous dealings with consultant psychiatrists over the years and told him that he would be an excellent one for many reasons, one being his high level of abstract reasoning and kindness. It was for this reason that she decided to ask him about Sam.

They chatted about the situation for a while and came to the conclusion that Sam needed to respect Charlotte. She wanted to know why he didn't and promptly told Kurt that she would ask him.

She found Sam watering the house-plants and asked him over an array of green why he did not respect her. He smiled sweetly and thought about it for a while, because he could see that she was serious. He came round to greet her and said that it was probably because he did not respect himself. Charlotte put on her biggest, little girl eyes and sweetest of voices, because she really meant it, and asked him if he could learn to respect himself, because it would make her life a hell of a lot easier. She saw the man in him smile with warmth, and ran back up to the end of the garden.

Sam swiftly followed, as she had asked him to mend a tap for her. He came to join her and Kurt with a large, gold washer that he disconcertingly kept placing on his wedding ring finger, whilst jesting with Kurt. They talked about respect briefly, before Charlotte took one look at the packet of plant food which they were liberally dousing the clematis with, announcing disparagingly how the picture had been so obviously airbrushed. "But that's not very respectful, is it Sam?" she commented after him as he walked away. He acknowledged her remark and walked on.

The CEO did not arrive.

108

The next day was more of the same; up with the clematis and other climbers at the far end of the garden. Charlotte and Sam were working hard, having renewed respect or perhaps wariness of each other. Kurt came to join them. Charlotte could not help admiring his features as he drew closer and wondering what sort of man he would become, which Sam became immediately aware of and backed off emotionally. It was rather a tense and timid atmosphere as they all got to work, which Charlotte did not help by popping up from behind the hedging and asking noisily; "Taxus; is that Yew?" She kept repeating the question, not noticing the political connotations until both boys had, and Sam had edged her closer into weeding a bed with him.

He said to her very slowly, so that she could understand each word, the Maggie May song by Rod Stewart;

"You led me away from home,

To save you from being alone.

I lost my heart

And that's a pain I can do without"

They stood up and admired the climbers. Charlotte pulled a label on one, saying how much she liked it. It just happened to be called Exchorda, or The Bride. Sam took an inward breath. "This one's nice as well", she said, pointing to a blue creation. He rubbished her on that. "I'm going to take my lunch now", she said flippantly, and walked off lightly down the garden path. She could feel his heart behind her, watching, waiting. Neither of them knew what to do.

The only other time this had happened was in the first two weeks of knowing Sam. She'd told him that he looked like Zorro, and when he came in with more facial hair than usual was a little perplexed. She had asked him how his mind worked, and told him that she mainly read the signs. At that moment, unbeknown to them both, she happened to be holding a patio rose called, "Lovely Bride". Sam had thought about it for a while, made loads of references to fairy tales and prince charming's. She had retorted that she was Sleeping Beauty because she still had that dream playing around in her head, where she was married to that man at the end of the table, who was certainly not Sam. Sam was tall and slender and told her that he had the body of a gnat.

Anyway, the day continued in its usual vibe of growing love and affection, with Sam delving into a vat of irritation. She stood by the doors of the shed explaining in great detail to Sam and Abigail how she wanted to go home, but did not know where home was. Charlotte really meant it, and got lost in a sweet lament, only to find the two others laughing hysterically in her face. She was a bit pissed off at that. Sam attempted to save the day in a mildly valiant effort by telling her that his home was at the garden centre, but slightly lost the good intentions by singing love songs to her in a vaguely testing way, which hurt her to the core, so that she stood up at Tom's compliment, telling him it was Kurt who had done all the work, and marched off leaving Sam in mid-song, gazing wonderingly after her.

The following day she had to herself, with no irritating boys around testing her nerve. So she plotted and schemed in her head until there was no further room for it, and she picked up her mobile, marched to the end of the garden, plonked herself thoroughly down in a gazebo and rang Tom's number.

He himself was having a day off, and was slightly surprised to hear from her, even more so when a torrent of ill favour came hurtling down the phone towards him. To give him his due, he handled it extremely well, fielding off the varied and many lists of complaints that Charlotte had so thoroughly put together and rehearsed. She was impressed.

They talked for nearly an hour, or at least Charlotte pushed so fucking hard that Tom had trouble not falling off the end at times. But he did it, and she imagined his face flushed with the exertion. She was careful not to mention the word "sexual" before "harassment", and also stipulated that she would like to keep the complaint unofficial as she did not think that it would be constructive. She felt Tom's mind wonder at this point. She ended the conversation by muttering the word, "Ratscallion, ratscallion", under her breath. This was her private name for Sam; one she used in her mind whenever she referred to him. Zoe had politely pointed out that she had rather ratscallion tendencies herself, but she did not care to think of them too much. She was going to get married to a psychic healer after all.

The next day she rather tentatively crept into the office to find the two boys falling over themselves trying to help her. Tom reeled out a list of information that was supposed to make her feel important, but instead made her feel a little silly. She was sent off with Sam and a strange device called a CTCD which booked in all the arriving plants. She sat on the floor of the entrance, surrounded by green, deciding it would be safest to be very vulnerable, as she felt Sam's eyes regard her with an absolute sanctity for her health. They made their way through the booking in of the goods, pretending to be mice, and doing a very good job of it. She was sorry to have made such a fuss, but quite relieved that she wasn't being mindfully bonked again.

Luckily, physical activity relieved the strain, as it so often did, and as Sam stood, waiting for his instructions on how to proceed, they began their dance again, which would continue in tempo and vibe throughout the summer.

But the heat wore on. The summer was not doing too good a job. It hadn't stopped raining since she arrived. The hole in her heart that Sam had ignited was beginning to flare with such certainty and desire that she had trouble keeping a lid on it.

Unfortunately Sam had not yet worked this out, or rather he was enjoying the chase too much, for she led a hell of a trail. She went down to Devon to visit her mother, and the familiar feelings of dread that accompanied her return led her straight to the phone and onto Sam. She told him that she was going to book herself into a residential rehab for sexual abuse, which was the only route the psychotherapists had given her as they felt that she was in too high risk of suicide or self-harm. Sam listened, and inwardly sighed.

The following morning she crept back to work. So many were the occasions when she had gone into work on her day off to buy a hammer or some plants, and her hands had been shaking so violently on trying to pick up her coins from the till, that she had sworn blue murder in fright and marched out of the shop, trying valiantly to keep her head above water. Every time, Sam's heart or loins felt a stirring of emotion she felt it like a kick in the stomach. She could have opened a butterfly sanctuary. But there was no sanctuary. Just this on-going bizarre sort of therapy; sexual healing in the most platonic of ways; so far.

Sarah, bless her, had decided to take her under her wing, mainly because she was standing at the entrance of the garden and telling all that she "must improve my bust". Charlotte had shouted to her that she didn't need to, and this had fuelled Sarah's humour, coupled by the blue suede cowboy hat Charlotte wore in all weathers, which had the double job of hiding her eyes and legitimately allowing her to rev up the volume a little.

Sarah took Charlotte to one side one day, as she was racing outside the door to write off a whole load of plants which had died. She showed Charlotte a poppy head, full of seeds, and explained that if you rubbed it, it would release chemicals which alleviated the pain of cancer.

Charlotte had been ringing Matthew sporadically over the last few weeks, saying "Help", and asking for healing. She felt it come in waves. She really wanted him to come over and give her some lessons in psychic defence, which she desperately needed, as she could just not seem to get this man out of her head. He had not responded to this request, so she decided to take the matter into her own hands.

She had managed to solicit Sam's telephone number out of him; a fact that he was not best pleased with. They had a new manager at the garden centre, and she had set them the task of wedding the entire place; Sam doing the shrubs and she the perennials. Poppy had made it into a competition, which she knew Sam took seriously. Tanya, in the conservatories, came and wound them all up. Charlotte called her a handicap, so she went to talk to Sam, which gave Charlotte time to think.

She had told Tanya, standing in the August sun and watching the clouds go by, that she would like to get married on her 34th birthday. Sam happened to be listening, perched on a flower bed, with a smile on his face. Tanya then started leaping around excitably, nudging through the air at Sam, whose smile grew. "You'll have to find a husband then!"

Charlotte hadn't finished her story, and waited for Tanya's alarming display of emotion to quieten, as did Sam. She then informed them that she wanted to travel the world for fifteen years. "And come back and retire", finished Sam with a smile.

They both wandered off. Charlotte was busy dead-heading some asters, when the thought, "This shouldn't be too hard", made its way towards her, accompanied by Sam. "Ha" she thought, and listened to him wrap him round a pole and proclaim his virtues, and how the garden centre group could not possibly be running without him. Charlotte made a disparaging comment about monkeys and disappeared from view.

Meanwhile, she had destroyed the shed at the end of the garden. It had sat there, looking a mess, for a year. She was fuelled by the very first conversation she had ever had in Henton, with a lady who had told her of a friend who had worked extremely hard and built a shed at the end of her garden for aromatherapy.

She'd taken a hammer to the last one, and Joe, the boy that lived next door, had climbed over the fence with some friends, and given her a hand. Unfortunately, excitement levels were so high that Joe had promptly stood on a nail, which she had spent five minutes telling him not to do, and he'd had to hobble home supported by his two friends. Paddy did not help matters by bumping into Joe at the front door and saying that he'd had a nail right through his foot at his age and to stop being such a weed.

Charlotte had also met her other neighbour in these proceedings, who was 87 and called Ellie. She had been a land girl in the war and her whole garden was full of vegetables. She told Charlotte to wear sun cream as the sun was not what it used to be.

So Charlotte sat there one night. Zoe had left to buy her own house and given Charlotte and Paddy a bottle of wine called "The Growers". Charlotte had stuck a candle in it and sat there, in a half demolished shed, looking up at the night sky.

She didn't have to ponder long, and egged on by a voice which was becoming strangely familiar; she picked up the phone to Sam and said that she had something really embarrassing to ask him. He allowed her the space to continue, so she blurted out; "I really want to have psychic lessons, but before I do I need to have sex, and I was wondering if you could help me out with that".

It was a rhetorical question. He had giggled, and she informed him that he could tell her the next day at work, and hoped that he wasn't offended.

Needless to say, she was a little concerned about the outcome. She had sat with Sam only days previously, hiding in the perennial beds, swinging their feet. They had been talking about ponds, as he had just constructed one in his garden. She had been describing hers, and how it had lain stagnant for many months, only to mysteriously evaporate in this, the wettest of summers. The sexual connotations crept their way back into Sam's mind, only to hit Charlotte into exclaiming that she had spotted a monkey puzzle tree the other day, and run off in search of more information. Needless to say, that is when she bumped into Sarah and her poppy seed.

Such was the state of affairs that cloud cuckoo land was not far away. The song on the radio that morning as she turned into work reminded her that it was a perfect day, but Poppy's tone of voice on arrival did not. She was drawn into the office for a chat.

Tom, Poppy and Sam had all been hiding in the office previously and it was obvious that Charlotte was the subject of their conversation.

So Charlotte got told off. The main cause for concern was that she turned up at Sam's house uninvited (which she had only done once, and felt he had wanted her there). She was also told off for phoning him. Charlotte felt a little shell-shocked. She remembered something Paddy had said to her about how her bosses would be interested in hearing how Sam talked about his sexual antics to her, and had done so as recently as Monday. So she said that, and some other things.

Sam was called in, and stood scowling at her with defensive venom, whilst Poppy re-iterated her points fairly, giving them both her number as a help line if required. It became obvious that Sam and Tom had been discussing the supposedly precarious state of Charlotte's mental health, without bothering to examine that they might have been a factor.

Poppy asked if there was anything else. Charlotte turned round to look at Sam, wide eyed and shocked, and said very quietly; "When are you leaving?"

This slightly caught Sam off guard, causing him to splutter a bit, as he had not considered this possibility. Sam was only on a temporary contract over the summer.

They then went about their business, but spent most of the day talking to each other, although Poppy from now on had given them separate tasks. Charlotte listened and Sam heard. They chatted quietly, wounded, but friends; a fact that Poppy, on catching them together, could not quite grasp. They only had a few days left before the new horticultural manager arrived.

They both had some time off before she arrived. All three of the new managers were women, and Charlotte was secretly looking forward to a female dominated society. Sam disappeared to celebrate his mother's birthday, which seemed to take nearly a week and Charlotte got to task on her shed.

It was a state of the art garden room which was to be situated at the end of the garden. She and Paddy had spent three hours bringing it in, piece by piece, from the road.

She'd got Paddy and Jamie to help her get started with the shed, running around enthusiastically and stressing them out until she could not contain her excitement any longer; fired them and finished the rest of it herself. She would be standing, hammer in hand, on the weekend, watching the clock turn to nine am so she could start work, and only stop banging about when she felt her neighbours really had had enough on this August bank holiday.

When she re-emerged back to work, five days later with a smile on her face, the shed was standing, electricity complete, but deficit of glass on the windows and doors.

Jasmine, the new horticultural manager, was there to greet them. Sam had an annoying habit of pointing to a memorial vase, on which was inscribed; "In Loving Memory". Charlotte had thought it was an ashtray, but Sam informed her that it was for when she died. There was a nasty smell of death in the air, and Charlotte hoped that it wasn't hers. She went for a cigarette to ponder the fact.

There was something about the ant that was running so precariously about by her feet that made her want to scream. Drawing an intake of breath, and hoping that God wasn't watching, she decided to kill the ant. Something inside her said that it was for the good of all, and her splitting headache miraculously transformed.

The vague notion that Sam could possibly be fired dawned on her, and after thinking about it for a while, she found herself wishing it true.

Jasmine, the new horticultural manager, was sweet, and they all got on very well. Unbeknown to Sam; Charlotte and Jasmine had been given exactly the same days off; something that when he did find out caused him much consternation. The new managers obviously did not feel it safe to leave Sam alone with Charlotte.

Charlotte's shed was nearly complete, and she very excitably went up to Tanya one day, and asked if she and Sam would like to come and visit. Tanya responded that she would ask Sam the following day. Tanya had invited herself and Sam to the shed when Charlotte had told them of her marriage plans. Charlotte had said that Sam was not allowed to come, but Tanya had been adamant that he was coming with her. Tanya had very sweetly given Charlotte a coffee table, and Charlotte had bought a cream sofa off her; both for the shed. She thought that she ought to dot her i's and cross her t's, so went to tell Poppy, in great joy, about the invitation she had issued.

Poppy was not altogether impressed, and went into deep thought, most of which was dangerous. Charlotte felt a splitting headache coming on, and went to complain to Tanya about the lack of respect anyone had shown her in the company. Tanya had listened thoughtfully. In the end, it all became too much, and Charlotte had to excuse herself on grounds of sickness, and made her way home.

The previous Wednesday she had received a call from Matthew, the psychic healer, and Charlotte was full of joy about this, namely because he was supposedly the man in the dream, and also she could really do with some back up. She told everyone she could think of that she was going to have psychic lessons, but stopped short, when Sam, who had heard that she had had a headache for two days, informed her that she'd probably have another one soon.

It seemed that Poppy had had a word with him about this shed visit, and judging from comments from Jasmine about dirty alleys, everyone was expecting them to get together fairly soon. Charlotte rang Matthew again for help, and he sent it. Something inside her told her to see Matthew first, before inviting Sam to her shed.

On Sunday, as Charlotte was putting the finishing touches to her new abode, a voice in her head, who she correctly judged to be Matthew's, urged her to go to the garden centre. She had some things to get, and logistically it would make a lot more sense to get them today; her day off. She knew that if she went to the garden centre she wouldn't exactly be welcome, judging from the electric atmosphere there between her and Sam, who she was surreptitiously ignoring; fed up to the back teeth of all this game playing; but she continued to listen to the voice.

It informed her that she had every right to go to the garden centre on her day off if she wanted to, and going off with shaky hands, but steady resolve she made her way there.

On arrival, she was greeted by a rude; "What the hell are you doing here?" by some of the teenage boys, who had far too much testosterone floating round their system. She then walked around the garden centre, completely ignoring Sam, and making quite a point of doing so, whilst collecting her purchases.

The reason for this rise in temperature was very simple. She had started to play the same game as Sam, and he knew it. When she had been told off by Poppy, she decided to go home and partake in the same nocturnal activities as Sam, not stopping until she heard his voice shout, "Get out!" in her mind. She was pleased and satisfied that at last he understood the consternation she had felt over the previous months.

She was also pleased that he had made comments in the last few weeks about talking to "oneself", with such intonation that she realised he was playing the same telepathic game as her. And so it wore on.

The arrival of Matthew bought much needed fresh air into the system and Charlotte was overjoyed to see him. He was an intuitive counsellor, and instinctively made her feel at ease, in contrast to Sam, who got her unbelievably psyched up, so that she usually ran for the nearest exit.

They talked, in her shed, and did some meditation. Charlotte couldn't help but flirt with him, which is not difficult to do with a psychic; a fact that she later pointed out to a woe-begotten Sam. Matthew politely told her to sod off. They also did some very useful psychic defence exercises. As Matthew departed he congratulated her on how well she had done that summer, seeing her as a warrior with a sword and she really felt that she had reached the level she needed to attain to be with that man in the dream.

A visit to her consultant psychiatrist later in the week confirmed his theory, although they were going to send her a female community psychiatric nurse to give her some support.

The sands of time had run out for Sam and she knew she'd played her part in helping them. By taking away her interest from him at a crucial stage she could see his credibility flounder and it was not without surprise that he told her in the following week that Poppy had asked him to leave, stating budget reasons.

She was not prepared for the emotional reaction she felt to this piece of news. The man she had spent the summer laughing and singing with had emotionally died, and his worn frame and lifeless eyes carried themselves around the garden centre in a manner which was hard to bear.

She knew she had to do something. This was not the justice that she hoped for. This was not the logical conclusion, when everything in her heart screamed for an outcome of a different kind, of which she was still not sure. So she told him that she would trawl her brain for a solution and promptly went home for lunch.

Not finding any post with extremely large cheques in, funnily enough, she went and bought the local paper, and was looking at it with zeal when something caught her eye. It was an advert for a post as a group worker at the Tale Centre; an extremely good drug rehabilitation centre.

Running back to work with glee, she informed Sam and Abigail of her valiance and his forthcoming good fortune.

The following day she promptly told Poppy of her decision to leave, hoping that she would obviously have to re-employ Sam, because after all he had been gardening since he was eight, had helped set up all the computer systems and been with the company ten years. Poppy responded by putting up very large adverts for weekend staff, prominently around the garden centre, having told Sam previously that she could not keep him on even for weekends. Charlotte inwardly thanked her for her support, but the effect on Sam was devastating. He took the next five days off sick, vomiting profusely.

Charlotte thought that he had disappeared for good, as he did not ring in. She took home his Siemens mug as a trophy, and sat looking at it. It just responded in quiet innocence and withdrawal.

She had given him a magnolia tree, a few days previously, as a voice in her head said to do that if she wanted to remain friends with him. But she couldn't get over the feeling of intense relief that she wouldn't have to see him on the shop floor again going through this perpetual song and dance.

It was with fear that she saw his car at work on Monday morning, but she needn't have worried. Sam was feeling sheepish, and still a little sick. He spent the entire day on the forklift truck. Both of them felt gutted. Neither of them liked to admit it. The love that had been burning brightly all summer was in danger of being lost, and Charlotte was beginning

117

to realise how she truly felt. He only had two more days left to go; the Wednesday and Friday, before the story closed.

Charlotte went to work on Tuesday and spent the whole day crying, hiding amid the tropical palms. Her nerves were shattered, her heart was raw. She spent the entire day arguing blue murder with Matthew. She demanded to know why this was happening to Sam; where was the justice in it. She called him to task on the subject of the dinner party dream, in which she was married to him. She called him every name under the sun, and he responded to her thoughts by looking ever closer at her affections.

It became clear that she had had enough of faith healers, witchdoctors; whatever you like to call them. People; who had taken away her power at a very early age, leading her to make some catastrophic decisions which she had inadvertently spent eighteen years trying to rectify.

She argued and bantered all day; until slowly the layers of the onion skin were peeled away and she was left with one truth. She had rushed to the post office at lunch, and two cards had caught her eye. One said; "wedding acceptance", and the other, "wedding regrets", but she still couldn't fathom out the truth in her heart.

In the end it boiled down to money, and her attitude towards it, which she could see reflected in Sam's eyes, but not in Matthew's. But the uncertainty screamed at her as she weighed her equation, which seemed hopelessly balanced on either side.

Sam arrived for work on Wednesday; an agonising day for all concerned. He had relinquished any emotional attachment to Charlotte, thinking her heart belonged elsewhere. It was only when she said she had spent the entire previous day crying that he offered her a biscuit with such hope. But she still could not take it. She ran out of the room squawking.

The rest of the day Charlotte spent trying to increase her levels of endorphins. She hauled one massive trolley after another, jesting with everybody on a high energy desperation. They teased her for having vodka in her drink, and Sam could only sit back and admire.

However, as the day ended, and her hope and betrayal sang bitter wounds, she stood by the till with Brett, letting him explain the thing to her. Sam was watching with affection. Charlotte could not help by let out the information that the letters, "P/B" on the till stood for, "Payback". Sam just ran from the shop with such hurt in his eye, for the first time showing his true depths, that Charlotte's interest was ignited once more.

They both took the day off sick on Friday and to all extents and purposes would never see each other again. Charlotte's mother said that she would probably do something stupid if she went in, and Charlotte's father came to help her finish her shed by putting the window panes in. As he hammered the final pieces into place he said that at last now she could keep things out. Charlotte looked around the garden to realise the elephant she had bought with a raised trunk, to represent Matthew, was out, and Sam's Siemens mug, which she had hoped to return to him was in.

The next few days were not easy, but on returning to work on Monday, she found herself relaxing and beginning to feel more at ease. She had talked to Matthew about it all, and he had at last advised her to stick with Sam. Sam had got a job in another garden centre, which to all extents and purposes was something of a promotion. She felt worn out and exhausted.

So Charlotte spent the next few days running around buying everything pink; two pink candleholders, two pink cushions like teenagers have, and two mugs with pink hearts that said, "Hello gorgeous" and "Hello sexy". She thinking about the ending for her story and decided to ask Sam to marry her in it. When he turned up in the garden centre twenty minutes later, looking all of the above, she ran off, on her lunch break and texted him that she didn't want to see him for three weeks as there was something she really needed to do.

She couldn't think what it was, as she had made her application to the Tale Centre, and finished writing up her story. She wasn't sure whether to show it to him yet as she was still working at the garden centre and didn't want to get into trouble. She decided that she wanted to become President, because after the summer she had had she felt that she could do anything. Three weeks was a very long time to wait.

This book is published with Sam's permission.

Charlotte continued working at the garden centre for another seven months. She was in deep depression as she missed Sam so much. She took her fork-lift truck driving licence. Her teacher was half Cherokee Indian. He had thirteen licences including a crane. She told him of the story of Little Big Horn, as he had left his tribe's teachings behind. Little Big Horn was a great chief. He went into a trance one day and foresaw a great battle. He was told by his spirit guides that his tribe would win, but that they must not loot from the soldiers. The battle came, and they won – it was an astounding victory, however, some of the Braves took from the dead soldiers. They looted. The cavalry were so overcome by the barbarism of the looting that they took force again, rounded the tribe up and put them in reservations.

119

PART 4 - THE PSYCHIC REVOLUTION

Being posh was the hardest thing Charlotte had ever had to be. Being psychic was the second. Being posh and psychic was a fine combination, especially when you're anti-establishment.

Charlotte didn't happen to be either. It was not until she was sent to an extremely prestigious girl's boarding school in the depths of Berkshire that she happened upon and rejected these ideas. (Charlotte would like to point out that she uses the term 'extremely prestigious' in a sarcastic manner – she doesn't want to sound pompous and due to events in the next chapter she feels that the meaning of these words have been misconstrued).

She liked school at first, and organised lots of pillow fights that she had read about in Enid Blyton books and heard about from her brothers, who also happened to be in the same predicament.

The years went by and she found she was quite good at learning and threw herself in it like a bull in a china shop, as there was not actually much else to do.

When she went home she would ride her horse and spend all day outside, dreaming. Dreaming of what, she did not know; but she would stare for hours at the plants and trees and get lost in a haze of wonder at the beauty of nature. She liked the patterns and the puzzles and the music of the spheres. She wondered at the divine nature of things and how nature was organised and whether she could find the equation that would explain the beauty of it all, and how it was managed. This management thing was something that she would look into in great depth, because she liked freedom, but always wondered nonetheless.

She would just go back to school for quick bursts of insanity when the time allowed.

As time passed, and she found she was growing up, and getting a grip on this thing that grown-ups called life she decided to cross refer to her horse Bluebelle about management.

Bluebelle, she had got for free from some family friends. Bluebelle did not like to be ridden and spent all the time that Charlotte was trying her out throwing her head around and causing havoc. But Bluebelle came to stay anyway. She was a grey mare, who had had a baby, and was extremely maternal. All Charlotte's mother's goats used to come and lie on or under her in the paddock. Charlotte spent hours with Bluebelle exploring, usually getting very lost, which was something Charlotte liked doing, as you usually found out more that way. She and Bluebelle had a telepathic relationship as they would gallop up the tracks outside Charlotte's house.

She'd had a little horse called Lady, who had very different ideas on management. Lady would hurtle round all the cross country courses at the rate of knots and then proceed to gracefully glide over and start to eat the grass. She was put in a paddock all by herself and escaped to find a cart horse pulling a cart down the road, trotting alongside him in glee.

Bluebelle was more of a dreamer and would point blankly refuse every jump, but on coming to the gate which Charlotte was supposed to open would just jump it to amazed sounds from passers-by.

It began to be quite a shock to her system when she returned to school to find the level of squawking and indecision quite so high. They were all put into different houses at school, and luckily for Charlotte, her house was full of quite rural people like her. But God, the place reeked of people from London who had very different ideals and liked to talk about them at the tops of their voices.

Charlotte had managed to combat it for the first four years, but her older brother, Ben, was having the same problem. He had been sent to Eton, which can be a blessing or a curse, depending on how you look at it. He was finding it a curse, and had developed a distinctly anti-establishment attitude and a mohican. He had always been very into anthropology, and getting different social groups together, and would always be found chatting to all the homeless people in the car park during shopping outings, and they thought he was wonderful.

His earlier attempts at bringing different groups together had not been so successful. He had stuck the cat in the fish tank to look at the fish, so the cat got wet and turned round and scratched him. He had also put the tortoise in the budgerigar cage to introduce them, but the tortoise had stuck its feet out so he couldn't get it back out again.

For now Ben was relieving his enormous state of anger by listening to punk music and feeding them gently to Charlotte during the school holidays on her request. Charlotte liked to look at the art work on the record covers. She was not so keen on the music as it was a bit loud, but she would read the lyrics and over the course of one or two months, suddenly became an anarchist. Her gentle little world of nature and harmony which she had enjoyed so much suddenly was blown apart with a global consciousness and immediately her mind became full of the problems of society and the world at large. Once this was acquired it was very difficult to get rid of, and all her imaginings of God and nature were predisposed by people, and poverty and politics on a global scale.

121

So she went back to her 'prestigious' girls boarding school, which her father had worked so hard to send her to and thought.

There were a few other people there who were having the same ideas. And Charlotte spent a very happy year riding about in Tasmin's gold beetle, taking a large amount of drugs with her and Claire, going to lots of festivals and generally having a good time.

It was not until they had all spent an evening waitressing at a party, that everything went horribly wrong. Charlotte, being an anarchist of very little brain, had deemed it necessary to fire a water pistol at all the guests, whilst she was serving them. Most of them thought that this was quite funny. However, on the way back home, something happened which was to change her life forever.

A turquoise mini came careering towards Charlotte and knocked her flat. Her bags flew in the air. Three ambulances appeared. Blood was pouring out of every orifice. The driver came and swore at her, and she thought that she was going to die.

She didn't, but something inside her did. And that was her will to live.

So she went back to her 'prestigious' girl's boarding school, and mentally lacerated everyone that was there.

Everybody who had built a social structure that was based on money and status, and everybody who didn't bloody well care. Only one girl asked her how she was, in six months. Everybody else was terrified of her.

She completely withdrew from society and destroyed herself with hatred for the English class system which completely surrounded her, completely suffocated her and completely destroyed her. She did not understand a society which did not care. And she certainly did not want to live within it. She hated that place so much. She hated the girls that were there. She hated their talk, and their values, it was vile. It was the most disgusting set of values she had ever come across. She wanted to destroy it so badly; she wanted to hurt these people so much. She wanted to stick their nose in the shit, and say look at that. Stop wasting your time you idiots. Don't you know that there is a world out there, with people, with problems, and you lot are so fucking intelligent, so fucking educated. Why don't you bloody well get your noses out of your pockets and do something about it. Don't you understand that we are all in this together? Do you really think it matters who you bloody well know, and how much money our parents have. Don't you think that you could get off your bloody arses and do something good for a change, instead of sitting around lining your own pockets and purses and trying to suck up to someone else because they happen to know the right people. Well, who are the right people? Who are the right fucking people? Don't you think that it matters what happens to this world, this planet, the people we live with. Don't you think it matters about everybody? You lot are so fucking elitist you should be burned in hell, because you lot who think you are going to run society are just in it for yourselves. You know nothing and you don't bloody care.

Charlotte went mad. But not before she had taken something for herself.

She was standing in a hall, with a large group of her classmates. One of them, a pretty, popular girl called Penelope was clutching a book. On it she had stuck a newspaper cutting. It said, "Leader of the Pack". Charlotte stood staring at it for some time, before she realised that it was nothing more than a concept, which did not have intellectual copyright issues attached to it. She thought she would take it.

A few days later she suffered a massive nervous breakdown and never went back there again.

Charlotte had inherited this desire and ability to care from her parents. Unfortunately social workers do not find it necessary to look after children who go to private schools; something that they made a joke about when Charlotte worked for the Fostering and Adoption panel, much to her irritation.

Charlotte's mother had been beaten by her mother, with coat hangers and hairbrushes, which broke on the impact. As a result, she created an oasis of love, peace and harmony within the family home, filling it with animals and spending her days sewing and gardening.

Charlotte's father had been living out in Argentina, and his mother had been homesick and wanted to return to Wales. They did just that, but soon afterwards all the people my grandpa had been working with in Argentina suddenly became multi-millionaires. He found it difficult to find work. My father spent his days on ponies trying to escape from it all. He did very well, and won the national polo championships when he was sixteen, on a Welsh Cob rather than a thoroughbred. Added to this confusion, my father was sent to live with relatives in Argentina, and then sent off immediately on his return to boarding school, which was not explained to him.

My mother was a titled. Something she did not realise until well into her teens. Their title had come from battle victories in the fourteenth century and I think they had about fourteen generals in their family. My mother wanted to live a gentle, rural life, with animals and children, and created a very beautiful idyllic childhood for us all.

My father worked his butt off. He had been in the army, but my mother wanted to settle somewhere. He studied hard for his law exams and then took off.

My mother now lives down in Devon. She can see the sea from her garden. She has just got some ducklings, which she is really excited about. Her friends are people that live in caravans, or who have Aids. They are caring people. That is her domain.

My father now lives in a multi-million pound house in Mayfair with his beautiful and gentle new wife Annabel. People come up to him all the time to thank him for giving them their first break. He is wonderful and I am very proud of them both.

Before she went to Durham, Ben sat her down to watch The Princess Bride, a story about True Love. Charlotte was drawn to the story of The Princess Bride because of all the conquests that had to be made. There were three near impossible tasks, a test of strength, a test of ingenuity and the final test where the hero has to come back from the dead to complete his task. Charlotte liked it because of the impossible challenges that it held and the spiritual adventure that it intervened. There was nothing that she would not do to complete this test as she wanted the adventure, the courage and the resilience to do something in the spiritual domain. Her school desired academic achievement from her. They pushed her too far with their ambitions, but she wanted God. She wanted to know God and to understand more about the mysteries and purpose of life.

Charlotte had a wonderful tutor at Durham called Professor Knight. He found her a milkman and taught the History of Science, which was all about how they decided to set up scientific experiments in the 1750s when science was just getting off the ground. Einstein said that intuition is the highest form of intelligence. That is what she was testing. She wanted to test the psychics. She wanted to be psychic. She really wanted to be a Native American Indian as she liked their spirituality and horse skills. She even liked their smoking habits. The peace pipe was full of tobacco.

She chose Jerry as she recognised him from the dream that she had had when she was 7. He was the perfect bait. When she arrived in Durham she was deeply scarred from her relationship with Sid and suffered complete and utter anxiety and low self-esteem when it came to the small subject matter of sex. She was just too ashamed and over-awed by Jerry to admit that she did not know what she was doing sexually. Being a teenager was hard. The expectations are very real, especially when you are totally in awe of someone.

Jerry was slightly overwhelmed by Charlotte and her rather extra-ordinary dress sense. Not only that but the colourful array of friends that she had collected. Charlotte had just been raped for two months and needed him to be her friend. He pushed her away every time. He didn't understand why she would not go out with him. Charlotte was terrified of sex. She wanted intimacy with Jerry more than he will ever know but her fear prevented her from getting close. He pushed her away some more. She searched the hemispheres looking for a connection that would bring them together. He pushed her away more, all the time jeering at her because she couldn't cope sexually, which hurt Charlotte to the core. She was desperate for affection after the ordeal that she had been through and she looked to Jerry for support. He just tore her to shreds but she still loved him, still believed in him, because he was the object of affection – the Test of True Love. Somehow she must get through to him how she felt, but she was inadequate sexually and that was the only language that he was listening to. The house resounded with techno music and drugs. Charlotte stayed clean. She began believing that she was responsible for earthquakes in India as she had opened her mind up to such an extent to try and get Jerry to be her friend. He just pushed her away. She downloaded all the information that was ever available to man or beast in an all encompassing effort to get close to him.

Charlotte had become psychotic, which is when you become intensely sensitive to what is going on around you. You lose touch with reality and enter higher states of awareness.

Jerry began to hate himself. He knew that Charlotte liked him. She made that blatantly obvious but he knew nothing of the rape that she had been through in the previous year and had even moved in with her rapist in a blind effort to get close to her. Charlotte could not believe that he had done that but would never tell him, so afraid was she. Jerry was her ever present nightmare and her reason for living. He would be round at her house every day like clockwork, smoking dope with Mick and dealing to all the dangerous looking men from Newcastle who came to their house on a regular basis. Charlotte had no sanctuary. They took over the whole house and her bedroom was tiny. (It had turned bright yellow and pink in her effort to stay positive). She did not want him in her house every day. It destroyed her sense of peace.

Jerry had no idea why Charlotte would not commit to him. He did not understand why she had been out with Chris and not him. He hated it when Charlotte was chatting away merrily to a full house on a Friday night, and he, in his inebriation, could not muster any conversation at all. He began to resent Charlotte, because he saw her getting close to other people; why not him? He did not see the real panic that was behind the verve.

Charlotte occasionally looked down on Jerry, because it was the very same inebriation that had caused her to get raped in the first place. Well, to be fair, that was her responsibility, but it was that inebriation that had caused Jerry not to come looking for her, not to care.

She was very angry with Jerry as he represented to her her only friend amongst a sea full of devil worshippers, who had only wanted money and status.

She occasionally took the opportunity to make him feel uncomfortable, just a fleeting moment here and there. Her anger at him was apparent, but well disguised by mania. She just wanted him to know that she could make friends, while he found it so impossible. She had been totally reliant on him and she wanted her bid for freedom.

She gased away to all and sundry; colourful, eclectic characters that seemed to frequent the house. But she was not interested in them, per-Se. Her only interest lay with Jerry and making him understand, making him believe. He was out of his depth, poor soul. The burden of isolation and regret had become too much for Charlotte and she was looking for someone to save her. Failing that she was looking for someone to blame. The only person that mattered was Jerry. The scores of people she met did not matter. She was on a mission and it was 'Do or Die' for her. She was Testing True Love and her test was failing miserably.

All the friends who had gone out of her life seemed to resonate bitterly, their rejection flaring in her heart with a bitter sense of loss. Jerry was the only one left and he had failed her in the most horrible way. She must make him see.

If she failed this test she had failed God. She was not worthy to be. She did not see that her sense of worth lay in her social functioning; in her ability to draw a crowd and bring people out of themselves. All she saw was the nullity in Jerry's eyes as he watched her chat animatedly away to yet another colourful character. She saw his loss and made it her own.

Jerry began to be so insecure. He was expecting Charlotte to come on to him, she threw him so many life lines. He did not understand why she wouldn't seal the deal. It seemed that she had failed her Test of True Love. It seemed as if the test had been in vain. She had thought it was a brilliant idea. She did not know where it would lead, but she liked the conquest and adventure. She knew that it would lead somewhere, if only she could understand. Jerry all this time took the easy line and began to believe that Charlotte was being a snob because she would not sleep with him. The girl had just been brutally raped. It was not fair on her. She would have loved to have been with him. She wanted to marry him. But it was too late. The dream was taken from her and she was given a nightmare to replace it.

This was the worst case scenario. Charlotte had absolutely no ability to create a loving relationship between her and Jerry and now it seemed that she had failed her Test of True

Love. Jerry thought that she was being a snob by not going out with him and yet it was totally beyond her capacity to get close to him, or to get close to anyone. She could not bear to be hurt again. Her ability to trust had been shattered. Shattered by those girls at Downe House School who never did anything to help her but turned their backs on her. Shattered by her loss of all her friends who had coldly calculated that she was not worth the effort in their devil worshipping schemes, and now that she had found her one True Love, a man who was good and kind enough for her to trust and enjoy being with, he too had turned against her in a cruel and callous way because she had been horribly raped by a man who knew nothing else and Jerry, in his naivety had become his best friend and barred the way for her to tell the truth because she was so outnumbered by men who wanted to use her only for sex.

In later years she began to understand. A psychic healer had told her mother that Charlotte would be a very powerful psychic if she came off her medication. She was not on any now. She had not even been diagnosed. When you are psychotic, as Charlotte was, two things happen. One, you lose the ability to reason and see things logically and two, you are totally over-sensitive to other people's thoughts and feelings. This was the first time Charlotte had become psychotic and she did not understand it at all.

Jerry had made it impossible for her to have a relationship with him. He came round to her house to smoke dope with Mick and to laugh at her. He was jeering at her inadequacies. He was laughing at her failures. He made fun of her inability to get close to him, even though she would have liked nothing more than to be with him, she just could not get round her fear of talking honestly about her fear of sex. He drove her mad with his taunts, his ever present company and his complete dominance of her house.

Charlotte eventually in her desperation for friendship and security left a dead mouse outside Jerry's house, supposedly symbolic of Jerry's reticence. He wanted to call the police, but Mick telephoned Charlotte's mother and she was called home.

Charlotte was left alone with her mind that was shattered, her body that was psychotic and her emotions that spanned the emotional spectrum and fell off every end that could be imagined. Her mother loved her throughout.

After four years her medication was stabilised, so now although her mind was still in pieces, at least her emotions were not so violent.

She began to see what research she could do for herself.

Affirmations began to play a large part in her recovery, and she said them every second of every day. She was taken to a Christian summer camp, where she said she did not want to play, but read her pagan book. She heard voices from the clouds, shouting at her; 'God or Die'; 'Artist of the Era'; 'The Importance of the World to find a Bride'.

She read a book about a consultant psychiatrist who had gone on a shamanic journey and went back to work, to realise that her mentally ill patients might be telling the truth about their visions and their realities. They were indeed having spiritual experiences rather than mentally ill ones. It was similar to her experience where rape had off-set mental health problems, but there was a lot of spirituality going on too. It was hard to tell the difference sometimes. She later thought that if any of the doctors asked if she was hearing voices she would accuse them of spiritual discrimination.

She experimented, and decided on the affirmation, 'God'. She would later change this to 'Jesus', as her concept of Jesus was altogether much softer that God.

Her brothers came to visit occasionally but she would fly into a rage and hold a knife to her wrist. She was desperate for them to help her. She wanted them to rescue her.

All the time she prayed to Jerry, she wanted him, she asked him, and she just said his name. He was her true love and she believed that she had wronged him. She would have done anything to get him back, and she did. By totally destroying everything in her life. Everything had to go through the filter of Jerry first, and if it did not pass, it was destroyed. That did not leave very much.

Charlotte's father had kept a long rein on all of this as he could not believe what was happening to his beautiful daughter. He came up trumps by producing a healer called Will, who had worked with John Denver. Charlotte went to see him, and he suggested, that at some point, she could come off her medication.

She took him literally, and stopped taking her pills that day.

Within hours she was seeing ghosts by the river. A whole field of ghosts wanted to talk to her. She made them sit on chairs and gave them all a note pad and pen. She then moved on.

John Denver came to talk to her, and asked her to send an acorn to Will. She did so, and included on the letter the information she had heard that day on the radio, that oak trees only produce acorns when they are fifty and look after 187 living creatures. Will was about fifty. After she had posted the letter she went up to her bedroom and saw on her John

Denver CD that he had died three years ago to the day that Will would get the letter. Will was very pleased. Charlotte nearly got sectioned under the mental health act.

She had a lot of psychic experiences after that, but her one burning desire was to see Jerry again. He was her Prince of Peace, and she had elevated him as such, such were her attachment difficulties. What she did not realise was that he was consistently destroying her. He had told her to do better than him, so she set about seeing what she could do.

Charlotte got a series of very low income jobs. And her life continued like that for eight years.

Something inside her was burning, but she was not sure what it was. She did not know the truth. She only knew that she had wronged Jerry and she must pay for it. She must find out why Jerry felt like that towards her. She must find out how he felt so that she could understand him. She must understand him, because she was testing True Love and it had all gone so horribly wrong.

As the years went by, Matthew suddenly appeared. Charlotte loved it as the first time they had met she went into anaphylactic shock and started hurling tea on the lawn. He was deeply distressed and wondered what past lives they had had. It was only later that he realised she liked him. He was the most humble and caring man she had ever witnessed and she loved him from first sight. Little did she know that he was celibate – something he took very seriously as part of his spiritual practice.

Charlotte had had numerous problems at work with men. She suffered huge panic attacks. Sometimes her body would be in shock for over an hour, every limb shaking uncontrollably. If that happened three times a day it would be fairly exhausting. However, she soldiered on. She had absolutely no trust in men whatsoever. They were terrifying to her.

However, the long days of isolation were causing Charlotte to imagine once more. Matthew had always told her to listen to her voices. He had come to exorcise a ghost once from their house. The cat basket had moved ten foot across the kitchen, and Charlotte and her mother had gone round the house, spirit leveller and hammer in hand to see who was there. They found no-one so drank whisky instead. Matthew had said it was the ghost of a girl called Caroline from the big house, who had fallen in love with the farmer, from the cottages that they were in. She was pregnant with his baby, but he would not marry her, so she committed suicide. Matthew got cross with Charlotte for not talking to her. He said that she found Charlotte's mother maternal.

She crawled into the garden centre one day for more fun. It was in meeting Sam that she realised that all this mental illness might just be an illusion. Sam was someone that felt that same way as her about so many things, and thought the same way as her. He had a very creative, scientific mind, and as the months passed she realised that the connection they had was extremely telepathic. He cared for her in a way that no-one else had, and she was beginning to release stories that had plagued her for decades.

She knew that he loved her, and yet time was playing tricks on her. There were class issues once more. Charlotte knew that she had to do something when she heard that he was not working full time, and there were a bag of cakes in the staff room. She took them to him. Matthew was shouting at her not too, and a vision which had plagued her for many years crossed her mind. It was of a girl in the French revolution crossing a river. The revoluting pheasants, for want of a better word, were staring at her. She looked very beautiful in her blue dress and they were full of awe. They thought better of it, and decided to kill her. She was murdered.

That flicker of an image crossed Charlotte's mind whilst Matthew was shouting at her not to take the cakes. Charlotte knew that Sam would appreciate them. He did not have money to buy food. So she gave them to his house-mate.

Needless to say she got so badly bullied as a result that she ended up shouting at her female manager and went home. She had a vision which got her off the hook. But once ignited the storm started to boil over once more. Matthew was helping her again, and she decided that it was a cosmic probability that she would get a safe seat as an MP.

She joined the Republican party, joining Percy Piggins's (the leader) constituency as she had wanted to move to Stricken at the time. She did not know whether she wanted to be Republican or Democrat. She wasn't bothered which party she wanted to join as she was only really interested in Environmental Issues and it didn't seem to matter which party she joined. She didn't really know much about politics or what party stood for what. She wanted to go to Percy Piggins's party all the same as she did not want to pass up an opportunity to meet the party leader. She lived in a Democrat seat, the only one for miles around.

Victoria, her house-mate, came to Percy Piggins's winter party with her, wearing a tea cosy on her head. They got there late, as Charlotte was nervous, and wanted to ask Percy Piggins if she could have a safe seat. Percy Piggins was in full swing, telling his constituents how wonderful the Republican party was. Charlotte was collecting her tickets from the desk. The man behind the counter said that he owed her a pound, but he did not have a pound, he only had two pounds. Charlotte said that she had a pound, so that if she gave him her pound he could give her two.

The man behind the counter did not seem to understand this, so Charlotte explained it to him again. His friend started to get quite outraged and started screaming at him; 'Give the girl her money'. This went on for several minutes, during which time Percy Piggins's winter speech had been totally drowned out and people came rushing to the door.

Charlotte got her ticket and strode in to listen to the leader, who flushed. The room was full of a lot of people, wearing a lot of pearls.

Charlotte hadn't quite given up on this idea yet, and spent a few months avidly watching the parliamentary channel. She thought that the Green Party were doing the best job, as they actually put forward some well thought out interesting arguments with substance. When the House was full the two main parties just slagged each other off, which was a complete waste of time and tax payer's money. She got really irritated with Timothy Tailor, who made the comment that all the Republican MPs were only interested in helping wealthy people. She thought that if she became an MP she would have him done for political incorrectness and have him banned from the house. Little did she know.

Samantha, her cyberpunk house-mate decided that she would like to be Charlotte's secretary when she was an MP. Samantha was one of the most emotionally intelligent people that Charlotte knew, and always looked beautiful with her long pink dreads tied up in self-tying bunches. Samantha had really helped her get herself sorted out with the story she had written about Sam. Charlotte had been walking along the street, and every man that she bumped into seemed to resonate Sam's energy. Samantha was always absolutely squeaky clean in her relationships with other people, and who owed what to whom. She was a godsend.

Charlotte ended up losing her job at Green Fingers garden centre as she was absolutely exhausted from juggling endless balls that seemed to be flying off in extra-ordinary directions. She retreated to Devon, where she sat for two months in a black mood. She reapplied to the company, and they thought about it for quite some time. She knew that she wasn't the easiest of people, but they had become her family as she had unwittingly dumped quite a lot of emotional baggage with them, and they seemed to care. To a point. But they had healed her, Sam in particular. When she had met him she wasn't allowed to see a therapist as they felt that she would commit suicide. Sam, and everyone else had taken a fair degree of that pain from her.

Janice, in the village, kept popping round with the important piece of information that if she wanted a job at the Social and Health Care garden in the village she would have to go now, as it was changing hands. Charlotte didn't really want to go, as she liked working for a big corporation, which had a big network. She didn't really want to go back to Social and Health care, per se, as she had spent fourteen years ill, and wanted to move away from that to a more business environment and do something more creative than just healing. So she held out.

Sarah rang her a few times, asking how she was. Charlotte said that she was at the end of a line, a very long line. Charlotte tried to work during the day, but was so stressed that she didn't actually get a lot done, and snapped at her mother who was trying to tell her how to root geraniums, whilst actually knowing that it would have done her a whole lot more good to listen.

She took herself off to the Green Fingers in Gaydon and spent a few hours happily browsing. She bought some stuff. As she was nearly home, her intuition told her that if she went back and bought this key ring she would save a year. Charlotte considered it for a while, as it was a twenty minute journey back to the garden centre. However, in the grand scheme of things she thought that she would return and go back and get the key ring that said, 'Welcome to My Garden'.

She also did a bit of shopping in Queenshill, stopping in on a hippy shop and buying some little elephants on a string, which had good luck attached to them. She bought a rune, which she later saw represented the destroying of spring crops, but it was supposed to be part of the natural cycle. She also bought a little purse.

She had decided, before leaving Green Fingers, to become a Master Gardener, doing the Royal Horticultural exams. She thought that this would be quite fun. All through her head, as they were putting out the Christmas trees for sale, she kept thinking about being a Master Gardener, and in equal measure a voice kept telling her no, she had to be Head Gardener. Charlotte didn't want to be Head Gardener, as you usually worked at large estates, and the work itself was quite backbreaking. She enjoyed the retail environment. But every time she said Master Gardener, the voice would change it into Head Gardener.

Sarah rang for a third time, and said that people had been asking after her. Charlotte constructed a vision of herself and Sam, working on an allotment and ran back to Henton thinking that she was wanted. Things happened very quickly after that. She was invited for an interview at Heningham, and the reference which had not been pending suddenly was offered.

She went for the interview with Billy at Heningham. He questioned her quite strongly about what had happened in Henton, but did not pry. He looked at her, trying to take stock of her. She felt that she was sitting at a festival and smiled at him. As the ABBA song, 'Winner Takes All', was playing on the radio the recruitment agency rang her and told her that she had the job. They bantered a bit regarding wages and then all was settled.

She had fought Sam so badly at Green Fingers. She had played him her Levellers song, 'Fifteen Years'. 'They don't believe in Heaven. They don't believe in Hell. I don't believe what I'm seeing. This is no game can't you tell.' Sam had not realised how sensitive she was. She ended up playing a trick on him, in order to save her own job. They were both loaded; seeds that had remained dormant, but suddenly sprung into life. Her dormancy period had been fifteen years. But life had become so dangerous for both of them, so incredibly strong. She knew in her heart of hearts that she did not want to go out with him, because she was too scared to, and did not feel that he really was the right person to look after her. She did not want to have continual relationships and was only after one man to keep for good. She did not have the confidence to do otherwise. But the electricity between them was like being in an electric chair, and yet it never turned itself off, because it would continue at home too.

He felt it too, and felt equally uncomfortable with it. Both their minds were extremely sensitive and both of them were extremely telepathic. Charlotte could feel his moods, feel his breathing, feel his every gesture from the half mile that separated them at home. When he read her book, she could feel his growing anger; she woke up from her sleep. She knew exactly what time he finished reading, and she could see him go through the book, and each passage that he was looking at.

This was inverted NLP. Or the beginning of psychosis? Or both?

She liked Sam so much because he understood her to such a degree. He was so incredibly kind to her, and sensitive to her needs. He healed her more than anyone else she had ever met, and in the short three and a half months that they were working together she felt the benefit of his presence so completely.

But Charlotte had not had a male friend for thirteen years. Charlotte had not really had a proper, local network of friends for thirteen years. The degree of empathy between them was extra-ordinary and something that she had difficulty coping with.

Billy, her new manager, came to the rescue and Charlotte adored him at once, because he had saved her. She sat adoringly in their first staff meeting thinking he was great, and happy to be back working at Green Fingers. All the other staff were very nice to her. They had probably been given express orders not to be nasty after some of the troubles that she had had previously. Some of the younger ones wanted to talk about art because they knew Charlotte was into art. Mary, who was going off to do interior design, was looking through the cards at work. There was one with a mother, and a baby at her breast. Someone was trying to pull the baby off. For some reason it reminded Charlotte of Sam, probably because the baby had black hair. Charlotte turned round and looked at the card, saying, 'I wonder who the artist is'. The artist was called Billy Husband.

Charlotte did not like to see those two words together. She did also not like it because she believed in Jungian psychology rather than Freudian. Jung made his symbols universal, so that they meant the same to everyone. Freud made them specific to individuals. Sid was studying Freudian psychology, which was very analytical and did not suit her mind at all. Jung suited Charlotte's mind completely, as it was all about symbols and talking to your subconscious. This was not a good state of affairs and Charlotte was not happy at all. She was very unhappy indeed.

Billy was married with two small children.

Charlotte tried to ignore the card she had seen for some time. She believed that she was picking up on his thoughts when she looked at the card. He had already flirted quite strongly with her on a number of occasions, really pushing his point, always when there was no one else around. He had read her account of the garden centre with Sam and was taking advantage of her. She did not want to get involved. It was too dangerous. It was illegal in her eyes and certainly immoral. He was married, but she knew that he had started something that put her in a very difficult position. She had no experience with men and was desperate for affection and a sense of belonging. She was so isolated in her home life and did not like doing the things her lodgers did. Samantha went to Slimelight every weekend and Victoria liked to hang out in the Elrig Road. Charlotte wanted something a bit more cosy.

She threw herself into her work. She'd spent the first two weeks there getting a grip on things, as it seemed that most of the staff there had read her book, 'Cocktails at Dawn'. They were all very kind to her, and she made some friends. She did not like this situation at all. All she ever wanted in her life was to be happily married and have an interesting job. Well, she had got the job she wanted, and how the hell was she going to balance this equation. She'd look at Billy and hurry off. She decided the best thing to do would be to stop thinking about men completely. She decided on a different concept. She thought about home.

Some of Charlotte's friends thought that she was Jesus. This was quite a promotion! They had read her book, 'Cocktails at Dawn', and when she disappeared down to Devon for the Easter weekend everyone at work thought that she would not be coming back because she would have ascended to Heaven. Charlotte thought that they were quite disappointed to see her again on the Tuesday morning.

She spent the Easter weekend with her mother and two brothers, and friend Beth, all who were of spiritual intent. Beth decided that it would be best for her to become a nun, which is something that Charlotte did not like the sound off. They all thought she was bloody marvellous. Ben told her that what she had done was 'Priceless!' Will decided that they all had to get up at four o'clock in the morning to go to Pyle cathedral. Charlotte reckoned that this was about the time that Jesus got out of his tomb. As they were leaving, the cat, Sammy, knocked over the ash tray and it broke. Charlotte thought that if she was Jesus she would have to give up smoking first for it to happen.

She did not talk to Jesus directly as she was only just becoming aware of the power of prayer, but Matthew over the years was teaching her a lot.

Charlotte decided that there was absolutely no point being Jesus and ascending into Heaven. She thought that it would be possible, but would serve absolutely no practical purpose whatsoever. She decided that if she was Jesus she would stay on earth and make heaven on earth.

Charlotte did not really know what her idea of heaven was, so she decided to think about the concept of 'Home'. She asked other members of staff, and they told her home is where the heart is. Charlotte told them that her home was scattered into a million little pieces. She started to listen to her Wizard of Oz CD, but did not know whether she had to visit the wizard first before she went home. In the end, she thought she would do what she had always done and just say the word 'Home' and it would miraculously appear before her.

She went to tell Billy this.

Billy thought that this was a great idea. Other staff members had started to pick up other ideas from her book, 'Cocktails at Dawn', which were fundamentally based upon the principle, 'In the beginning was the Word'. The power of stories in our society. That's why Charlotte never watched TV, and that's why she wanted to make a TV program.

She started to run around and have some fun, and share some stories.

Her concept of home grew and soon they were doubling budget.

She motivated all the young teenagers and soon they consistently hit sales of £22K a day at the weekend, rather than the aimed for £11K. £17.5K of that was in plant sales. She was the only full time member of staff outside. Plants, in Spring, were averaging at £3 each.

Charlotte was told that this was the Deb's party that she never had. She ran away in her van before she had her Deb's party, even though her father had gone to the trouble of printing out invitations for her. She wanted a Deb's party that was more inclusive, less exclusive and more fun.

Charlotte was selling, but she didn't consider that she was selling plants. She was selling a lifestyle, a feeling, a sense of heaven. A sense of what she considered heaven. And quite a lot of people bought into that. She liked the garden centre as it contained people from all walks of life, with one common interest.

She thought of the healing power of nature, and how it had healed her of so many ills, as she walked for hours every evening after work in those long dark days she lived with her mother.

And she thought of Jerry, and what he had told her. The books he had given her about changing society by changing ourselves. The creative power of all our minds and how it would infiltrate the world in which we lived, heal it and change it.

And Billy, by and large, thought she was doing a marvellous job.

Soon everyone was running about like excited electrons and business was booming.

Charlotte found people to heal, and people to heal her.

However the one fundamental core principle which she could never get round was staring at her in the face.

The harder she worked, the more Billy appreciated it. The more he appreciated her, the further she came off kilter. Her balance was being skewed.

His feelings were feeding straight into her Achilles heel and she did not know what on earth to do about it.

Her feelings and stories became increasingly unbalanced, and instead of giving out good things she found that she was beginning to tell tales that were increasingly deviant. She was slipping from her holistic spectrum into a realm that was pure fantasy.

But it was a fantasy that they both shared, and he hid from her.

Soon it was no more. She was spiralling and the only way he could hold her was to reprimand her. She lashed out at him.

She had been thinking about being made horticultural manager all morning. In her mind's eye she could see the contract being given to her. She signed it, but the words Charlotte White came up on the page; Billy's name. She frowned, and they disappeared, to read her own name. This was his conscious intention that she was picking up on and it frightened her as she knew how many people would be hurt. She had been told psychically that Billy was chosen to be her manager because he was a good father, and he would never leave his two children. In her mind she had come to the conclusion, in between so much pain, that it was his choice. It was up to him. She could not chose his happiness. It was his choice. As long as she did not go out of her way to flirt with him, if he decided to leave his wife to be with her, she could pass no judgement on it. But it was up to him and she tried to keep very much out of the way. She could not hide her feelings though, try as she might. She was absolutely besotted by him and everyone knew. They were all treading on eggshells.

Her house-mates were getting increasingly concerned about the morals of the issue. Charlotte was as well. She tried to study and concentrate in the evening, but her mind was askew.

She started to understand the stress that her father had been under when she was small. She felt that stress now. She was on the minimum wage and yet paying for all the bills on a house with three lodgers. They were paying nothing but very cheap rent. She became very short with them, never rude, but indirectly she was scrambling in a pit of despair, trying desperately to keep her head above water. What she must have been like to live with, God only knows. She thought of her mother and gradually the crystallisation of her early life was beginning to make some sort of sense. She could not afford to lose this job, she had no other means of income. What was being asked of her was impossible as she could not find a way to express herself in front of Billy that was not fear or passion. It was not unrequited love and yet the bars were drawn very much against her not only by her house-mates but by her heart.

She found a lighter placed outside her shed, on the bench near her pond. The lighter read, 'Now piss off and buy your own lighter'. On her way back to work she went into the garage. The newspaper headline said, 'Now this is a Real Crisis'.

And so she fired, the best bullet she could muster. She said to another manager that Billy would only give her the horticultural manager's job she wanted if he slept with her and was escorted out. The following morning she received her letter to say that she had been fired, and funnily enough felt extraordinarily relieved.

She went back to work the following morning to return her clothes. She bumped into Billy and the other managers. Everybody was hurt.

She felt awful. She had lost the job she loved, and she saw from Billy's burnt frame that she had hurt him too. She wondered why he had employed her, and sent him a letter telling that she was going travelling. She saw him read it in her mind's eye, searching and stopping at the word 'kindness' she had used to describe him. She could see in her mind's eye him and her going off together around the world. She wanted him so badly and yet was struck by remorse as he was already taken.

So she wrote to head office to tell them that she had thought it best to leave. She was dropping all charges. He had never done anything wrong. It was just that she thought it best to go.

After she had sent the letter about going travelling, she heard the 'whole' of Green Fingers discuss it. They thought she would never survive. They thought that she would get raped as soon as she set foot outside the house. She loved listening to the voices of Green Fingers. How people cared about her, how they knew her. How they hated and loved her. She could see some of the faces of the people that she knew as they discussed her.

She started thinking about writing an account of it. 'The Buck Stops Here' was the title that first suggested itself to her, but that was replaced over the next few days with 'The Psychic Revolution.'

Her brother Ben dictated an email to her asking for a job. He cheekily suggested that she ask to go back to Heningham. She sent it off, and could hear the whole of Green Fingers laugh and think that this was funny.

She heard the voices continue in their discussions, and one of the managers said that she owed Billy an apology. So she sent him an email apologising and hoping that he was ok.

She saw him read through it quickly, sighing heavily, and sending it off to head office. She didn't really know what was going on.

Her friend Emily, from school, came to visit. They went out for a walk together. Charlotte was very quiet and subdued. She wasn't sleeping at all. Some nights she went without sleep completely. All she could hear were the voices of Green Fingers and they were all arguing. She couldn't really make out what they were saying. After she sent the last email off to Billy the voices got so loud that they were unbearable. They were shouting and shouting, arguing about the rights and wrongs. Charlotte was beginning to become extremely traumatised. She had not slept properly for three weeks. She sent a text message to Sarah saying sorry, and telling her about the voices that were ringing in her head. Sarah knew Billy, and she imagined she might pass on the message.

Charlotte in medical terms was extremely psychotic at this point, but what would Matthew say?

The voices stopped, and all she could see was Billy standing by his desk, saying all he had to do was wait for the paperwork. Charlotte wondered what the paperwork was. She got her P45 the next day, and her reference the day after.

The voices didn't stop screaming though. She opened up her emails to find one from head office. They had sent out a really aggressive email to all store managers saying never to employ her. They were really angry with her. Charlotte cried when she read it.

Billy obviously felt bad too, because she saw him talk to another manager, one of his friends. He told her that Charlotte had done nothing wrong; she was just reading his mind. The manager urged him to tell head office. A cry went out: 'phenomenal', they said. The girl that had sent out the nasty email was upset and embarrassed. This started the Green Fingers voices once more.

Charlotte asked Matthew, her psychic friend, in a psychic way, if he would help her. He said that she could either go for silver or gold. Charlotte said that she wanted to go for gold. Matthew said that gold would be more expensive. Charlotte said that she wanted to go for it anyway. Matthew said that she could do it herself but he would be there for her if she needed it.

Once Billy had admitted that Charlotte was reading his mind, things changed. But not just for him, for her too. And this is where the story closes. Because it was not just this psychic revolution that was thrown into question but the entire nature of Charlotte's life. She had seen things going on with Sam, but now that it had happened again...her maths teacher at school, said, 'Once a possibility, twice a probability, three times a certainty'. This was the third time this had happened, and Charlotte began thinking very strongly about Jerry.

These thoughts were subconscious at first. She had told her consultant psychiatrist that she was not working and was going to become bankrupt. He said that she wouldn't become bankrupt in two weeks so she decided to prove him wrong. She went to Rose Ash, a RHS garden and spent a fortune on two pots and olive trees. Her intuition told her that it was very important to have these.

She thought back on everything she had gone through with Jerry. How for years he had thought she was being a snob, when in fact she was terrified of sexual intimacy having just been raped. How it had completely destroyed her, and her family life. How her brothers had not had a mother for the best part of a decade, and how they had become meditation teachers as a result. She thought of her mother in Devon, and how she had suffered so horribly during those eight cursed years. The same years Sid had spent cursed. She wondered at spiritual authority. She wanted to find an answer. She wanted to find a fault line so that she could heal it.

Billy wanted to find a fault line too. He stood by her in friendship and soon her mind became full of questions. He wanted to know how many sexual partners she had had. She saw him beating up Sid in his mind. He watched over her as she slept at night, looking at her and making sure that she was okay.

The Green Fingers voices picked up again, and Charlotte's mind became full of possibilities.

Billy cared for her in his mind. Now that he knew, that she knew, they talked to one another. He went through every aspect of her life. Of all the relationships she had ever had. He solved them, he healed them. She went and bought him a Superman t-shirt.

She spasmed throughout. Her whole body was taken over by muscle spasms as she was releasing tension that she had felt for fourteen years. She sat and studied her horticultural notes but the pain just kept on coming, releasing, healing. Billy took the image she had of the French aristocrat being murdered. He killed the townspeople and took her into her home. He built a huge iron wall around her home, and invited all her friends for a party. They all came in their cars and they danced.

Anyway, the Green Fingers voices continued, and so did Billy. He was brilliant, and for every thought he gave her she would spasm out some more pain, because the nature of the relationship between thought and matter was becoming very apparent.

Billy, having punched Sid and talked to her a lot about how she felt, decided that the issues she had with Jerry were between her and him. Charlotte held onto Jerry so strongly. She would not hear, or think anything nasty about him, but it totally destroyed her too. She didn't really know where this all fitted into her ecology. She had been reading about pests and diseases and came to the conclusion, that although some animals exist they can by nature be extremely harmful to other animals. You could always try and denature them, but Charlotte did not really think that that was going to happen. With all the people she had met, and some of the people in mental hospital were very hurt, the only group of people who really hated her were people like Jerry. And that was an equation she would have to balance. Jerry fundamentally hated her, because of who she was. And try as she might, she could never change that. She could destroy everything in her life, but she could never change her genetic make-up. And that was something that she was going to have to live with.

The class system in this country is something people don't like to talk about and yet it is something England is famous/infamous for. At the end of the day, Charlotte wanted to marry Jerry but couldn't get past her sexual insecurities which still plague her life. She is sorry (for Jerry) that things turned out this way and wishes him every future happiness.

But this is twenty years ago. A lot has changed and the class system has been broken down; Thank God. People are more into aspiration. My aspiration was to Test True Love and ultimately gain a sense of belonging. Jerry very much made it clear that I did not belong with him such was his dominance and control over my house, destruction of my education and annihilation of my circle of friends. He was the push that sent me into mania. Something that has taken nearly two decades to resolve.

I know he fancied me now. Friends have made me realise that, but at the time and for twenty years after, all I saw was a dominant, controlling figure who seemed intent to do me down. Even as I drove home, to be sectioned, my lasting memory of him was sitting in my house resonating with dominance, pleased to have cleared the rubbish away at long last whilst he went on to get a first in his degree.

I do think that there is a strong element of chauvinism in all of this. I had been to an all girls school and grown up with brothers, and treated men as equals. I was not prepared for the sexism that seemed to abound with his every gesture and the knowing that if I did not possess sexual confidence and use it, I was worthless. Maybe I am being a bit mean on him, but I have to exorcize him somehow. At the end of the day he was immature and naïve. I'm sure he did care a lot about me. Why else would he move in with Chris and be at my house every day, but because he was doped up he could not see the reality and pain of my situation, instead laughing at it and treating it with humour.

And everything Charlotte had done in her life was trying to get authority. She'd lost her mind, so that she could understand it. She'd become psychic, so that she could understand why Delia had given her such strange advice. She'd met people on their terms, in order to understand. But she found it very difficult to take her authority back off Jerry, because she loved him.

She thought about it a lot and asked him to lunch. She'd sent Emily a copy of her book, who had spread it round the circles of her old school friends. Not much had been said, but as she went to sleep one night, the book was handed over to her. The book that Penelope had, saying, 'Leader of the Pack'. Charlotte wanted that book so badly because to her it represented a set of values, and she wanted the values to be held by caring people, who she believed she was. She did not want to the book to be held by self-interested people.

Her house-mate, Samantha, said that she was from the future and here on a very important mission to save the planet, by finding a book.

That is what Charlotte thought about that book. And that is why she did what she did with her life. Because it mattered.

Charlotte wondered actually whether it was possible to denature people. She would certainly give it a go. It would probably involve some sort of self-harm, however, so was a no-go area. In the few weeks that she had been spasming, and being held by friendship, albeit of a psychic nature, but that is sometimes how nature intended, she felt changed. She felt free. Her worries and woes had been discarded violently from her body and now were only held in her third eye. And the more she wrote the more they left her.

Victoria, her house-mate, had bought in Special Forces, namely in the form of Stuart, who was a physicist. Charlotte always used to read books on the scientists and the sages, and how they were basically all saying the same thing. They used to draw parallels between quantum psychics and Buddhism. She told Stuart about the people from M15 who came to her school, and told them that every contact leaves a trace. She said that she had gone through her mind like that, and seen who had affected her. He told her that it was no wonder that she had gone mad.

Charlotte knew that the time had come where her survival depended on letting Jerry go. She could be spiritual and thank him for what he had taught her. Which was quite a lot. She had experienced life in a way that she never would have come near to if it had not been for him. And that is all she needed to know. She had the book. He was only part of the story in getting it. He was just a tool, and not the master.

I actually found Jerry really boring and I would not go out with him anyway. Not only was he a drug dealer, using my house to invite all the dangerous looking men from Newcastle to come and score. Not only did he dominate my house and completely take it over – treating it as his own. But he was boring. He'd continually pass out when I was in full swing so I would be left talking to nobody, and he didn't have any gumption, get-up and go, or drive.

He fancied the pants off her. He'd moved in with her rapist and spent all day, every day with Mick, dominating her house – his house, and all he could do was pour scorn on her for her sexual inadequacies – his sexual inadequacies.

And with that she destroyed him. Totally, certainly, definitely. We always have the power to change ourselves and create our own lives. Something Charlotte had been doing for some time. But what she had learnt through working at Green Fingers, and working with Sam and Billy, is that people have to answer for their own actions. And Charlotte wasn't going to answer to Jerry any more. She was doing all she could to survive for herself.

When Charlotte was at university she wanted to become a professor of philosophy, love of wisdom. She would decorate her walls with pink or purple, with white spots and teach a philosophy accordingly. She felt that she had done that.

Now she wanted to live in peace.

She had done the affirmation, 'World Peace' for an hour, a few days ago. She had lain on her bed spasming horribly as visions of sexuality came before her. But she released what was necessary. And now, according to the doctrine, her own peace.

The words peace and piece are very similar.

Charlotte had gone and bought herself lots of union jack things whilst on a trip to London. She had two key rings and a mug. She thought about this country so much. She didn't really know what to make of it. She knew that a lot of people in Henton had read her book, because people that knew her from Snoopy would tell her to 'take care' when she was in the shop. The man in the computer shop, who looked just like Jerry, smiled at her kindly, and for the first time she was beginning to feel truly loved for what she had done, not who she was, or was not.

So she thought that at the end of the day, when there is nothing left to work on, which is singularly true for someone who is unemployed, has a terrible reference and no qualifications, she would try and do something amazing.

She would not test true love anymore. She had experienced true friendship.

She would go back to Billy in her mind and ask him to forgive her, thank him for his kindness and see how the cookie crumbled.

(And hopefully the Green Fingers voices will be a little more peaceful this time).

P.S. As Mary would say, it's the thought that counts!

PART 5 - TRUTH OR DIE

To my beautiful mother.

I am only just beginning to see the gifts that you have given me. Thank you for the wisdom of your patience, the kindness of your love, your amazing sense of humour and your endless good grace. And for always being there for me.

To my industrious father.

Your life has been a constant reminder to me of proving the impossible and what fun it can be. Thank you for sharing your dream with me. Thank you for always doing the best by me. Thank you for showing me that integrity is the most important thing in the world. Thank you for being there.

'The truth shall set you free.'

Charlotte was at her wits ends. Or rather she did not know where her wits started and others stopped. She had just exploded a big love bomb, that it seemed was travelling around the world, and the feedback mechanism which she had created in her mind was giving her a drip feed of information that had her rocketing.

She was not really in a very good way. She'd just lost the job she loved and been forced to move out of her home due to economic circumstances. She was a shaking and quivering mess, and had gone to live with her Mum for a while. There was a fair degree of concern about her colleagues whom she had left behind, but it seemed that all roads were barred to them, and she could do nothing to precipitate the ongoing storm of confusion and insanity that plagued her mind.

Except that there was nothing remotely insane about it. It was a working mechanism that she had tinkered with for several years and it seemed as if there was a lot of truth in it.

But it did not seem to offer much sanctuary now. The sense of loss was unbearable. The losses that she had incurred over the last several years seemed to weigh heavily and account for a complete and utter collapse.

So she stayed at home with her Mum, listening to the sounds and voices of approval, concern and outrage and went and sat in a shed and painted pictures, all the time hoping for some peace, and a way out of this web she had created.

People had come up to her a lot in Henton, knowing that it was she who had made this funny new tune. She was a little bit concerned. Her heart was being ripped from her chest, as she had lost all that she loved, again.

So she went off to see a friend of her Mum's, who lived on a big old farm. He had ponds and log cabins and loads of animals. He had two beautiful, bold, black horses which pranced around his fields in a magical way. He had a goose and a dog and a sense of enormous peace.

Charlotte spent a very happy few days in the sunshine, in his field, surrounded by dock leaves, pulling them all out. She had intermittent conversations with him, as they sat eating their sandwiches and looking at his pond. He sat with her, and let her just be.

Her Mum came up with solutions: seeing a spiritual therapist as an outpatient, three days a week. Her Father was also well on the case, and found a residential rehab that offered psychotherapy. Charlotte thought about it for a while. She loved the idea of staying with her Mum, and seeing a spiritual therapist, but there was something inside her that said going into a residential setting would get the job done more quickly. She was not massively happy about it, as all the times she had seen a psychotherapist in the past, they either said that she was mad, or shouted at her, or worse still refused to treat her. She didn't think psychotherapists did intuition or spirituality for that matter. She'd never lasted more than three sessions, and had actually never had any consistent professional help for anything in her whole life. She was still pondering it on the way to her father's house, when she saw a sign, which said that 'Every Venture tells a Story'. She still wasn't massively happy.

In truth, she wasn't massively happy about anything at the moment.

Outside her house, before she left she'd seen a bright orange van. It had 'total reclaim' written on the top, and 'demolition' on the bottom. It reminded her of a book she had, years ago, with a huge sculpture of an orange hand reaching to the sky with just one word on it; Change.

She had sat in the garden of her house. Her paternal grandfather had come up to her, in spirit form, as she sat on the bench, and told her not to do an experiment with Time, as he said, when you die, you just go into a different dimension anyway.

Charlotte's dreams were extremely vivid. She'd lie there every night, in full on lucid mode. All these people would want to come and talk to her. A whole load of psychics would gather round her and peer inquisitively at her. They told her that they were not going to hurt her, but they'd be just staring at her, their faces right in hers. She'd get up, huff and puff a bit, and make a cup of tea. When she went back to bed they were still there, peering. Someone sent some birds. Some really big birds of prey to protect her.

There were three consultations in all.

During second consultation she met Jon who was to be her residential therapist. He was a scruffy, comfortable looking man, who seemed not to be able to look at her. She had had an hour to kill before the meeting and spent it in a charity shop decking herself out in a very beautiful silk coat covered with flowers.

The third consultation she met Sylvia, who was to be her therapist. Sylvia informed her that she was desperately sad, and expected some sort of response to this. She actually found this quite irritating, and informed Sylvia that there were two billion people in the world without access to clean drinking water, so what did it matter if she was desperately sad. Sylvia would not move off her base. Charlotte continued to find her irritating.

Eventually the great day approached for Charlotte to move into the rehab. She was terrified, as all she had heard about from rehab's is that people shout at you a lot. This, of course, is not strictly true in every case, but she thought it best to be prepared. Her father dropped her off and Charlotte thought that it would be a good idea to protect herself from the obvious onslaught that was bound to happen and started shouting. This was not actually a very good idea, because in the meantime she was terrifying herself all the more. She was holding her cards very tight to her chest.

They all had to sit down as a house and eat. There were three residential therapist, and four or five guests. Charlotte sat quivering at one end of the table, unable to eat as she was so scared. Jon, who had sat down next to Charlotte was entirely non-committal to her welfare and basically turned his back on her throughout the whole meal. Charlotte informed him that every healer needs healing. Carine, one of the cover staff, thought that this was funny, and changed it to the wounded healer, but Charlotte was adamant and told Jon again. He turned round and shouted at her. 'This is MY house', he bellowed. Charlotte shut up and looked at her plate. She did not think that this was very friendly. It may have been his house but she was paying the mortgage.

That being over, they all went to bed. Charlotte was put in a huge room called Sunflower, which was the size of two stables. She lay on her bed, which was stupidly covered in a bright red duvet cover and thought.

The next day they all traipsed into a house meeting. The other guests did not say much. Charlotte decided to ingratiate herself to all the other guests and told them that she had seen far worse and far braver. This caused a reaction. She knew loads of people who could do with a stay in rehab, and would really use the space. She didn't quite know what to do with it herself, because everyone was very quiet. What she began to realise was that all the other guests were actively either self-harming or suicidal. Her levels of aggression, which were based on fear were causing an extreme emotional reaction in the other guests.

In the first week of her stay all of them had had to go to hospital.

Lottie was the first. On Monday, the day after Charlotte arrived, she took herself off to a hotel room and took a massive overdose. No-one knew where she was. She rang Jon and told him of her actions. Jon then spent a frantic hour on the phone to her, trying to get her to tell him where she was, as the pills would be kicking in and it was imperative that she get to hospital. Lottie eventually told him, and an ambulance was called.

Paula was next, on Wednesday, taking a razor to her arm and carving a hole that went right down to her bone, and ten centimetres across. She took an hour to do it, and it needed stitches in Accident and Emergency. This was a fairly common occurrence.

Jenny was last on Friday. She also took an overdose and had to go to hospital.

This terrified Charlotte to such an extent that she decided to stop shouting. All the other girls were polar opposites to her, in that they dealt with pain in the way they did. She tended to deal with pain usually by channelling it into work or exercise, but since she was redundant the excess energy and frustration caused it to come out as anger. She was told that it was not her fault that all the other girls had gone to hospital, as they had to take responsibility for their response to her anger, but it did really unnerve her and make her think 'help'. She spent the weekend outside in the pouring rain, in her dressing gown, her feet and legs getting covered in mud. Staff would come and try and talk to her and offer her some tea, but she did not want to talk to anyone, and lay on the wooden decking, getting soaking wet, trying to find peace. After two days she came back inside, but did not say much.

She kept hearing this voice in her mind, saying 'Death or Glory'. It just repeated itself. Charlotte thought about it. She thought that there were some very good things about Death, metaphorically she meant in this case, and that there were some very bad things about Glory. She could not decide, and mulled it over. Death represented to her Change. Jon had a T-shirt on with a skull, so she nabbed it and wore it for a few days before deciding to give it back. She didn't want to choose Glory because she felt that it would return her to her Deb lifestyle which was very superficial.

She went into her therapy room, which was a small room known as the second office. She sat down in her chair and looked at Sylvia and Jon. Sylvia was wiry, with blond hair. Jon was gentle and kind. Sylvia started attacking her about wanting recognition. Charlotte listened to her, slightly perplexed. This continued all week, as they had three sessions a week. Sylvia would become more and more adamant, and vindictive about Charlotte wanting recognition. The recognition that Charlotte wanted to was to go and have a drink with a friend, which had so far eluded her for over 15 years. Charlotte continued to look at her in a slightly bemused way. She said nothing, and let Sylvia continue with her theories, wanting to know what was going on. Jon said nothing, but sat and observed.

Charlotte asked Sylvia if she had read her two stories about the garden centre which she had emailed in to the Managing Director. Sylvia refused to tell her. She knew Jon had read them as he had referred to them, and she even caught him thinking that he wanted a free go. Charlotte needed a sense of belonging. She had not lived in a community for 15 years and had very few friends.

Charlotte found a newspaper article which said, 'In reality she has no more hurdles left to climb'. She cut it out and gave it to a homeless woman who scurried off.

At the end of the first week Charlotte had a dream about Sylvia. She was Glenn Close in the film, Dangerous Liaisons. Sylvia was in the scene at the end, where she was taking off her make-up, having been discovered for her part in a really serious manipulation. She had used her male friend to sexually manipulate a young girl, causing her downfall. They had been found out, and her life in the French court was over.

After the first week, Charlotte was making a huge effort to be nicer to everyone. She was washing her hands in the bathroom, when she noticed blood on the floor, and went down into the kitchen and in a sunny manner informed Paula and Jon that there was blood on the floor, whose was it, and could they clean it up please. Paula became embarrassed and quickly went upstairs. Charlotte went to help her. Jon came up the stairs behind her and she could feel his eyes on her upturned bottom, and the resultant chemical reaction in his groin.

It was a few days later, as she was going to sleep at night, that suddenly an oval diamond appeared in her vision. It announced to her that it was Jon. Another oval diamond appeared and tentatively went to join him. This was a representation of Charlotte. They formed a band of gold that went round the entire world.

Charlotte immediately became very emotionally attached to Jon, as this representation she had seen told her of his heart, and she liked it a lot. She loved it in fact. She had been searching for Truth for so long, and this man, Jon seemed to have all the answers. She puzzled and pondered over it for a little while. She desperately needed a sense of belonging, having been out of action for so long; stigma and mental illness making a social life impossible. More recently she had been turning to men for this sense of belonging, which was not altogether a healthy option as she tended to get sexualised.

Josephine, one of the other residential therapists, took it upon herself to make a series of extremely bitchy comments to Charlotte, based on sexual jealously, as she had designs on Jon herself. Charlotte was upset by this and felt very threatened, especially as she had read Josephine's mind, as they sat outside having a cigarette. She had heard from Josephine; 'You think we're just here to cook and clean up after you don't you'. Charlotte thought that this comment was totally unfounded and based on jealously. She really did not like Josephine, and found her a huge threat, since she seemed to be incredibly malicious and cruel.

Jon continued his sexual fantasies. Charlotte could see them through her mind's eye as she fell asleep. She could hear the thoughts of the entire house as it drifted off for the night. She was becoming really worried, because this was not fair. This was not fair at all. She could so easily fall in love with this man. In fact, in reality she kind of already had. He was not that sexually inspiring, but the seed had been sown, and her sense of loss was so great, so enormous. And this was a man that she could never have, because he was her therapist, and as the professional regulations stand, she would not be able to stay in contact with him after she left.

She knew that, and yet her heart was beginning to be broken. Because in her mind they were beginning to have a relationship, which would never flower past their imaginations. And her emotional reserves were so low; her heart was already so broken. It was never meant to be, and yet it killed her, because she would have liked it so much.

So, at the end of the second week of her stay, she put on a white outfit and red shoes and went into her therapy room. Standing behind her chair, she told Jon and Sylvia that she had been a health care professional for eight years, and never in her life had she come across anything so unprofessional in her life. She was really adamant, she was really upset. He was totally crossing professional boundaries in the sickest way possible. She asked Jon to stop what he was doing. Please. He just smiled.

Jon went away for a two week holiday and she was left with Sylvia.

Sylvia, not being very imaginative, had still not moved from her original base and continued her onslaught about Charlotte wanting recognition. Charlotte continued to sit in silence and listen. She was getting really annoyed by all this. She thought that it would be lovely to live in a world where everybody was treated with recognition. What was wrong with recognition anyway?

In hindsight Charlotte realised that Sylvia probably was against her hurting other people to get recognition, and Charlotte agreed. What Sylvia did not realise is that they had put her in an impossible situation, and to be quite frank, it was Sylvia's job, in her position as therapist, to understand and resolve this. Sylvia made absolutely no attempt to get to know Charlotte. She asked her nothing about her childhood and in no way made an attempt to construct a therapeutic relationship. She just attacked.

Charlotte looked at the emotional content that came with Sylvia's repertoire, which was not very broad. She was more like a screaming harpy than a therapist. Charlotte told her of a psychotherapist she had massaged once, in a nursing home. This therapist had done a lot of good work in her time, and even in her nineties was continuing to write. But one thing that really struck Charlotte was for all the intelligence this woman possessed, she had really troubled, deeply shadowed eyes, and precious little heart.

Charlotte looked at Sylvia and saw the same kind of woman. Her heart felt paper thin, and seemed to lack emotional nutrition or reserves. And for all this shouting about Charlotte wanting recognition, all Charlotte could hear was this poor woman screaming for the need for recognition for herself. Of course there is nothing wrong about wanting recognition, but not when you are trying to destroy someone else in order to get it, something that Charlotte had tried desperately hard not to do and failed, but not through want of trying. She believed that Sylvia had only taken her on to fulfil this need she had for recognition, and the therapy was more about Sylvia's needs than her own. So after four weeks of this onslaught, with Sylvia practically lifting herself off her chair in her enthusiastic and adamant display, Charlotte just turned round to her and said; 'Fuck Off!'

This was on the Friday before Jon got back, and by the time he returned to the therapy room on Monday, Sylvia and Charlotte were engaged in a very heated debate. Full on slagging off match more like. Both of them just hurled abuse at each other, Sylvia in vicious attack, and Charlotte in extreme defence. Jon was bemused.

Sylvia proceeded to tell everyone at the staff meeting on Wednesday that Charlotte was a complete snob, based on what she had read in Charlotte's two books about the garden centre. Charlotte knew this as Sylvia would flinch when she mentioned details about her home life, so much so that Charlotte felt that she could not talk about them anymore. Sylvia also had rather an irritating habit of mis-interpreting events and circumstances based on her own bias. Sylvia's counter transference was huge and to Charlotte, who knew about such things, her jealously was very apparent. Counter transference being where the therapist projects their own issues onto the client, and makes out that they are the client's issues. There are not an awful lot of ways to get round this as a client, and it is up to the therapist to reach the conclusion themselves, which can take some time, as they need to work it out, and are not always gracious enough to admit it if they do manage the recognition. After nine months, Sylvia eventually did and apologised, but by then the damage had been done.

Charlotte realised that she may have pissed Sylvia off. On her arrival at rehab she declared that two of the residential therapists were not up to the job, having only done art therapy training. Time proved her right. She had a dream of Jon putting her in prison for twenty years for saying that, and not being allowed to get out. This was hardly a rehab where free expression of speech was invited. The other fault she found was the shared bathroom. Some of the guests covered the tiles in suicidal writing. Charlotte did not feel that she had to put up with that. It was a shared space and legally she had the right to complain as she was paying to use the house. Sylvia hated her for getting her own way.

Sylvia ignored Charlotte's stories about the jealously of her house-mates in Henton, Jon picked up on it as a pattern. Her first lodger was Irish and an academic at the university. She exploded in fury at Charlotte when she found out that Charlotte was from a titled family. She showed Charlotte a picture of a lake in which a million Irish people had drowned in the potato famine. She made it all Charlotte's fault and became so aggressive that Charlotte started shaking in her presence and had to ask her to leave. Her latest lodger was extremely jealous of her and on numerous occasions had been rude or threatening, but Sylvia was having none of it. In her head she was determined that Charlotte was a snob, and would speak of nothing else.

Charlotte did not think that she was being a snob. She wanted to achieve. All the evidence Sylvia had for Charlotte being a snob was contained within her book, 'The Psychic Revolution'. Freudian psychotherapy did not seem to take into account intuition or spirituality. That's why Charlotte preferred the Jungian model.

She had said to Fred the gardener that she liked practical people, because practical people solve problems in a way that had to work. He had replied that she should be careful of the sexual interpretations to this, which was his interpretation not hers, but that's Freud for you. Everything that she said was interpreted on, but usually wrong, as the therapists, led by a very zealous and bigoted Sylvia were heading down the wrong track. So caught up in their own theories that they would try and squeeze the reality into the box that they had created, even if it meant killing Charlotte in the meantime, because their theories, however much they loved them, did not fit.

Charlotte had just spent the last fifteen years on, or just off, the minimum wage. She couldn't actually afford to see any of her friends, as they did not live near her, and had therefore lived in isolation, as she had been so ill that making new friends was extremely hard. Buying a DVD in Tesco's for £3 was a luxury that she usually could not afford. She often got up in the middle of the night, desperate for food, and drank gallons of milk to try and get some fat into her. They didn't see this.

She'd spent years shouting at her mother, desperately alone, wanting friendship, and the only way she knew how to do it was to get a better job and be among like-minded people. So far, it had eluded her because of the panic attacks she suffered at work. She was confused because Sylvia seemed to get mixed up with the difference between aspiration and snobbery. Charlotte was very ambitious. She wanted to do God's Will. She had had no consistent friendship since she left Downe House eighteen years ago. People had come and gone in her life and the friends that she did have she saw only a handful of times a year. It was not enough to nurture her. Everything got thrown back on her mother, who had a be a carer, best friend and mother all in one go. She milked her dry. Matthew had always said that she needed two or three friends that she saw regularly. This was not possible. Her friends in Henton were her lodgers, who did not know anything about her past, making it impossible to have a meaningful relationship with them, and her old friends had turned their back on her, knowing nothing about her illness but scarred her with their ideologies. The only person in her life that she trusted and talked to was her mother, and her mother was dangerously ill as a result.

The reason Charlotte was so angry at rehab is that she did want recognition. She wanted friendship and she still had the dream of the TV program going round in her head. There was nothing else to cling to. She wanted to fulfil her talents and her creativity as she had been taught that that was the spiritual thing to do. Her time at Camberwell had been destroyed by Class bullying by a tutor and she was fed up with her life chances being annihilated by jealously.

Josephine and Sylvia both got hysterical with Charlotte as they thought that she was rejecting Jon because of class. Charlotte thought how odd, because she couldn't have him anyway, and she was protecting her already broken heart. She just could not bear any more loss. She used to get really annoyed by their bitchy, brazen cruelness, in a situation they knew nothing about, but they were using as a vehicle to attack her with, and enjoying the attack so much they did not bother to think of their motives. The only way she could think of to deal with it for now was to shout at them, which did not do an awful lot of good, it only fuelled their desire. Josephine had huge issues to do with class, having come from a hippy family that never worked. She internalised Charlotte's attack on her as being personal, not professional, and thought that it was her God given right to undermine Charlotte as justice for her own woes. Charlotte was desperate for help, but every ear in the establishment was dead to her.

As Charlotte said to Josephine in a house meeting, 'I am within my rights to shout at you Josephine. You are not within your rights to bully me'. Josephine was treating her as a sexual rival, and had her claws out, and used Charlotte's fear as a means to attack using Class as a weapon. Charlotte had lost everything in her life, including her mental health for the same reasons.

After that Charlotte barely said a word to Josephine for the rest of her stay, because every comment Josephine made to Charlotte was laced with a barely concealed jealously. Charlotte felt a pit of fear in her stomach every time Josephine came into the room.

So that was two residential therapists who were playing silly mind games, working against her rather than with her, and as a friend of Charlotte's said to her, 'Gilly, the third residential therapist looks completely ineffectual.'

The thing is Charlotte readily accepted that all the staff there were only human; it was just that they didn't! They thought that they were deities who always thought that they were right. They took no responsibility, and indeed, were quite blind to the fact that they could ever be human, and had the capacity to make mistakes.

After a particularly gruelling period of many months Charlotte turned round to the Managing Director and said to him that this Class bullying had got to stop.

Charlotte went to bed one night, dreaming of some girls from school. They had put a round wooden table out in a field and were showing her some blue china rabbits. Charlotte knew the rabbits as her mother had one. She also knew that they were very expensive. The two girls were showing her how much they cost, as if to say that they needed them and that they were important. Charlotte became furious in her dream. Suddenly the table disappeared, leaving field after field after field. Each field was separated by eight foot stone walls and Charlotte was climbing over each one. As she did, this enormous, charging, black horse just galloped over every field and sailed over every wall. The horse would not stop galloping. There was a powerful energy to it.

The Capitalist world was beginning to collapse. The biggest bank in the world, based in Britain, had gone from being worth £4,000 billion to £20 billion. Germany had the next biggest bank, and then the US. The fourth and fifth biggest banks were UK owned.

All the guests had sat together, in the first few weeks, at a leaving party for one guest. They had been discussing the idea of 'Shining the Light on the Shit'. They were talking about how difficult it is to get better, and then go back into society, only to find that society does not support people in their emotional difficulties or recovery. It is just something that is not talked about. All of them were in their early twenties, or early thirties, and all of them had spent half their lives actively suicidal and self-harming. There were four beautiful, talented women sitting chatting about how emotionally unsupported they were and how they feared they would never lead a normal life if they survived at all, which was not unrealistic.

Charlotte used to talk a lot about measurable results, at which point Josephine usually started screaming at her. Simple things, like racing round a guest through the busiest part of the city for the whole day, when she had been in hospital for two years, and was totally disorientated, they really didn't get. Of course it was going to confuse and upset the guest. It seemed pretty obvious to Charlotte. They just used to get irritated with the guest, which made her even more depressed than she had been already. She took to stabbing herself in self disgust on a far more regular basis.

Jon had lived in a Buddhist monastery for a year. He used to try and do some different work with the guests, involving deeper emotional work, empathetic heart stuff, which the guests responded too, but he was too busy with the day to day running of the rehab to put much time into it.

The residential therapists were timetabled for a minimum of 29 hours out of a 35 hour working week. That meant they had precious little time for the guests. They would often stay up until midnight, listening to stories, but at that point they were working for free, and not giving it much thought. They became quite resentful. Charlotte very much felt like it was her responsibility to ask the cover staff for help as she felt that the residential therapists did not actually want to help her, and made her feel bad for asking, if they did not shout at her, which Jon and Josephine took the liberty of doing at every given opportunity. Jon would scream at her regularly, right in her face. He had quite serious issues of unexpressed anger towards women, and he used Charlotte as a vehicle for his own recovery.

However.

Charlotte kept dreaming about Buckingham Palace and going out onto the balcony with hordes of cheering people in front of her. She was given the keys to all the churches in England. She decided to fill them all up with homeless people. She was carried around on a platform and put down and told to say something. She didn't really know what to say. She kept dreaming that she was clinging on to a particular type of Pittosporum; the one with the pale leaves. She would not let go of it, although people were trying to move her on, for her own sakes.

The cover staff were wonderful. Damien, an extremely attractive Italian, used to engage Charlotte on some really interesting discussions, that usually had them laughing at some intellectual loophole. He was very into the nature of creativity and would follow up Charlotte's ideas so that he could understand them with her. He was particularly supportive with everything that was going on in the house, and raised an eyebrow when Charlotte told him that Jon incessantly burned incense in his room.

Carine was an extreme star. She loved walking and nature, and they would often set off, fast walking, and fast talking for hours, coming back invigorated and relieved. Carine loved concepts, and they would break things down together, whilst standing by an oak tree in a forest, sharing stories and ideas and making mincemeat of insanity. Carine had read Charlotte's books about the garden centre and she said that the first one was re-writing the Garden of Eden story in the Bible, where Adam was blamed for their downfall rather than Eve. She'd eat endless lettuce leaves and lentils and dress like an Egyptian goddess, always swathed in purples and golds, with an accompanying pair of long boots. She'd take Charlotte out shopping, which was probably not a good idea, as Charlotte would come back with a host of pink, fluffy things which were not entirely practical.

Carine told Charlotte about the Swarm Effect in ants which had recently been discovered by scientists. The ants would not have their own mind but would work together in a collective mind which drove their actions. Charlotte thought how many similarities this had to the ideas which she was working on. She was only a beginner, there was still so much more to learn.

Nicola was a very petite Egyptian, who cooked up the most amazing feasts and was kind and delightful all in one go. She was an existential psychotherapist, and a DJ. She was amazingly caring and loving and in a very peaceful way guided Charlotte through the pitfall of errors that was there.

Madeline too, was a star. She was the only counsellor there, all the others were psychotherapists, and her kindness and humour was a real treat and joy. They used to cook and chat together, she peeling away all the layers of a purple cabbage, until they found the heart.

She could not have survived without them.

She had a dream about six weeks into her stay of Sylvia. Sylvia was going through room after room, desperately searching. All the rooms were empty, but decorated beautifully in yellow, with high ceilings and white cornices. Sylvia just could not find anything.

Eventually Charlotte took pity on her and decided to help her. Her dream continued and she went into her therapy room and took off a long, black leather coat, the insides of which were covered in knives and other weapons. It was heavily laden with very fine instruments. As she put it on the table between them the door opened behind her and she heard a voice say, 'Take these'. She was handed more weapons. She obviously felt the need to be protected from Sylvia. Therapy with Sylvia and Jon was like stepping into the lion's den. And she shook like a leaf throughout.

She would stand in the kitchen, in front of the Managing Director and Jon, and shout at them that she was the only person who was telling the truth in this house. Jon quite often would shout back at her, his face in hers, telling her that she did not have that much power. He was losing his cool. And yet at the same time he would torment her by talking in the house meeting about the incredibly strong bond that they had between them, which was not altogether appropriate in front of some of the other guests, who treated Jon as the only reason they were staying alive.

No one believed a word she was saying and no one heard her. Freudian psychotherapy did not leave much room for spirituality or understanding of the power of prayer. In a place that was costing a fortune to be in, and to be listened to, Charlotte never stopped screaming and asking for help for the next six months. She said that she was the only person in this situation who was telling the truth, and indeed she was. Jon never said a word to help her, and only laughed with Sylvia when she described his sexual fantasies to them.

Charlotte was not getting to sleep until four o'clock every morning. She would lie awake every night thinking how on earth she was going to get out of this situation. The loss of yet another man was something she could not bear. In the staff meetings they would discuss how Charlotte could not cope with sexual desire. It was not that. It was the unbearable sense of loss she was already suffering at the loss of Jon, which was inevitable. Sylvia and Jon used to find it funny and treat her heart like it had no feelings. Every night she would see his sexual desires flash across her mind's eye and for all the shouting she did at him to tell him to stop, he ignored every word. If she did mention details of her rape in the therapy room, he would enact them out in her mind's eye in bed that night. She was aware that she was in severe danger of being sectioned. She would scream at Jon and tell him that she had been suicidal for eighteen years, and this was her one chance to get better, and that he was totally standing in her way. He just used to get angry with her. Very angry.

She complained in a house meeting, that her therapy was more about his best interests than hers. Jon just turned round to her and said that he thought it was in both their best interests. There is not much room for mis-interpretation on that, except Charlotte knew that he was in control, he held all the cards, because only he could say whether he would make it real or not. It killed her.

She had spent most of the first four months in the house meetings screaming abuse at Jon, calling him an abuser and all the names under the sun. No-one was taking her seriously, and the effect on the house was chilling. There was a complete breakdown in relations between Charlotte and the other guests, and Charlotte and the other therapists. She was causing havoc, but she had no-one and was being completely isolated by Jon's antics, disbelieved by everyone, and in mortal pain. Seriously suicidal.

The other guests all wanted to help Charlotte, although her shouting was unbearable for them. Slowly evidence began to creep out that she was telling the truth, and they supported her on this. Expressions on Jon's face and other such material, were all picked up on by the other guests, and the tide began to turn slowly in Charlotte's favour. She no longer became so isolated and slowly company crept in once more. The guests suggested getting Jon an Anne Summers catalogue. She had lived for six months in a situation where everyone was treating her like dirt for telling the truth. The therapists continued to completely ignore everything she said. Even when she was pleading in mortal agony for help. They had been told not to believe her, help her, or engage with her on her level, and it left her desperate and suicidal.

Josephine continued to make bitchy comments, always trying to put her down, on a range of issues regarding careers, sex, and friendship; anything that she could get her hands on. She started to have panic attacks and uncontrollable spasms in Josephine's presence.

Charlotte had taken to going to one of the big churches in the centre of London. She would go there religiously two or three times a week for the first four months of her stay. She loved it there, and found a droplet of the peace that she was looking for. She asked after the services if she could go and live in a convent for a while. They put her in touch with a nun, who she emailed.

After three weeks of not getting a reply she went back to the church and stood there, in her mind, screaming; 'I want a job with the church'. She kept on repeating this, until she had a reply. 'Check your emails', were the words that came floating back. So she went home and did. There was an email from the nun, which was three weeks old, and it was inviting her for further correspondence. Charlotte began to realise that the clergy used the same techniques as her. She saw in her mind's eye as she went to sleep at night, thousands of teenagers, all wearing bright orange hoodies, amassing outside the church.

For all the months that she went to the church, the Head of the Church and the other clergy would be lovely to her. They wanted to talk to her, and be nice to her. However, she was terrified, and as soon as the service was over, would bolt out of the church as fast as her legs would carry her, usually before they got to the door. It was not unheard of for Charlotte to walk the streets of London in floods of tears, weak as a kitten.

It came as a source of great relief when she began to see the Father in her mind's eye come and protect her. She hid within the church at night in her mind, to escape the roving dreams of the rehab. The arguments Charlotte and Sylvia had continued throughout the night, as they both battled with each other were huge and exhausting. Charlotte just felt that Sylvia was trying to get complete dominance over her. Sylvia did not believe anything Charlotte was saying, about her and Jon, and Charlotte was fighting for the truth.

The Father kept Charlotte safe in his sanctuary of the church, and invited both Sylvia and Josephine in. He questioned them thoroughly about their motives. Charlotte saw him tie both of them up in a chair, and beat them up, violently and thoroughly, as he obviously felt their envy towards Charlotte. Jon was not allowed into the church, and if he was, Charlotte hid behind a nun. The Father obviously felt that he had no evil intentions towards Charlotte.

The nun had asked her in her email for her calling. Charlotte thought about it long and hard, and the answer came in a dream, where she saw the inside of the House of Representatives and through one door appeared the Leader of the Republican Party who wanted her to help in motivating teenagers. The prospective Leader of the Democrat Party came out of another door and wanted her to help in foreign affairs. She did not feel capable of helping either of them at the moment, and prayed some more. She sat out in the garden, by the pond, breaking the ice for the little family of plastic ducks that she had. A song came on her portable radio, given to her very kindly by her father. The lines, 'For all that we've been through, I will make it up to you. I promise too' came on, to which she sang along at the top of her voice. She decided to help her mother. That would be her calling. She would help her mother with the environment and healing and all the things that her mother was into. That is where her heart lay. The nuns however, where not impressed and declined their invitation to the convent.

The next day the new President of USA of America was announced.

Charlotte remembered a science fiction film she had watched once, years ago. All the scientists had built a rampart through the forest. They were time travelling into the past, or the future, she could not remember which. Anyway, the scientists were told not to move from the rampart, so that they would not destroy any of the wildlife, as it would have a cause and effect on the ecosystem and effect the present day. One of the scientists fell of the walkway and squashed a butterfly. When they got back to the present day, they found that not only had the language changed slightly, but also the President of US of America had changed. I suppose this became known as the Butterfly Effect.

Charlotte had been sitting a few years ago in her attic, in which she was painting a huge oil painting, in yellows and purples. A Red Admiral butterfly came flying straight towards her painting, like a suicide bomber, and went splat into the thickly laden oils. Charlotte did not know whether to be a Buddhist and not kill it, or a Christian, who she thought might be compassionate, and kill it, since it was destined to die anyway.

She danced in her room for three days after they got the new President, and rushed about smiling at everyone. Everyone was really happy. He was their President too and he was going to look after them all.

What Charlotte found most ironic, is that Jon and Josephine pretended to be such hippies, and proclaim peace and love and they were acting in the most competitive, jealous, damaging way possible. Charlotte frequently used to feel a pit of fear in her stomach when Josephine was in the room. She would frequently start to shake or spasm, a reaction to a threat, which of course was being mis-read as illness. Sylvia was pretty certain that Charlotte should do another two years in residential care, which apart from being a complete waste of time, would have cost a fortune. Charlotte was in extreme danger, and Sylvia held all the cards, as her clinical judgement on Charlotte was a bit like God's. Every member of staff did exactly as she directed them, and she had the power to section Charlotte or detain her in residential care for as long as she saw fit. The fact that Sylvia was totally missing the point, and actually creating illness, or rather bullying Charlotte, did not dawn on her. Charlotte's family was kept completely in the dark about Charlotte's treatment, and only given advice by the Managing Director, who was totally under Sylvia's wing. All that was seen was a screaming, tortured Charlotte. The real reasons behind this were unseen, except by Sylvia, who seemed to be enjoying every ounce of the pain she was inflicting on Charlotte, and helping herself to more at every episode.

But going back to jealously, which was the theme of that moment. It was pointed out to her by one of the other guests, that those who experience jealously are usually jealous themselves, whether they are aware of it or not. Charlotte thought about what she might be jealous of. She thought of all the problems she had had as a result of being raped, and how they had stopped her being promoted at work, or having any form of social life. All she really wanted was to go and have a glass of wine with a friend in a nice wine bar and feel friendship once more.

She thought about the economic theory of happiness, which says that once you get past a certain point in salary, an increase in salary does not equate with further happiness, indeed it starts at a level to decrease happiness. Once you get to the point that you can go out and enjoy yourself once in a while and see your friends etc. and have security of a home, without having to worry about money, any increase in wealth does not actually constitute for an increase in happiness. You just go to more expensive places, and buy more expensive clothes; it doesn't actually make you happier. And once you get a really big salary your levels of happiness decrease, as you're so stressed and do not have time for your loved ones, and space to relax.

Charlotte thought that the therapists were being stupid in attacking her. Jon and Josephine had a good salary of at least £18K a year, free accommodation, free high quality food, at least 29 hours a week of free therapy and tuition. They all had good support networks and people that cared. They were on a fast track in their careers and they had good prospects. The rehab cost her father £80K over a nine month period and that money had to be going somewhere. The food was good.

Christmas was fast approaching and Charlotte was exhausted. She had not stopped screaming for five months, and had not slept a wink. Not one person at the rehab was engaging with her on her level. They were all treating her like a complete idiot. There were constant threats of her having to leave. Usually they were from Jon. She thought that this was a bit rich, and she would tell him that she had been suicidal for eighteen years and he was totally getting in the way of her healing. And no one believed a word she said.

Sylvia sent her her notes after her stay. She used the words 'She who had been born into everything', to describe Charlotte. Sylvia knew nothing of the stress that Charlotte had grown up in. Her notes mentioned absolutely nothing about rape or fear of men, or mental illness for that matter. Her tone suggested one of extreme hatred and jealously. She didn't realise that I was living in one of the rougher parts of Henton, on the minimum wage, paying the bills on a house of four people and housing an alcoholic, a suicidal psychotic lesbian and an ex-heroin addict in my vain attempt at a rehab.

None of the guests were particularly overly enthusiastic about Christmas. There was a deep depression over the house. The residential therapists weren't really very enthusiastic either. They all wanted to spend time with their own families. All three of them got very sick over the two week period. They had spent hours decorating the tree, and wrapping presents, and spent a very large quantity of money on some lovely food. They were watching TV and the song 'Hallelujah' came on, sung by a girl in a gold dress. Just at that moment the Christmas tree fell straight into Charlotte's lap. Lottie got hysterics and couldn't stop laughing. The horse chestnuts that they had put in the oven caught fire and started burning, exploding into another guest's face and getting her hair covered. Suddenly all the guests started to enjoy Christmas a little more.

Charlotte spent hours wrapping up all her presents. She decided to write a card to the Managing Director, even though he didn't like her very much. He had shouted at her in the face calling her vindictive, being furious with her, because of the way she was behaving around Jon. She had smashed a mug on the floor, and put her face right in his as he screamed at her, frightening him away with her defiance. Countless mugs had been smashed, and always for the same reason. Jon had watched her clear it up, having set up the situation in the first place. She just said to him, 'Why did you do it?' He just looked at her and admiringly appreciated her figure.

She wrote endless letters to the Managing Director, except that from where she stood, nothing was done. The pounds signs were ringing up in front of her in rather a sickening way. It was costing nearly £2000 a week to be there, and so far she was not quite sure what had been achieved.

When Sylvia and she were alone, Sylvia would turn on Charlotte and nastily tell her that she didn't like her, as if her opinion actually mattered. When Charlotte told her father about this, the Managing Director made Sylvia apologise. The endless letters that Charlotte wrote to the Managing Director were not heeded, and Charlotte's parents were out of the loop, as they could not get involved in the treatment. Charlotte did try and bring friends in to help her but they were powerless. Charlotte had no one to go to to make a complaint, or who would listen to her.

Of course, her mood had massive ramifications across the house. The other guests level of self-harming and suicide attempts increased dramatically with Charlotte's pain. Her mood was severely affecting the recovery of the others, and sending them all into complete regression. This was her worst nightmare, the insanity of the mental health system. It was do or die for her, and for others as a result. This was the situation which had always given her the most dread. She had been diagnosed as mentally ill, with bipolar disorder, for sixteen years, when in fact the root cause had been rape. She felt raped in this situation in the most horrible way, because she could not prove it, and he knew it. She was in a situation which could section her, could write her off as insane, and keep her within a residential rehab situation for another two or three years, so that when she came out she would be too old to have children, and she had absolutely no way of proving her sanity.

This is the situation which had terrified her for so long, because she knew in her mind that she was right, that her perceptions were real. She was dealing with a bunch of people who rationalised and removed reality a few steps all the time from life. They drew inferences, and conclusions, but they were always based on their own perceptions of reality and could not draw the distinction. They refused to put themselves into the equation, which was their fatal mistake, because they had this insane belief that they were right all the time, that somehow they had transcended human emotions, and were in control of themselves to such an extent that they were beyond motive. Sometimes Charlotte thought that all these people were using their position to act out their prejudges and fantasises in the most horrible cruel way. And they did. She thought of a therapist she had seen once, who had risen off the chair when she had talked about intuition. She had called Charlotte mad, in the rudest of terms. Charlotte had told her that she could report her for that. She had replied, 'Well who would believe you. You are mentally ill'.

In physics, it has been proven that the results of the experiment will change if the experiment is observed. The observer does have an influence on the results. In this situation, no one was observing the observer. And they were drawing the most terrifying conclusions, because Charlotte was working in a system that was out of their parameter anyway. They did not understand the logic and certainty of her mindset and they were ripping her heart to shreds.

Sylvia later said that Charlotte was cleverer than her, in a manner which made Charlotte think that it really hurt her to say that. Charlotte was a bit confused by all of this, as she rated being clever as number five on the list of attributes. She rated being kind as number one. Charlotte thought Sylvia was a bit stupid. She liked to provoke Charlotte. Charlotte thought that this was to cover up the fact that she didn't know what she was doing. And she honestly believed that. Sylvia was turning Charlotte's therapy into a personal battle for success. And Charlotte was not going to let her win. Because she was a bitch, and she was doing it for herself, and trying to destroy Charlotte for her own ends. She did not care two hoots about Charlotte's health.

Sylvia and she did not stop screaming at each other. Charlotte would stand in the therapy room, screaming at Jon. 'That man is an abuser, and you are a perpetrator to abuse'. Sylvia would respond by mirroring her. Charlotte was mirroring her initial aggressive performance when she was talking about recognition not to mention Jon's sexual aggression. The decibels raged and nothing was done. Nothing was achieved. Charlotte waited for Christmas to come.

Charlotte passed by a shop, just before Christmas. She did not go in at first, but only later when she was with her brother. She found a mug there, which said; 'Man of the Match'. She bought it and decided to give it to Jon at Christmas.

Charlotte did not know whether to leave the 'Man of the Match' mug by Jon's bedroom door, or to leave it under the tree. She would not be there over Christmas. She knew the Managing Director was coming, but was told that he was coming on Boxing Day. She discussed it with some of the other guests so as to make sure they were not hurt. They seemed to think that it was fun so she decided to leave the mug under the tree.

As it happened, the Managing Director changed his plans, and came on Christmas Day instead. Jon opened his present in front of him. Charlotte knew this as she could hear the absolute fury of the Managing Director telepathically from where she was many miles away in Devon. From what she gathered from the conversation the MD wanted Jon to give him the mug, but he refused. The MD was furious, absolutely furious, because in his mind, everything that Charlotte had been saying had been proved correct. Jon adamantly refused to give up the mug.

Charlotte had used this tactic before. It worked by stopping aggressive sexual advances and promoting peace. Whether or not it was actually serious did not matter at the moment. She needed him to calm down and it worked, to the benefit of all.

Charlotte asked Jon for the mug back when she saw him next. He just screamed in her face and refused to give it back. This was all about him, not her. At, coming up for the maximum of three years, he had been too long in that rehab.

When Charlotte next saw the MD he was trying to be extremely nice to her, in a very apologetic way, whilst at the same time wiggling the wedding ring finger of his hand in a suggestive manner. She had had a dream before she went to the rehab of him trying to touch her breasts, so she was not a massive fan of his.

Jon accused her of trying to intimidate him.

That she found quite ironic.

It seemed as if the place had fallen apart over Christmas, whilst she was away. The other guests had been having a very difficult time.

The next few months were very, very painful for everyone. Lottie and Paula both were sectioned and had hospital stays of a month each. Another guest had burnt her entire arm to third degree burns, which is until she cannot feel any more pain. She had plastic surgery on it, and spent two months in hospital as it was felt she needed round the clock attention.

Charlotte was managing to coast a little. She found it easier to be in love with Jon than to fight him. Jon mentioned in passing that he had just spent the last four months with his supervisor telling her how he was in love with one of the guests.

She asked Jon to go out with her in one of their therapy sessions when Sylvia was away. He became extremely defensive and asked her whether she had just come to the rehab to find a man. She did think that she had come to the rehab to deal with coping with men's sexual fantasies about her, which she later pointed out to him, explaining to him in no uncertain terms how on earth he could construe any other meaning from the words, 'Fuck Off you Bastard', other than those intended.

So she asked him out. All the other staff started running around in glee. They were delighted with the situation. Carine would point out that the pots that she had got for the garden had her name on, and the word 'sold', as well as mentioning smugly to Josephine that she had been trumped. When they all sat and had lunch all the cover staff would try and raise their glasses in joy, in a toast to the unspoken situation, of which Charlotte knew nothing, was told nothing, and in real terms her heart was being shredded. This was rehab?

Alex, the art therapist told Jon in no uncertain terms that the brush he had picked up, in his words, thinking that it was broken and wanting to see what it did, was not actually broken, it was a special brush for a special purpose. Charlotte felt totally used.

Jon had sat in a house meeting saying how when he went for his first psychotherapy interview his interviewer had told him how he had had to choose between his job and his wife. Jon turned round to Charlotte, and said, 'what do you think of that Charlotte?' in front of everyone.

Charlotte stopped trying to look beautiful, and ran outside to get her coat, which she hid in.

Jon made repetitive comments about wanting to find a wife, and as someone pointed out to Charlotte, always when there was no other staff around. He would flirt with other guests, just to annoy Charlotte. These were all vulnerable, young women and he was completely playing with emotions, creating jealously between them and illness. One of the other girls tried to commit suicide and left the rehab permanently as a result of his actions as she was so vulnerable and dependant on him. Charlotte told this to Sylvia and Jon in the therapy room, and they tried to blame her for it.

It was not until she stubbed out a cigarette on her hand that the staff immediately realised that this was a new pattern of behaviour, and eventually began to relate to her on her level, and actually engage with what she was saying. Sylvia still seemed to think that she needed another two years in residential rehab. At the end of January, surprise, surprise, when Sylvia was alone with Charlotte in the therapy room, Sylvia leaned forward maliciously from her chair and informed Charlotte that she did not believe a word that she had been talking about in the last six months. She went on and on, in a really evil manner.

Charlotte just picked up the lighter she had in her pocket and in an equally evil way, said; 'Don't you, Sylvia? sneering at her, whilst proceeding to burn the palm of her hand in front of Sylvia. This rose into an argument, with Charlotte continuing to burn her hand to piss Sylvia off, for twenty minutes, with Sylvia's tone rising into panic. Charlotte couldn't give a fuck anymore, as the system which was supposed to be helping her was tormenting her beyond belief. She just couldn't be bothered. Sylvia wasn't helping her at all, and was actually damaging her with her blindness and jealously. She was being tested beyond extreme.

Charlotte was racked by uncertainty. She was terrified of asking Jon whether he wanted to stay in touch with her after she left, as she was scared the answer would be no. She spent months trying to build up the courage to ask him, but found she could not, as he had become her world. This was the situation she had anticipated and dreaded, and was the reason she was trying to make him leave her alone. She did not know how she was going to cope.

The atmosphere at the rehab had noticeably changed. Something was up.

In February Charlotte was overcome by a voice. The voice kept going round and round in her head. It was talking about her becoming a residential therapist. All of the other guests had commented that she was better at helping them than the residential therapists.

The voice kept going round and round.

Charlotte took herself out on loads of walks to listen to this voice over a two day period. The words; 'part time, permanent, residential therapist' were the most important ones.

They had been discussing plans for resettlement at the rehab. So she decided to write to the Managing Director about her plans. She asked him whether she could become a part time, permanent, residential therapist. She wittered on about government spending on the NHS, and money due to sickness at work but really she was padding out the letter.

She gave it to Sylvia. Sylvia was obviously not allowed to open it. Charlotte said that she had asked for a job. This sent Sylvia into overdrive. She was furious about the situation. She wanted to know what was going on, but the Managing Director did not tell her. He drew Charlotte in for a chat, and said that he would like her to stay and help him grow his flowers, (as bait), but also added at the end of the conversation that he would give her a big leaving party when she left, (as a security policy, just in case his plans did not work out). Charlotte knew he was playing mind games with her. He would not give her a straight answer, and he was just playing her, which she thought was a bit stupid when she was in his care. He teased her, as did Jon, with uncertainty. And her sense of belonging and trust was shattered.

All the time that he was playing her, Sylvia had got a bee in her bonnet. Charlotte could hear her with the MD in the room below her bedroom. They talked for an hour and a half, and Sylvia was giving it all her wellie. She could hear her loud protestations. Charlotte could not help but smile. She kept leaving little notes for the MD saying how Sylvia's jealously was destroying her career.

The thing is, for Charlotte, this whole balance was being destroyed by uncertainty. And the uncertainty of Jon fairly much blew things apart. Sylvia just seemed determined to destroy her. Charlotte was not that concerned whether they gave her the job or not, it was just an idea that she followed up on. Jon told her that it would be in both their interests if she made an extra effort to get on with Gilly and Josephine.

All the other guests knew about this. Lottie found some confidential paperwork that said that they were considering a fourth residential therapist. Charlotte continued growing her flowers, and they all seemed to be blooming. The guests had really taken to Charlotte, and leant on her a lot more than the residential therapists.

Sylvia continued to be furious.

Jon was kind, and a source of great comfort to Charlotte, but in total denial as to his motives or actions. Charlotte was left in the dark by the very people who were supposed to be supporting her.

She told Jon that it was a very strong wish of hers, ever since she had been sectioned, aged 20, to bring the psychiatric and psychic worlds together. The government were trying to standardise alternative therapies, like aromatherapy, but were finding it extremely difficult to scientifically prove their validity. There are some things which do fall outside the realm of science, but as she took great pains to explain to Sylvia, it does not necessarily mean that they don't work.

There was a grapevine that was growing into the conservatory. Jon liked it. Charlotte kept trying to pull it down. She said that it would destroy the building.

Fred, the gardener, was a beautiful hippy who was also a therapist. He would talk to Charlotte for hours as they sauntered round the garden discussing plants. He told her how Capitalism had been set up by a psychotherapist as a marketing system, who had used things like crowd control, herd instinct, competitiveness and greed to create a consumer culture.

For her birthday Jon and Carine were spending hours making her a bright pink birthday cake, decorated with an enormous pink butterfly, which she had asked for. She had been told to go out into the garden whilst she waited. She sat by the pond, a very favourite spot of hers. She had been trying to find an identity over the past few years, and had taken on being an oak tree. She did not like this as it was extremely tiring, as you had to support loads of people. She had also tried being a sunflower, which was fun, but also exhausting as it required high energy. She had heard that peonies do not like to be moved, and had spotted two peonies by the pond, both still in bud. She waited for them to open. One opened loads before the other, as the other was dappled in the shade of the big trees. As the peony came into flower, with its deep magenta hues and folds of beautiful petals she suddenly was struck with identification. She was the peony and all the other flowers; the cascading white roses, the pale blue ceanothus, and the hoards of white wild onion. They all took a place in relation to her and each other. And then came the buzzing of the bees and the insects pollinating all these plants. The squirrels and the birds feeding. She felt total peace and serendipity in her place in creation, and the supportive structure that was looking after it, nurturing it and sustaining its growth and development.

Lottie had given her a beautiful T-shirt with 'Nurture Nature' written on it.

She had taken to weeding the garden just before Christmas. She knew that really it would be best to leave it, but deliberately misjudged the fact that gardens are supposed to be aesthetic. Fred put her right, as he pointed out that all the dead leaves that she had collected were put to best use by putting back down on the beds as the plants could use the nitrogen that they contained.

And so it was that Suzy, one of the cover staff, who only came in every few months, bounced into the room. She had just been in handover with the other members of staff and had been filled in on all the news.

She leapt up to Charlotte and said the immortal words; 'So you have been reading Jon's mind, and then you have been reading the Managing Director's'.

Charlotte grinned at her inanely and agreed what a wonderful thing it was.

It actually took a few weeks for the reality of what she had said to sink in. And when it did she was very pleased.

She had proved it academically, medically and legally.

She waited until the eighth month, when Sylvia, under extremely heavy duress, allowed her to make the decision to leave and then explained it to Sylvia in very simple terms. When you have been through the mental health system and been treated like shit by doctors who are overworked and don't have the time of day for you. When you have had countless rejections and social stigma from all those you used to love and hold dear. When you have lost everything in your life, because society deems you to be unacceptable, and the way you think to be mad beyond belief. When you have lived that life for nearly two decades, and been isolated, alone, confused, uncertain, shivering and quivering in what is deemed insanity. When you have been totally degraded and unfit for use, or purpose of any kind. When you are stigmatised so much for your thoughts or beliefs, which do not hurt anyone, but are deemed different and therefore unacceptable.... Actually Charlotte wanted to say it a lot stronger than that, and she did. She held up Sylvia like the Spanish Inquisition and told her straight out.

What Charlotte was actually trying to say is that she had proved her own mental health against one of the most rigorous, logical, academic disciplines in the world, Freudian psychotherapy. They had validated her sanity. They did not see fit to tell her directly, it had to come out by accident, but she had grown used to their callousness, and defensiveness of anything that did not fit their parameter.

She had total, absolute peace of mind. Job done.

She was reminded of something that had flashed through her mind in the very first session she had with Sylvia. It was a scene from the film 'Rob Roy', about a Scottish Highlander, about 800 years ago. He had had to fight a last battle, with this really irritating expert swordsman from London. The man from London was devious and mean. He was manipulative and cruel; a complete bastard in fact. Rob Roy was not really trained as a swordsman, but this man was an expert. They were fighting; Rob Roy was hurt anyway, and in great pain. He had already fought an excruciating difficult battle and was on his last legs. The Londoner got him to the floor and held the sword to his throat, leering at him. Rob Roy was certain to die. He decided not to, and put his hand on the other man's sword, blood pouring from his hand. He just lifted the sword away from his throat, and with a great cry of fury grabbed his sword and bought it slashing down on the man, cutting him in two.

He walked off, saying it had been a matter of honour.

That's what Charlotte felt about this fight.

Those records that Sylvia had been so neatly keeping could have been used in a court of law against her at any time. Charlotte really should have been in psychiatric hospital rather than rehab as her psychosis made it impossible for her to do any work and she needed a stronger level of Olanzapine, an anti-psychotic drug. It was eventually put up from 5mg to 20mg which stopped the mind reading and made her much more logical. Sylvia's aggression towards her led her to long term unemployment and not being able to leave the house for two years with chronic anxiety which has crippled her ever since.

Sylvia apologised for her jealously towards Charlotte. She admitted to her jealously and said that it had been subliminal, using terminology that Charlotte had introduced anyway. Charlotte was totally unimpressed by this. She had not slept for months, lived in a permanent state of terror and fear, and never come so close to death in all her life. All because her therapist was jealous of her. She had constantly complained to the Managing Director about Sylvia's jealously, but was told that nothing was wrong. There was absolutely no perception that the staff may ever have been in the wrong. Charlotte was talking to a brick wall most of the time, a brick wall that had her verging on a breakdown.

Josephine thanked her when she realised that there was nothing left between Charlotte and Jon. He was hers to play for now. Charlotte blamed him for standing in the way of her therapy which as she constantly reminded him, she had to wait 20 years for.

Charlotte thought about the reason why she had started to write in the first place. She had read a book ten years ago, about a woman who lived in LA who was a dealer in Native American Indian art. One day a Native American spirit guide came to see her, and told her her mission was to get a marriage basket. The woman had to fight a dangerous spirit to get the basket. She eventually won, but nearly died in the process. The spirit guide came again; telling her that if she wrote a book, it would change her life. She duly wrote a book, and as a result got to go to live with the Native Americans. Those words, 'Write a book and it will change your life,' touched Charlotte all those years ago. It didn't change her life, so she kept on writing. She thought that this time her spirit world had become real, and she was at last where she wanted to be.

When she got home, her GP asked her if she was still hearing voices. I know that there is a great overlap between spirituality and psychosis, but Charlotte really did feel discriminated against, especially in view of all the work that she had done. Jesus later said to her that if her book was published he would like her to do a PhD on the spiritual side of psychosis.

My old friend Beth told me that she knows when people are praying about her. What Charlotte felt that she had proved was the power of prayer. Scientific studies are done in the USA which test the levels of crime when people are praying for peace. They fall dramatically.

Of course, all good stories have to come to an end. As if by magic, a room came up in her house, so she was able to return home.

In aromatherapy it is said that about 85% of the effectiveness of the treatment is due to the therapeutic relationship; i.e. how safe and how much you trust your therapist. Charlotte felt totally unsafe and completely threatened by Sylvia, who she felt was trying to destroy her and the rest of the rehab didn't score very highly either, apart from a handful of shining stars.

She did agree that she had made enormous progress at the rehab, namely in losing her anger, which she realised was utterly futile. It was pointed out that it was she who had done the work.

She was extremely grateful for what she had learnt.

Nicola came to her in her mind as Charlotte thought back on her experiences, and they smiled together. Nicola said that she had not just proved it to herself, but to them too, for themselves. The Busy Lizzie that Nicola had given her from a cutting was beginning to flower in the most gorgeous shades of pink.

She thought that it was important to point out that in the UK rape by definition is when a person does not consent to sex. They do not actually have to vocalise this.

She thought of the story of the mole catcher, who used to catch the moles, but leave the babies behind so that he had work for the next year. She had told Jon in January that this time she was going to catch all the moles, even the babies, because she did not want to have to do the same work next year.

Charlotte felt that it was important to tell the truth without fear.

Two years later, as she was still unable to leave the house due to the chronic anxiety she suffered because of her treatment, Charlotte sent over 2,500 emails of complaint to the rehab. It has subsequently closed down. The emails were useful as they allowed Charlotte to work out her own psychology and so she at last felt that she had got her money's worth.

What the rehab eventually did was make her realise the level of hate in this country towards people like her. It made her realise where she didn't belong. She made the move into a Republican area, but not before she tried and tested the reaction in her house first, which was in a strongly Democratic area.

It was sad really, because the rehab was in a beautiful part of London. There were some very nice people there and she enjoyed getting on with all the other guests. It was a shame that Josephine and Sylvia had made it so much hell. You can't force love. It's got to grow naturally. She probably would have got together with Jon if it had not been for the pressure that they had put her under and she would have liked to work at the rehab. But it was not to be. Maybe it was 'silver' that Matthew was talking about? She had yet to find 'gold', but she did know that it was proving to be very expensive, both emotionally and financially. She hoped that she could find her path. The jungle was quite thick and she did not have the tools to clear a path.

The ring with the two oval diamonds she kept. The two diamonds fell off, and left the ring of gold.

Charlotte would like to say thank you to everyone who supported her during her stay at rehab, with special thanks to her father who paid for it all, and had done the best for her, in the knowledge that this was recommended to him as one of the best rehabs in the country. The good wishes and support of everyone really helped her.

## PART 6 - THE CONTINUED ATTEMPTED MANSLAUGHTER OF CHARLOTTE DAY; THIS IS AN ELECTION ISSUE

I'd just come out of rehab, or rather, forcibly removed myself. My therapist had wanted me to stay another six months, which I felt was not entirely in the interests of my health. In doing so, I lost a job working for my father's company, which is something I'd always wanted to do.

I'd been in London for 9 months. I had very little contact with anyone back home, and was going to stay living in London as I'd spent a fair amount of time with old University friends there. However, it was my old lodger, Matilda, who encouraged me to come back home.

I did so, and died.

There was nothing, there was nobody. There were only the two girls who rented rooms in my house, who after five minutes of trying to encourage me, gave up. They had no idea of where I'd been.

I'd been to hell and back. I'd been screamed at for nine months. I was a quivering mess, who didn't trust anybody. I sat alone, trying to make sense of my world. I felt impending doom, and clung to the fury and injustice I felt as it was the only logic and reason that could recompense the pain I felt.

One of my lodgers, Daisy, took a different view. She started tormenting and bullying me. Calling me names with a passion and fury that I could barely understand. She called me posh, elitist and words to that effect with a barbaric viciousness. She had read my books about the garden centre. She tried desperately hard to undermine me and ridicule me. She did it with such force and passion that I could barely understand where she was coming from.

Eventually I had to let her go.

I'd been to see my mum for a few weeks, and started screaming and stabbing my hand with a fork, drawing blood and a shocked expression. I said that I didn't know anyone in Henton; there was no-one I could talk to, and I was being attacked again about class, through no fault of my own. It was their own jealousy. I had had a very strong voice in my ear telling me, before I went into rehab, that the two girls I shared a house with were not my friends. It was a warning, of which I took heed and did not share any personal information with them. They took it upon themselves to ridicule me for all manner of things and I took it upon myself not to notice or care. I had been warned.

It did still hurt though; the way they were treating me. I could not believe anybody could be so cruel or so callous. They were deliberately trying to hurt me. I started self-harming as a result. If only they knew. Would it have stopped them, or would they have enjoyed the hunt and caused yet more pain. I only saw them as stupid. Unbelievably stupid. Cruel beyond words. And yet they enjoyed it and dug in some more. They were just renting rooms off me. There was no more to the contract than that. But they would not let me be and found fault in everything that I did.

I only knew two people in Henton, and did not see them very often, as they were busy - perhaps once in two months each. I had known quite a few people, but the stress of the last few years had broken all contact.

My mission was to become an MP, but I had yet to have a party to choose. I wanted to stay in Henton and join the Democrat party, taking over from Tom Woodwood in years to come. However, the moot point was that it was becoming impossible for me to stay, as my inadequacies were not mine and evil activities were afoot. They did everything in their power to make my life miserable.

My mother had three major operations in the last three years; two of which were life threatening; a hole in the heart and a blood clot. It is actually a miracle that she got through the last one. She came a hair's whisper away from having her leg amputated. She looked after me when I was seriously ill for eight years. She gave up her whole life after her divorce to care for me and guided me through some of my darkest days. She did it single handedly. She is a brave and heroic woman. I really enjoyed the eight years that I lived with her. They were the best years of my life. We had such fun in the garden. She was always making me pretend to be a tree, so that she could design the garden correctly. She was endlessly nurturing, endless giving and great fun to be with.

The last eighteen years of my life amounts consists of psychic bullying, and my mother's near death.

I took to the psychic world to solve my puzzles and create connections in a very barren world. For three months I sat motionless in the garden, tidying up loose ends, at some considerable emotional cost. I mentally said goodbye to quite a few people; which hurt. One of which was Billy. I spent hours at a tapestry shop in Wrentham. I wanted to get a tapestry of a duck but to me it resonated with feelings of being a 'sitting duck'. I chose instead the barge and canal scene which reminded me of Billy. It even had his name on one of the barges. I dutifully completed the tapestry over the run up to the election. It was my only thread I had left to him.

For some bizarre reason I decided to set up a website. After much faffing about, and asking silly questions, I managed to get the hang of it. CharlotteDay.com was born, and I uploaded all my recent artwork.

Matthew had been supporting me. He said that it was like drip-feeding an anorexic. I was absolutely dead to the world, and could not relate to anyone, but would sit quivering; staring into space for months. If I had to go out to the shop, it would take all the will in the world not to stop shaking as I did my transaction, which was something I could not often manage, and I would have to return home hungry. Matthew was the only meaningful connection I had in the world, and I clung to his psychic direction with an implicit trust, as he had got me through some very sticky situations before. I trusted him with my life, and it is due to him that I am still alive. I never saw him. It was all done psychically.

My father was incredibly generously supporting me, as, because I had an income from my lodgers which paid my mortgage, I was not entitled to any benefits. He has always been really helpful and it certainly took an awful lot of stress out of my situation.

I lived in a haze of psychic past, putting my memories into order.

There was also the small problem of rats. Before I had gone into rehab I had pulled up the carpet, which was rather dark. The sitting room did not have a window directly into it and I wanted to expose the floor boards. I pulled up the ply boards under the carpet too and put on a finishing polish. However, when I returned from rehab I heard the deadly news. The house was full of rats. They did not take to the poison that the Rat Man gave them, but they did eventually begin to drop off with the blue poison that I liberally scattered. They would appear from under the sofa as I sat on it, and amicably move to me if I sat in silence for too long. The sound of them gnawing the wood, trying to make a hole, filled my being with fright, and to this day I still startle at the sight of a shadow crossing the room.

It was getting very cold outside. I had to move inside. I wanted to ask the man who I talked to in the High Street to come and live with me. He was homeless and I had a spare room. I thought about it quite a bit and asked my father. One of the girls who was in the rehab at Christmas had been rescued from the street by a very kind woman who took her in. She was able to make a pretty good recovery. I later had a dream that he was coming to rape me, so I thought twice about it.

I had seen an advert on TV when I was at rehab of a punk dressing up as an aristocrat. My therapist, Sylvia, told me that it was because of the work that I had done. I told my brother that, and he put his finger to his lips and just said, 'be humble'. I stopped reading the papers and watching TV after that, even though I could see in the headlines that there were some blatant referrals to what I had done. I wish I had read them now. It would have kept me better informed so that I could make a more balanced decision about what to do.

It made me think of a text I had sent in January when I was stuck in rehab. I had told a friend about the recurring dream I had; being married to a man at the end of the table, with a dinner party of guests, and the occasion had been my birthday. I had shown Matthew the dream, years before, and he had gone very quiet. He later told me that the room had been Draughts; the President's country house. I had reckoned that I was forty in the dream. 'Happy Birthday to my beautiful wife'.

I clung onto that dream so hard. Some of my deceased family came to help me. They had all been Commanders in Chiefs of Armies, and there was a large part of me that could not find expression in where I was living. If I wore a smart coat out to the local shop I felt and feared attack. I was finding that I was constantly being called upon to be diverse, and yet no one was extending the favour to me.

All this time rumours were circulating around Henton. There was great consternation about the fact that I was not going out and integrating. People were getting quite shirty. I would have loved to go out, but I knew only two people and they were not that available. I just needed someone to support me. I did not have anything to give. I was still dangerously ill, and quite frankly getting quite irritated by the lack of understanding people were showing me. I had not gone out over the last fifteen years, because of being raped. I felt shit enough as it was without hearing what the people of Henton had to say about me. They didn't know anything, and they certainly didn't bloody care. After what I had been through at rehab I was in no mood to take any more shit, but that is all I got. God I run out of patience sometimes. Attempted Manslaughter attempt number two, and it did drive me to the point of suicide, knowing what rumours were circulating. It was as if everyone was talking about me, but no one was talking to me. Daisy was going out of her way to be rude about me. I was not being a great landlady and she had no compassion or understanding.

Charlotte became more and more deluded as one by one her life lines disappeared. She had no friends to speak off, her house was a hostile place and it seemed as though her community too was turning not just barren, but aggressive. She was deeply traumatised from her time in rehab and had no-one to turn to. Her home was her only sanctuary.

She clung to the Republican Party and Percy Piggins as they represented safety to her in this barren world. She was being attacked and she had no reserves or defences apart from solitude. Percy Piggins represented authority and safety. He would see her through. He supported the heroin addicts and those living in poverty. He knew about the ills of the world. He had lived in one of the roughest council estates in Henton purely to be able to understand the problems that they faced. She held onto him so hard because he was the one voice of reason. Everything that he said resonated with her and she looked to him with hope for a better life.

Help came one day to Charlotte. She had been sitting by the pool in semi-darkness for months. Her long, black hair had become matted and the stench of sweat and body odours had almost become too much. She was dangerously thin, and had just taken to starring out across the shrouded lake. A few pretty water lilies showed their heads and were beginning to flower, and fish occasionally darted before her eyes, but she saw nothing. Only darkness, loss, pain and no way out.

The Compassionate King sat down on the bank. He had been watching her for some time and was unsure of how to approach. He had been calling her name softly to her, and the occasional tilt of her head showed him that she must have heard.

He sat down beside her and slowly she began to realise he was there. He had a beautiful, gentle presence. It was very calming, very reassuring. It was authoritative but gentle and she found herself warming to him. He did not say anything and nor did she. They sat in each other's presence and she could feel him taking the weight of her pain. It was a shared pain.

Charlotte had not thought about the dream about the man at the end of the table since she had told her friend the year before. In her mind, she had been the President. It did not seem to have much significance, and she let it pass. There were more important things to contemplate. Life and Death being one. However, she did join the Republican Party.

Since she had a lot of time on her hands she took to reading the Republican Party Policies on their website, and sending in her views and opinions, which were slightly tongue in cheek. She began to hear telepathic feedback from this, and was beginning to see that the life she left behind was over and that the new life she had entered had a slightly different format. After much conversing with Matthew, she decided to send in the book she had written, 'Truth or Die' to Percy Piggins. The only thing she was worried about was that it would be kept confidential, and Matthew assured her that it would be.

Charlotte was becoming more and more psychotic but she delighted in contact with the Republican Party. She wanted to feel that she belonged, she wanted to have some part in this great drama that was unfolding. Her opportunities were bare, she had nothing to give, so she deluded herself into thinking that she was important, that she had a part to play because in reality she had negative resources. She clung onto the Republican Party because she knew how dangerous the world was and she wanted their support. She was terrified of leaving the house and often had to come back to the house empty handed because she had too much anxiety to buy her food. The Republican Party offered her some sort of sanctuary in an increasingly bitter world.

Fantasy was being carved from reality. She relied heavily on Matthew and derived meaning from her senses. She could not tell whether she was right or not, but it gave her a guide. Her intuition took her to a place that she could only imagine. And she found that she carved her reality there. Fantasy took over, but it was a comfortable place to hide from the inertia and pain of the real world. Who knows how much of what happened is real, but Charlotte started making connections and relying on people for their approval and judgement. Whether or not they were actually aware of her or not is not the question. She relied on the politicians as she trusted them and wanted their approval. She was looking for authority after rehab where those in positions of authority had been so unkind to her. She was looking for a mentor, looking for guidance and looking for support. Whether or not they were aware of her was not the question. She wanted answers from them, so she made it all up as she went along and imagined their responses.

Charlotte began spying on the Republican Party. They were after her for some reason, and she did not know why. She had countless dreams of Percy Piggins in the village hall that they had met in, asking her to marry him.

She saw the TV advert again. It implied that Percy Piggins would win votes if he had Charlotte on his side. She began to be suspicious, and stopped watching TV after that. She usually averaged about 6-8 hours a year of television viewing anyway, so it was not great loss.

But she couldn't help but love him. She had first heard about him when she had been friends with lots of ex-heroin addicts and been in a spot of bother. She had heard that one of his close friends had been a heroin addict, and knew immediately that he would have full understanding of the issues involved. She knew that he was the trustee of the heroin rehab. She was failing so badly with her boyfriend at the time. She became terrified of sex. They had moved out from the stud cottage that he was living in. She trod on a newspaper and picked it up. There was Percy Piggins standing next to an old school friend. She was his PA. They looked so happy together and half of her liked the picture of the young, dynamic, positive man she saw in front of him and half of her hated the girl, because she represented the school that they had been to and the lost opportunities that she had had as a result of their failing to pick up her illness for 6 months until she was so far gone there was no return. She has always wanted a career; for the money – she could not afford to see her friends, for the stability and for the friendship of like minded people. It had been denied her. She always worked with very old people or very young people on the minimum wage. He was the answer to the prayer that she had been repeating like a mantra for so many years, whilst her life was being ripped away from her. But she didn't even know it. He not only knew the issues, but was in a position to do something about it. She had been desperate with her ex-boyfriend. She had felt that she had disobeyed God. She would have done anything for help.

Something inside Charlotte let off a very bizarre chemical explosion. But she was unaware of the certainties. When she had received a recurring dream about being married to a man in Draughts on her fortieth birthday she also had a recurring dream about a State Funeral in which she was floating as a spirit above. She thought that something serious was coming, or at least that is what they preached at Henton University. The last person who had had a State Funeral was Sir Winston Churchill, and he had had to win a World War. She thought that she had to do something. She thought that God was calling her to take part in politics and it was of the utmost urgency. She had prayed so hard for a career and now this was the result. She did not give much thought about which party to join, she only knew that she had to do something. She thought the environmental issues of the world were going to prove catastrophic.

She couldn't quite believe it when she received an invitation in the post one day for the Republican Winter Party at the village hall in Medstead. This was the same venue that she'd been to two years previously, and she'd stormed into the hall, wearing a bearskin, totally interrupted Percy's speech, and made him flush.

But this time the invitation was handwritten!

It was all butterflies and fairy dust, and Charlotte rang up her brother in a great state of excitement to tell him that she had a handwritten invitation!

She put the phone down, mooched about a bit, made a cup of coffee, and sat down and looked at her invitation and realised with slight disappointment that it was computer generated handwriting. She did not even know that this existed. She did try to explain, in high excitement, a few more times, with a few more people, but they put her straight and dampened her spirit. However, as far as her brother was concerned, Charlotte had a hand written invitation to the Republican Association Winter Party.

Charlotte only knew that a state funeral was going to happen. She did not give a moment's hesitation to going to the Party. She knew that something was afoot. She deluded herself into thinking that she was important and that she had a part to play, for everyone's benefit.

She wanted more than anything else to do God's Will and it seemed at long last that God had a plan for her!

She wondered what it was all about.

Suddenly it dawned on her. She thought about the dream with the man at the end of the table, which was supposed to be in Draughts. She suddenly realised that this might have been common knowledge by now. She suddenly realised that it was her 40th birthday in the dream, and that she was not the President, but Percy Piggins was. Shit! She suddenly realised that she was married to the President; she was not the President herself.

Fuck!

She suddenly realised that everyone must know, and how it must have annoyed Percy Piggins. He was happily married with a very beautiful wife.

Shit.

She decided to keep everything secret, which in turn drove her parents mad, as they thought that she was being incredibly deviant and not doing anything.

Shit.

She called in Matthew!

Matthew was his usual attentive self, and catered for her every whim and desire. He began to call her the perfect student. Charlotte started to occupy a strange space of non-existence and took to listening to everything that was being said. She did not think at all, and if she did think she asked Matthew's opinion on everything. He told her the only rule was 'Listen, Listen, Listen', so she obeyed. He looked after her, and guided her through all the telepathy that she was hearing. He told her when to listen, who to listen to, have you heard this, don't say anything, shhh! He was always there. He completely took over the reins, and she was extremely grateful.

She had sent in her story 'Truth or Die' straight to Percy Piggins, marked 'Addressee Only'. Needless to say, within a week, she was hearing feedback from her book from all the Republican Party and some of the Cabinet MPs. They were all really shocked by what she had written, and she thought they were quite impressed too. She had sent it in as part of a job application, which was quite a strange thing to do; but she got to know some of the characters of the Republican Party and enjoyed hearing their comments on her work.

She took to listening intently to everything that they were saying.

Charlotte was now dangerously mentally ill. She had totally lost touch with reality and was living in a dream world. She thought that she could read the minds of those in power – those people who she perceived to be talking about her and she sat up day after day, night after night, with who she perceived as Matthew, reading their minds.

The Great King lowered his head and drew a picture in the earth, so that Charlotte could see. He drew the world, and in the world, he drew a smiley face. A smile lingered on Charlotte's features. She couldn't believe anyone could draw anything so simple, and yet so perfect. She touched the ground on which it had been written. He signed it and put her name too.

Charlotte kept starring at the picture.

It was beautiful. Tears welled up in her eyes, but her heart was smiling.

'Welcome Home', he said to her.

She could not believe it.

She didn't believe it and withdrew further into her shell. Her long black hair flooded down the back of the long, black velvet dressing gown that she wore. The rats drew ever closer sensing her vulnerability, kinship and distress.

Matthew told Charlotte, exasperatedly, on more than one occasion, that there is no point being psychic if you don't believe what you are hearing.

She had sent in her CV when she had asked for a job. She had wanted to study International Studies but had changed her mind as she had gone to a lecture at Henton University entitled 'Climate Change; Leadership at Local, National and International levels.' All that she had learnt is that due to man-made chemical confusion in the atmosphere, politicians had ten years to evoke changes, otherwise the climate would change irreversibly and we would enter the Androcene Period, that is the extinction of man in 100 years.

Charlotte hurriedly wrote into the Republican Party headquarters and asked if she could help.

The Great King sat with his advisors. They were watching Charlotte, but they could not touch her. She exuded a strange, deathly chill which meant that they could get nowhere near her.

The King's Foreign advisor was looking through her sketches on the website with the King. The King was concerned; 'They are very sexual', he said. The Foreign advisor was a chirpy, lively man, 'but look at how considered they are.' The King scrolled down through Charlotte's sketches. He stopped briefly on one of a big oak tree, which she had called Mighty Oak. It was covered in hearts, big and bold. The King sighed. He had still not got any further to working out how to break the spell that enshrouded her.

Matthew happened to mention to Charlotte one day that it would be a good idea to email her father to tell him what she would do if she made any money from the sale of her book.

She sent him an email late one evening.

She wanted to start a school for entrepreneurs in an old disused pub. The entrepreneurs in question would come from one of the rougher housing estates in the constituency.

The King's special advisor got quite hysterical at the suggestion.

'I don't want Charlotte teaching all the hardened criminals of the world to mind read the Government', she declared.

Charlotte's face began to smile, but she still listened.

Charlotte went shopping to buy some new books. She had placed all the books she had ever owned in her life on one book shelf and now was in search of some more. She liked writing about issues; but now she wanted to write about more global issues so she went to Machrie's in Henton; the most academic bookshop she had ever been in and tried her luck. She was a little nervous of the books, but came out with a book on poverty, global migration and world poverty.

She ploughed through the first one. It was heavily academic, and full of stats and some very obvious facts. The second one on global migration was slightly easier, but quite repetitive, and the one on global poverty was full of passion and written by a man who really knew what he was talking about from a lifetime in the field.

Then Charlotte began annoying everyone by asking for a job. She'd been asking for the same job for years and no one seemed to want to give it to her. Anyway, she asked Oxfam and Cafod, to name a few; if they could send her on a plane to a remote country so that she could write about them.

They didn't want her to. Her bid for freedom kept failing, so she kept on listening to the racket that was going on in her mind.

Percy Piggins's Winter Party came around. She had invited two friends to go with her. She didn't know what to wear, but had heard the Republican Party discuss her. They had all been made to read her story, and other members of the party were getting quite annoyed that Charlotte was taking up so much of the Republican Party's time. Charlotte didn't mind, as they were healing her. She used to listen in to their discussions of her. They were always very nice, methodical and intelligent, looking at things from lots of different points of view, without judgement. She found herself liking them. They all thought that it was very important Charlotte was dressed smartly at the Winter Party.

The photo on her website had been taken when she was just out of rehab and visiting some crop circles with her brother and his wife near Avebury. She was looking as scruffy as could be, and running gleefully down a hill, grinning like a Cheshire cat. She was not really making life easy for herself, although she knew Percy Piggins liked the photo. She had also put a photo of a cow's udders and calves, which she thought was frightfully funny.

She didn't know how tall Percy Piggins was. She wanted to wear her long, black boots with heels, but that would have made her nearly six feet three inches. She decided to go for it anyway, and wore her long, black velvet coat and a pair of jeans.

God, she was nervous. Luckily her friend was nervous too, and her nerves counteracted Charlotte's.

Charlotte had long been told that in order to publish her book, 'Truth or Die', she needed to have a boyfriend, as it would make her too vulnerable. The Cosmic Wisdom held, but as she was five minutes away from the Winter Party, the spell was lifted and Matthew said she could go ahead with the book without a boyfriend.

That lifted a pressure, and Charlotte went into the party mildly relaxed.

She spotted a table in the corner and went and they went and sat down there. Tim arrived and got them drinks and they all waited, thinking that this was all quite fun.

Low and behold the Great Man arrived. After meeting and greeting some of the guests he came straight up to us. Luckily he was about six foot four. We all stood up. He asked

Matilda where she worked. She gabbled away merrily. He knew her housing association and told her they were good people there.

Then he looked at me, with a large degree of apprehension and wanted to know if I was working at the moment. He said it in such a manner that made me think of my father, and I felt like I was being told off. I thought that this was quite funny, as I wasn't working and felt really naughty, so I pulled a comical face, said 'No' and promptly collapsed into my chair. I found his manner very intimidating.

Matilda swiftly saved the day and we started giggling.

Percy Piggins found this all rather nerve-wracking and started to heavily question Tim.

Percy Piggins gave an extremely passionate speech, which got the blood going, and we all went home happy, or sort of.

I had to step around a man on the way back from my cigarette. I passed Percy, who was sitting on a chair on his own, thinking about life. He had a face of such depth, compassion and utter unknowing on him. He thought to himself; 'I want to get elected on merit, not because who I am married to'. As I raised my leg to get past a chair I showed him my heel, not just to show him how smart they were, but also how dangerous. I was frightened at the connections that had been made. I was frightened about what had gone on when I was in rehab and I was stepping into a world I knew nothing about.

It was his face of understanding, confusion and uncertainty, of perhaps wanting to get to know me, but unsure how to – whether I would be worth it; which I carried with me, and conversed with for several months.

Charlotte saw that an email had been sent to her the afternoon of the Winter Party from Percy Piggins's Long Green email, inviting her to look on the Republican website for work. There was a job in Henton over the election, looking after a team of volunteers, and for two months after it, with the possibility of an extension.

What Charlotte was really passionate about doing was be in a position to write issue books about the affairs of the country. She was using, or rather, clinging on, to Percy Piggins, as a vehicle to do that. That was the real reason she found him so inspiring. He didn't quite come up to measure on other accounts. She had great dreams of writing for the Commonwealth, about issues and problems and perspectives that would educate others in their foreignality and bring this small world together in a rich, illustrative account of diversity of cultures and similarities of humanity. She kept looking at her tobacco pouch, which said

'UK DUTY PAID', and longed of adventures overseas. Hair dye, contact lens and medication could have been a problem. But vanity aside, her heart was really in it and she longed for adventure and new cultures. She'd had her fill of it in Henton.

I was desperately unhappy and desperately alone. More than anything I wanted to get back to something familiar. I wanted to get back to a way of life I knew, and people that actually knew me well. I felt totally judged by the people around me, who did not know me at all. I was craving company and affection and something that could sustain me.

Yet again I was not sleeping. I had not really slept before 2 in the morning for the last three years. But in the last two years it had been consistently 4 am.

I felt so drawn to Percy Piggins as I knew he was thinking about me in a caring and compassionate way. I knew he was looking after my interests and knew that he was fully aware of the depths of sorrow that are possible. Unfortunately the aggression at the rehab had mortally wounded Charlotte. She had lost her trust in people and especially in authority. She looked to Percy Piggins for authority and kindness. He was going to help her and other people in her situation. He got up every morning full of ambition and audacity, every day, to help people like her. He did it because he cared, she could see that on his face. He wanted to make a difference in her life and in the lives of others like her. He wanted to change the world and make it a better place.

Charlotte began to draw in the sand too. She liked the King's picture. She didn't know what to draw because she thought his was really good. She made some little scratch marks, and turned around to show him, with a smile on her face. Her eyes showed warmth for the first time in years. He smiled back at her and took the stick from her hands so he could carry on the drawing.

His advisors bought some new clothes for her. They were clean and fresh. She was given a long, deep blue, velvet coat, and they combed all the knots out of her hair for her. They washed her and bought her food to eat. She only picked at it. She did not have much of an appetite.

The King said that he had to go. His advisors wanted to talk to him. He made a little bed for Charlotte to sleep in and gave her a safe, sheltered spot where she would not be disturbed.

He said that he would come back, and if she needed him, she could think of him.

She watched him go. The shadows settled in once more, and darkness grew. She was terrified of being attacked and started to cry.

The evil haunting memories of her recent past crept up to destroy her once again. She had not been sleeping. She never slept. She had vicious, recurring nightmares of being attacked and mauled savagely.

She had been a Princess in a far off land, and had fallen prey to a wicked spell. She had been stripped of everything that she had and been sent penniless, begging into the streets. Her former friends had spat on her and she had been kicked and bullied. She had been raped and had become a slave girl. She grew to love the life she had and was very happy, but the wicked witch saw that she was happy and sought to destroy her once more.

The wicked witch decided to turn everyone in her life against her by called her a posh, stuck-up Princess. Underneath the new velvet, blue coat that she wore, Charlotte was covered in lacerations and scars where they had attacked her. The scars were months old, but they still hurt her when she moved.

Every night she would go to sleep and see the wicked witch in her dreams. The wicked witch knew that the King loved her and so was determined to destroy her so that the King would not want her. The only thing that mattered to the wicked witch was that the King and Charlotte would not be together. The wicked witch wanted all things bad to happen to her.

Charlotte knew that the spell cast by the wicked witch had been cast far and wide. And she knew that the damage done to her by the wicked witch was nearly mortal. She was so scared now. All she could do was sit and be alone by her pond in the darkness, because she was so terrified that people were going to hurt her. She knew the wicked witch would be really pleased to hear that.

She felt really sad. She used to love her life, but the wicked witch had spoilt it all and made her afraid, and she could hear from the whispers in the trees that people believed what the wicked witch had said about her.

She didn't know what to do. She tried to get up and move but the pain was too great and she collapsed in a heap. She thought it was safer to stay put and wait. The King would come back, with his advisors, and they looked after her. They nurtured her by giving her attention.

She needed looking after, and there was no one else to do it for her. Occasionally a little boat would come into the entrance of the lake, and people in the boat would call to her, holding out a lantern, trying to find her. But she couldn't move, the pain was so great. If she moved, the wounds would come open and the blood would rush out, and they would have to start to heal all over again. She thought that it was better to stay put and let the wounds heal.

She whimpered and cried a bit, as she wanted to talk to the people in the boat. They had come to look for her, but she couldn't get the words out. She sat hugging her knees, and crying. Her throat had gone dry.

She waited for the Good King. He would come back. He would help her. He was the only one who could reach her. He understood what she was going through.

Except there was someone else there.

There were two people. One was the Sorcerer, and the other was her cousin Earnest who was long dead, but liked to look after her. The Sorcerer liked to call himself an Intuitive Counsellor rather than a Psychic as people tend to understand that better. Charlotte clung onto him as he was another man that she trusted. He had always been so kind to her and was such a loving man.

The Sorcerer went around the woodland clearing looking at the energy, feeling the magic. He would come and sit beside her and show her things. Charlotte liked what the Sorcerer did, but she did not know why he helped. He did not usually like the Great King and his advisors. He usually favoured the Opposing King. But he said in this case, the Great King was the best man, and his advisors were the best people to rule over the land.

Charlotte did not question the Sorcerer much, as he had ways and means that were totally beyond her disposable income. She knew that the Sorcerer cared for her. He had helped her in the past. She wondered what would happen if she and the Sorcerer fell in love, even though she knew the Sorcerer was celibate, for spiritual reasons. She thought that they would be very happy, although she was a little concerned because the Great King needed her to do something for him, and she was not quite sure what. She let the Sorcerer help her. She liked the Sorcerer, and relied heavily on him.

Earnest was the Commander in Chief of a Great Army. He was very concerned about Charlotte's health, and spent a lot of time making sure she was ok. He guided her on matters regarding the Great King as he had had experience of this. He watched all these proceedings with renewed interest.

Charlotte remembered back to when she was little. She lived in a house called Lower Mill House in Malham. One of the first books she had ever read was about a little girl called Charlotte, who lived in a village called Malham, and she worked at a hospital for badgers.

Charlotte had spent the first two years of her life, in the Army. She had been born in a British Army Hospital in Germany. She had enjoyed being in the Army, there was always lots to do, and her father was a Captain. He drove tanks, and tanks go through anything.

They went to live in Malham when Daddy left the Army. He studied for three years, and we all had to be very quiet. We were watching our pennies, and my parents made a huge veggie patch and kept sheep and chickens. It was really important Daddy got his exams, and there was a lot of stress in the house.

I woke up two years ago dreaming of this with tears pouring down my face, and uncontrollable sobbing. I dreamt the same dream a week later and sat bolt upright in my bed, hysterical and shouted, 'I want to PLAY!'

We lived near the council houses and my brother would always take me and my younger brother running across the cornfield. The farmer would get quite cross and chase us. We spied on all the boys from the council houses, who were much older and playing on their motor bikes in the woods. We called them the The Big Boys. I always wanted to play with them.

My older brother always had to be leader, and we all had to call him Captain. The password was always Castle. We would make mud pies with some of the younger boys from the council houses to throw at the cars, and they would call my brother Prince William.

When my older brother went away to school I was 5. He got bullied and didn't like me anymore. I didn't want to play with my younger brother because he looked like a monkey and he didn't look after me like my older brother had. He was a baby.

I had seven years before I went away to school as well, and I got to know some pretty strange characters in that time. They were all over the walls of my house.

Not much was said about them, and they were always downplayed, but they became for me legends, daring heroes with courageous adventures, and they turned my life into a fairy tale and my parents into mythical heroes and heroines.

There were two men in heavy red uniforms. They had a battle going on behind them, and medals on their breasts. One was a father and other was a son. I never really knew which, but they had fought in the same army and commanded troops and created legends. They stared at me from their heavy gilt frames as I sat having my Sunday roast as a little girl. I was daunted by them, and would lower my gaze, quite in awe of them.

I got caught up in the Changing of the Guard last year at Buckingham Palace, with all the horses with their plumes and the soldiers, and there was even a carriage. I stood next to a lady from New Zealand, who said she had seen it ten years ago, and had come back to show her daughters. I had tears of pride rolling down my face as I watched them.

Then there were endless black and white photos of men in army uniform. I never could quite manage to remember who was who, or how they fitted in to who was alive now, but they all seemed to be Brigadiers or Generals, or Commanders in Chiefs, and I so wanted to talk to them. I thought they looked really nice, and I wanted to see how they did things, because to do a job like that is no mean feat.

I milled about the house for 7 years, between the ages of 5 and 12, and this was my company. All the stories, all the legends, all the greatness. I just sat and stared, and it filled my head with chivalry and wonder.

I was at the village school with my younger brother, and we would go into the church and sing, 'I Wish I Was a Butterfly', with the vicar and do all the movements. But I didn't want to be a butterfly. I had much more important stories going round my head. I wanted to be like them - the men in the pictures. I wanted to be courageous and daring and just and loyal. I wanted to be a Medieval Knight on a Holy Quest.

Charlotte woke one morning hearing Percy Piggins on the radio. He sounded really upset by something. Timothy Tailor had attacked him unfairly about Class. Percy Piggins said that if Timothy wanted a Class war he could have one. In the Netherlands there are about 20 political parties and they are always in coalition. There are not two dominant parties like they have in Britain. Therefore their do not have the same class differences as we have in this country, and their Queen also rides a bicycle through the streets of Amsterdam!

Charlotte plotted. She was annoyed. She had been through similar stuff and had lost her entire life to other people's issues around Class.

So after a few days pondering.

'Don't mention mental health Charlotte, they will use it against you.'

She put pen to paper and sent in an email to Timothy Tailor, six newspapers and a blind carbon copy to Percy's email address.

Dear Mr Tailor,

I have heard that you have been making a series of highly abusive remarks to the Republican Party leader.

I, myself, have been suicidal for 15 years and nearly died last year because of the attitude that you are perpetrating.

You, in your position as President are making such an attitude acceptable to the rest of the country. If you were in any other job you would be fired on the spot. And I personally think you should be if you continue discrimination and inciting, what is at grass roots level, violence.

Charlotte Day
HENTON

The King said; 'Print that out and circulate it'.

Timothy kept quiet.

It turned out that inciting violence is a criminal offence.

Charlotte had a dream of her dungeon where she kept all the people who had offended her. They were all tied up neatly so that they could not escape. Timothy happened to be in the dungeon tied up. She went up to him and took a badge of his suit. It said '01'. Percy came down the steps of the dungeon and wanted the badge from her. She did not want to give it to him. He already had a '01' badge attached to his suit. Instead she pinned it to her suit. It obviously represented the position of President.

The Great King was delighted. He told his advisors of how Charlotte had swooned at the party. They loved it. The stories raged about Charlotte swooning. Charlotte sat at work getting a bit annoyed.

Charlotte called her mother that evening, and said that the Republican Party's job that they had shown her was a dead end job with no prospects, and she probably wouldn't get it anyway as she was not qualified. She said that she wanted to do her degree, as it was investing in herself. Charlotte's mother told her father.

The King said that he would throttle Charlotte if she didn't help him

Charlotte felt ripped apart and terrified. The feelings that she had had at rehab, where there had been no one to help her were resurfacing. This was mindless destruction. Her mental health issues had come to the fore. She had completely lost touch with reality. She was living in a dream world, where all she cared about was the order and authority that the Republican Party offered. She wanted safety, she was scared. They offered her peace and tranquillity. She felt so threatened where she lived and did not have any one to confide in. She was carrying the heavy burden of a state funeral and she did not know what to do with it. She thought she had to marry Percy Piggins in order for him to have a state funeral which would have world changing consequences. In short, she went mad, but not before she had got into serious trouble.

Charlotte decided that she wanted to leave Henton. She went into complete shock at the way she had been treated. She felt the gossip and the injury, the attacks and the humiliation, even though she rarely saw its face. There were extremely high expectations on Charlotte, but absolutely no support and all the Democrat voters delighted in destroying her. The reality was that she still wanted to be an MP, but the truth in fact was that she wanted to get back to living in the countryside and that was the only determining factor in her choice of political party. The Democrats only had one seat in the area and it was right in the middle of the city. She longed to return to nature.

Charlotte had been staring into her pond over the last few days. She was beginning to find it a little more interesting. The grass had grown a bit, and was looking particularly lush and vibrant. A great big bullfrog was croaking around beside her. She watched him do breaststroke in the water, his body lit golden by the sun. She was beginning to relax and shake away her cares. The trees were kinder to her now.

She thought of all the leaders of the world and how they were doing and what they wanted. She saw a tall man with a beard, wearing a turban and dressed in white. He said that he wanted her to visit his country and write about his people. If she came he would give her a horse.

He had visited her once before, when she was in rehab. She had stayed up really late into the night, smoking in the conservatory. Suddenly this great force of anger came beside her. It was him. He had read her book and had agreed with her sentiment. She felt his anger and began to cry.

Then a remarkable man from the Motherland, one of the most beautiful countries in the world. He told her he wanted her to write about the poverty, beauty and bravery of his country.

Charlotte sat by the pond. She was tired and it was dark. She let her mind idly wander to the Great King in the far off land. He was going to chop her up in little pieces. She was rather shocked, but listened on. He wanted her to come to his country, and then he would kill her and send her back in little pieces to the Great King. She didn't like the sound of this much.

She rang her mother, and asked if she could drive to Devon and spend some time with her. Her mother said yes, and that she would leave the key out. Charlotte thought she might wait until the morning, but as soon as she thought that she was violently sick eight times. She had to get out of the house. Her mother was the first person Charlotte had talked to about how she felt in months, and the stress and strain all came out. She was desperately suicidal. She couldn't sleep and did not want to live.

The Great King had left Charlotte. She was alone. She missed him so much. She missed the intimacy, the empathy and the understanding.

The Great King wanted her to be well, but she couldn't be well. He was controlling everything in her life. Everywhere she went, everything she did, the Great King would hear about it. And for all his kindness and compassion he was judging her and she knew that she was failing. She did not have the resources or energy to be the person the Great King wanted her to be, although she would have loved to be that person herself. She did not want to lose him, but she was losing the only person who had shown her real kindness, real trust and real understanding. She could not tell anyone about the Great King, because she thought that they would not understand.
'No', she screamed.
The Loss of the Great King was too much to bear.

Charlotte was so dangerously ill it was hard for her to keep on going. She was a nervous mess of anxiety, always listening, trying to get a sense of control. She never slept. She stayed awake all night, trying desperately to find out where she belonged, who cared for her. She wanted more than anything a sense of peace, but her only peace was her house and that had turned into a hell hole. It was not a place of safety for her anymore. She clung onto it and she clung onto Percy Piggins, because they offered the peace and the sanctuary that she needed and deserved.

Charlotte was given strong sleeping pills, and anti-depressants. She sent messages to people back in Henton, as she knew that they would have a wider audience. People were expected her to perform, when she badly needed some encouragement and love. She did not know what she was living for, apart from a dream. She caved in under the pressure. Nothing was sacred, nothing was confidential, and nothing was held. There was no nurture. She hated life.

Back in Henton, I told my house-mate of all my delusions. I needed the support. Percy Piggins had been coming to me in a dream since two months after I came out of rehab. I thought that he was asking me to marry him. I said that I felt totally spied on by him, and I was unable to do anything or get to know new people as he would be using them to get information.

I said to my house-mate, 'Did he mean it, or was it a vote winning exercise?' I said that I was going to join the Democrat party.

What I tend to forget is that people do have very strong political views. My house-mate, and most of the people I know in Henton are strong Democrat supporters. I live in a very safe Democrat seat. This did in fact influence my lack of recovery over the last nine months, although I was not aware of it.

My house-mate went and put it on Facebook, and it spread round pretty rapidly, and I joined the Democrat Party the following morning.

At my Politics evening class, I hid in the loo and cried at the break. I was terrified of talking to anyone. They told me in the class that I was feudal, and tried to make friends with me by inviting me out for a drink, but they were all men and I was scared.

My membership application to the Democrat Party did not go through, as I had not got my bank account details right. They wanted an 8 digit number, and mine was 16. They rang me personally whilst I was sitting at the doctor, telling him that I could not go on. The doctor told me to try. After a whole year of feeling suicidal I was only given one consultation with a therapist. I had never felt so ill in my life and I thought that the doctor was deliberately withholding treatment from me because of my supposed political views.

Whenever I start a new lease of life I go to the doctor and read a children's book. When I first came out of rehab the children's book had been Mowgli, the Jungle Boy, and how he goes into a village, and finds his tribe (humans), and meets a lovely girl. This time the story was about a Sorcerer and his Apprentice. The Apprentice has to do all the cleaning, and the Sorcerer does all the magic. The Sorcerer went away, and the Apprentice picks up his wand and tries to emulate the spells of the Sorcerer, but gets it all wrong and creates utter havoc. The Sorcerer comes back and clears up the mess, and the Apprentice has to go back to cleaning up the floors once more.

I had tried to cancel my membership of the Republican Party although I found I was still a member, since the details had gone through in November.

Charlotte heard the Great King call her a meddling little bitch. He was not happy. The Sorcerer had told Charlotte that the best use she could be to the world was to work for the Intelligence Service. He had said to her, 'Look at me and tell me what you see'.

She said that she saw a wise old man.

The Sorcerer told her that when he looked at her he saw a girl desperately trying to do something good for the world. He told her to text someone.

Charlotte texted someone she knew was a known leak, and said that Percy Piggins probably thought that she was a meddling little bitch, but she wasn't and she felt much better now. She felt that all her text messages and emails were being talked about. She blamed her friends for their lack of support, but later realised that she may have been being watched.

The Sorcerer told Charlotte that he always guided her to the best possible outcomes. He said that she had a very high level of telepathy, but he took her to what she needed to hear. She agreed. She loved the Sorcerer. She felt very close to him. After all that he had done for her over last few years, she would have been lost without him. He saw many worlds in one breath. She always did what he advised or told her to do, and she loved him as she had implicit trust in him. The Sorcerer reminded Charlotte of the words she had used many years ago; 'International Healer'. That is what she wanted to be. That is why she had taken the course she had. She wanted to write about Social and Health Care issues and raise awareness of them.

She'd had a recurring dream for sometime where she'd been sitting at a desk overlooking a Quad. The window was open letting in a lovely summer breeze. She'd been a professor at a university. She was very happy, having the world at her fingertips but the only thing that bothered her was her door. The name on it said Charlotte Piggins, and try and she might she could not get it off, or change it to another one. The other thing that bothered her was her future daughter who she saw as a teenager; desperately anorexic. With this in mind she decided to abort Henton and go and find a life for herself elsewhere.

Jesus stuck his face in Charlotte's and said that she had to have a happy ending.

Charlotte prayed for a happy ending.

It was the fairy that did it. The pink, fluttery fairy who been Charlotte's companion, but who had not noticed that she had been ill. She lived in Charlotte's nest with her. She spoke to her for five minutes a day and Charlotte always put on a brave face.

Charlotte started to show signs of recovery and began decorating her nest with water lilies and beautiful flowers.

The fairy was jealous.

She stamped her feet and said that's not fair.

She showed Charlotte that all she could afford was one flower, even though she had many in another forest.

Charlotte sighed. She told the fairy that the best piece of advice she had ever received was that if you always have a good intention things will work out alright for you in the end.

The fairy became self-righteous and told all her fairy friends that Charlotte had too much. Charlotte heard the rustle of the fairy wings. They thought that their friend was being stupid. Charlotte's father had given her the beautiful flowers and had said that she deserved them. Charlotte's friend told her that even if she had not earned them she still had the right to have them, and enjoy them.

The fairy had lived with Charlotte for years, and had saved a lot of money as Charlotte was charging her very low rent and was paying all the bills on a very low wage.

Charlotte remembered going to boarding school where there were people who were seriously loaded. Everybody accepted that some people had more, and some people had less.

What she couldn't stand was people not caring about each other.

Percy Piggins never stops talking about helping people in Poverty. Nearly every second word he uses is Poverty. Which is a good thing, as approximately 1 in 10 people in the UK are living below acceptable standards of living.

Charlotte was looking forward to seeing her friend from school who had lived in India for 8 years. She had stepped in front of a policeman who was about to hit a street child, and ended up setting up a school for street children, selling jewellery at Festivals in the summer. She was the only person Charlotte knew who had a picture of the Senate in her bathroom.

Charlotte squashed the fairy dead. The fairy had been with her for 17 years, and was the cause of her illness. The fairy was anti-capitalist.

Charlotte's father showed her loads of books a few years back about Caring Capitalism. There was so much Charlotte had been able to do, because of the wealth he generated, and it had meant so much to her. She wanted to be able to do the same for other people. She read an interview in the paper, about the best thing about money is being able to share it, to enable other people. She wanted to have something to offer.

Charlotte's personal view, not one that she had discussed with her father, was that the money that he generated in taxes went a long way to help people like her.

But was not always the money that mattered.

It was abundance; the Attitude of Giving.

For Sophie, my CPN, who told me that hearing voices in some cultures is considered spiritual.

And for all the healing power in Devon.

PART 7 - HONOUR BEFORE JUSTICE

Dear Sophie

This is my account of the last year, which you, as my CPN, have requested to see.

I am writing this account of being sectioned under Section 2 and subsequently Section 3 of the Mental Health Act for being a Fixated Threat to the Republican Party; as per the Fixated Threat Department at Welsh Yard.

I decided to write this manuscript, in my defense?, as you said that the police were going to visit me in hospital and if I had not been sectioned under the Mental Health Act, I would have gone to prison.

I am aware that I came off my medication - approximately 6 weeks before I was sectioned by the police. I felt spiritually guided to at the time. I realize now, that it may have been a good thing, as it gave me a watertight alibi. I would like your opinion on what you consider the best course of action is, considering my motives, which were in essence (at a very subliminal level) the transference of shame.

I would like to finish my Open University degree in environmental studies and carry on volunteering with BTCV, the biodiversity action team, (as they have very strong links with the social and health care world through their volunteers) and hopefully get a job with them, or in a related field. In 4 or 5 years I would like to apply for an MA in Environmental Policy and Management at Henton University. I may not get in; (not just) because of the events of the last few years. However; I would like to become an environmental academic.

I wrote probably 3000 emails to the rehab, many concerning the Republican Party. These emails should have been treated in confidence and within psychotherapeutic guidelines, i.e. I was allowed to say what I wanted, and they should not have been made public, unless I threatened to murder someone.

I made the mistake of emailing my MP, and other members of the Republican Party 34 times.

I was enraged by the media, who seemed to be having an anti-psychic campaign. I was fiercely protective of Matthew, the Psychic healer. That is why I started to defend my position and started emailing the rehab. Perhaps wrongly, but they had so curtailed my life and I was living in fear, with so much anxiety, that I found it impossible to move forwards except by writing to them. I did not involve my mother as she was too ill and I wanted to protect her. I had no-one in the world to talk to.

I was so weak after the hate campaign against me in Henton, inspired, in my view, by the actions of the Republican Party, that I did not leave the house for a year, except to go to the village shop, where upon I had a massive panic attack. I do not know what happened in the outside world whilst I was at rehab. It seemed that people had read my work, but I did not know who, or what they thought about it. People in Henton used to smile and wave at me and joke with me in the street. I did not know why. People I saw in on the streets would be quoting from my books. It frightened me and drove me underground. All I needed was a good friend, someone who I could confide in, but they were lacking. The election was destroying me as people became opposed to each other. One of the Democrat leaders, the head of the economy, used to joke that I was easily mistaken for a Republican Voter. So much so that men would come up to me in the street and shout in my face over the election. I had absolutely no-one to talk to, and a head full of nonsense to contend with.

I was living with my mum in Devon. I knew no-one apart from her friends, and she was seriously ill. Eventually I gave up, and decided to go to London, where I knew people. I needed the confidence of being with people who knew me, and knew how ill I had been over the last 20 years. I did not tell my mum about the emails, or anything else. We kept different hours, and I did not want to involve her as she had been so ill. I was up until 5am every day, sending the emails, imagining the response, and then sending another. The rehab has subsequently been closed down.

I only spoke to people a handful of times on the phone the whole year, and saw no-one, apart from one friend, who I got annoyed with as I felt she had been sending out detrimental emails about me. She was actually worried about my health.

I had been worried about death threats towards me, and I felt that my life was at risk on several occasions. Once in Henton, where I kept seeing in my mind's eye a man shooting me dead at point blank range as I came out of my house. There are guns in Henton. They were going to stake me out on Tuesday to see where I went and what I did and commit the crime the following Tuesday. I also had a recurring nightmare that I was being pushed off a cliff in Devon. I would be coming down the cliff path and a man would come up to meet me. He could see me from the bottom of the path. He used to try out several places on the cliff path to see where was best and then try and push me off. In my dream, I was stronger and I managed to push him off. I later heard that he thought that I was quite a nice person as I had said hello to him on the cliff path. These things were very real for me and have made me very upset. My mother was very kind, but still in recovery from a series of serious illnesses. I never confided in her. She cooked me delicious food, and gave me the space I needed. She helped me in every way she could, but I had lost my trust in humanity as a whole. I was trying to protect her by not talking to her as she had been so ill, but she could not have been kinder, helping me in every way whilst still very much in rehabilitation herself.

I subsequently moved up to London to stay with my cousin, who I had not seen since my confirmation, when I was 14 and hopelessly drunk. I was still very ill. She is lovely. I had a bedroom on the top floor of her flat and there was an immediate problem in that I could not use the loo after 9.30pm, as she would wake up. This did cause problems, especially after one weekend, when I did not sleep until 5am on both nights, and was supposedly crashing about.

When I was in hospital they wanted to drug test me, because I smoke roll ups, and would spend a lot of time in the garden, doing psychic work.

In the three months that I stayed with her I managed to see some friends, which was a blessed relief, as I am so much more confident and relaxed around people I know, who I know aren't going to attack me. I also felt much more comfortable in the company of men, when I had friends around.

Unfortunately, I was very aware that I was under an increasingly level of surveillance in Central London. It could have been seen as intimidation. I liked being in Long Green Abbey, near the Senate, and all the places the MPs hang out. I enjoy the atmosphere. I had dinner once at the Cafe, outside the Republican Party headquarters in Little Stretton. I had become aware of the surveillance as I could read the minds of the people watching me. It seemed fun at first. They seemed nice, and I would wave at the cameras and make funny faces, and do sign language. Unfortunately some of them (who shall remain nameless), were highly critical of my dress and appearance, and criticized everything down to the way I walked. I tend to stride rather than mince.

I became really fed up with them, but was trying to please them, as I had applied for a job in M16. I had become very frightened as sometimes the level of criticism was so strong that I feared my life was at risk. Unfortunately because I felt my life was at risk before I transferred that feeling to the M16. I became very paranoid. I have seen the level of security cameras in Henton. They are nothing compared to Central London. And why was I considered such a threat? They were seriously threatening me. I could hear what they were saying about me and one group of MPs said that they were going to gang rape me. I could hear them discuss me and the fact that they were going to send me to psychiatric hospital and dose me up on so many drugs so that I could never get out.

I could see who they were and I really began to worry that my life was at risk. The security men seemed fine, they seemed happy and supportive but I came out of Long Green Abbey one morning at 8am having not gone to the Communion Service there and they shouted 'tart' at me. I was totally confused, I did not understand what they were saying. I paced up and down outside the Senate not sure what to do. I was seriously psychotic. I found some sunglasses and put them on and then started trying to communicate to the security cameras again, to try and make sense of it. They did appear to listen, or at least their attention was held. But I did not understand that they didn't know that I was doing it on purpose. They must have thought I was mad trying to illustrate to them what I knew what they were thinking and trying to involve them in some sort of dialogue. My inner voices and my cousin Earnest always told me to take the side streets whilst I walked around Central London. I suppose because there are less security cameras there.

Matters came to a head one day and I drove down to Devon.

Where I was subsequently sectioned by the police.

I am going to write an account of my time in hospital. The people I use are real people, but for the purposes of confidentiality I will adhere to these 3 rules:

1. I will change their names.

2. I will not mention any personal details.

3. I will not mention the location of the hospital.

I hope that the following account is in the interests of patient care, and please forgive me if I am too explicit.

After about an hour, I was led onto the ward. It was high security, and covered in staff. Most of these were ex-army, navy or police, and very nice. I was totally shell shocked, and had nothing but the clothes that I had come in with. I was wearing my England t-shirt and a pair of jeans. The ward was small. I was led into a room, which had a bed, and very little else, and an ensuite shower room. The ward itself consisted of a main lobby, with a sofa, which also shared its space with a dining area, and lots of round tables.

I did not really know what to do. My father came in and I cried. He bought some more stuff with him. I did not know why I was there. I did not know what was happening to me.

It did not help. Ben and my Mother came in to say 'Hi'. We sat at one of the tables, and Luke, who I had got to know, sauntered by in his panama hat. I told him that he looked like he was going on holiday with the bright pink T-shirt that he was wearing. I was only on the ward a week. There was a very small area where we would smoke, and the walls were 4 stories high with no windows. It seemed more like a prison than a hospital. Luke decided to recruit me into the M16. I asked him if I had a choice. He said that I had no choice, other than a life time of misery, despair and loneliness.

Needless to say, I believed him. I thought that it could be a possibility. I began to panic, as I thought that the Government was trying to give me a diagnosis of paranoid schizophrenia, to get them off the hook for all the writing that I had done. One of the doctors, my consultant psychiatrist had been very rude to me, and said why did I think that Percy Piggins was interested in me, as if to sneer at me for being a mental health patient. I didn't. The last time I met Percy Piggins he came right up to me and offered me a job which I did not take. He had never met me before and yet he knew who I was. I call that some level of interest.

Luke told me that people do not get recruited into the M16 by being taken into a smart office and given a job. We had been smoking cigarettes at the time in the courtyard, and something inside me told me to be careful. I didn't know whether to believe him or not. I needed to check him out a bit more first. He told me that he had done a lot of psychic work for M16 before, and had had his own email contact there. He told me that he had been tortured.

Luke was about my age and very kind. He had an atmosphere of peace and security around him. I trusted him in many respects but wanted to get to know more about his illness. I told one of the young trainee doctors what he had said to me in a state of high excitement as I believed it could be a possibility. The doctor could not keep the smile from his eyes and his mouth. I began to realise that other people were ill too, which was a shame as it would have made a perfect tale of romance.

I was going to send him my ring. It was gold, set all round with tiny, circular freshwater pearls. I did not know what to do with this ring as I knew that he wanted it. I did not know whether to give it to him – in my mind, conjuring up images of The Lord of the Rings, or keep it – inferring The Bride of Christ.

There were some other lovely people there. A strange man who had fought in many wars.

Young boys who had taken too much ecstasy, and many other characters. I am not going to write about them directly as it is not fair on them.

One girl became very aggressive to me because of class. She would shout in my face, and intimidate me, for no apparent reason. I became very upset with a male member of staff, as I did not think that I should have to put up with that level of aggression on the ward. He laughed at me. And then I got very upset with him. The other male members of staff started to bully me and be heavy with me, as they thought that I was being abusive to the staff member.

I wrote countless letters for my file. I told them that this was supposed to be a hospital. Where was the treatment? I was in here for rape, and they were acting as abusers by shouting at me, when all I was doing was asking for protection.

Luckily, they saw the sense in it, and peace prevailed.

I did write a lot of notes to my file. But I also used the email. I had been told by one of the members of staff that I could email friends. This apparently was the wrong information. So I was quite happily emailing, with one of the other patients getting very cross with me, as he knew that I would be in trouble. The staff came down on me like a ton of bricks. I managed to press 'send', on the email that I was sending to my father, but I nearly was locked in solitary confinement for doing so.

I had emailed my MP to tell him that there was a patient hospitalised under Section 3 and from reading his letters from his solicitor that he showed me it may have been a permanent thing as he did not have the ability to communicate effectively. He had been a nuclear scientist during the Cold War and was terrified at how the Government had disposed of the radioactive waste. He was a darling old man who could not stop talking. A few days after I sent the email he was moved to a gentler ward for good and had some chance of recovery.

Apparently the Republican Party thought that I was a fixated threat. If they only knew how much danger they had put me in over the last few years. It is criminal. They did not like my response to the danger that I had been through. I had lost my home, my friends and my community. I would go so far as to say that my stay in residential rehab had been totally destroyed by their actions. That is how it seemed to me, and they showed me absolutely no compassion, only aggression. They knew that I was dangerously ill, and yet the media still continued to persecute. How was I supposed to feel, when every single life line that I had was wasted and abused by them. People I knew had been used to spy on me, when I was suicidal and desperately needed some help. I felt as though every single counsellor that I had been to in the last 2 years had deliberately not kept anything I said private. So I ended up by not telling them anything that was important to me. In the eyes of the world, I was very, very ill, and yet I had no help offered to me at all. Only persecution.

And all they did was sexualize me.

Which in my view, considering my problems, is the worst persecution of all.

There was a young chap, who was seriously manic. He used to leap around, talking nineteen to the dozen, always making associations, and never having a straight (in other people's eyes) conversation. He talked about Einstein and the Church, and how Einstein had destroyed the Church with his Theories of Relativity. He told me about a cat, trapped in a box, and whatever happened to that cat would have profound implications for the rest of the universe. He was lovely, and very athletic. He had been very seriously sexually abused by his father, and as a result trusted no one. I managed to get him to talk to me, on a few occasions, mainly because I am well versed in mania, and could get some, if not all of his symbolisms. And he liked that. He told me when I left the hospital to trust my instinct, and that is one of the best and the most valuable pieces of advice I could gather.

Not more so as I found a picture of a unicorn in the Sunday papers. There was a girl's hand, decked out in a long black glove and a diamond bracelet, giving the unicorn a mint. The caption said something about being discerning in your choice. One of the other patients at the ward, a lovely lady who had been sexually abused by her father all her life, told me that my choice would save my life. I started to panic after that, as all I had was Luke. And he seemed intent on recruiting me to M16.

After Luke told me that I had no choice I started to stress. I made sure that I talked to as many people as possible. I wracked my brains about what other choices I did have, as a lot of bridges had been burnt. I decided that the Church was a good possible option, particularly as if they did give me a diagnosis of paranoid schizophrenia it would immediately be revoked by the Church, as I thought that the psychic work that I did would be seen by them as prayer, which indeed it is. And the truth about my emotional fear of men would be seen rationally for what it was.

I had not been put on any medication, and for the first week, in the high security ward I was given none. I may have appeared slightly manic however, as I was desperate to create a new alibi, and yet at the same time keep Luke on my side, just in case he did have a shot to kill policy on me, which is what I was living in fear of before I came into the hospital, by M16 and the Government, such was their aggression. I had gone out on a walk on the cliff the afternoon before I was sectioned with my brother. I had told him that I thought that there was a shoot-to-kill policy on me. I feared everyone. I was not a paranoid schizophrenic, I was a paranoid psychic. I felt that my emails had been tapped into and my phone was being bugged. I may not be wrong.

So I went around and made myself a lot of friends. There was a ping pong table there, and we played lots of that, which is a great way of building up physical trust with the opposite sex. I did some drawing in a room with a girl who was being rehomed and given a completely different identity. She had lovely pictures, and I was allowed to use felt tip pens, which I love.

There was a television room, but I did not spend much time in there.

Luke eventually asked me out for a date. I tried to touch him, but it was difficult with all the surveillance cameras. I felt that I was being watched a lot, and played up to the camera a bit.

As soon as I saw him I knew that I had made the wrong choice, and maybe part of me rejoiced that I may have another. I saw this man, with deep, brown eyes, with long black lashes and black hair. He looked completely vulnerable. His name was Clive. He came and sat on the sofa with me. He had just been transferred to the ward.

I was moved from the high security ward, and taken to a lower security ward, for 5 weeks, where I finished off the rest of my stay.

It was such a relief. You were allowed to make tea and coffee whenever you liked. You could stay up after midnight if you wanted, and there was a bit more room. The down side was that the staff were younger, and not so experienced, and there were 32 people on the ward, rather than 12, so the close knit feel was not there.

But it was ok.

After a week, Clive came into the lower security ward. He was on a lot of drugs, probably Haloperidol and was very spasmodic. He walked around a lot, looking very lost. I was gathering my tools for my Tribunal the following day. I had been looking through the local paper and found a horse, called Paris, who was a good ladies hack. I was trying to make head and tail of the horse situation, with the unicorn, and I knew that I had to get this choice right. I started to write lots of letters to Luke, four in total, explaining to him in great detail why I didn't want to go out with him. Children were the obvious answer. He wanted 2, and I did not want any. He wrote me a love poem, eluding to the fact that he wanted a relationship but not marriage. I was quite scared of him, as before I had left I had this horrible dream of me being in his room in a body bag, and he was flicking through all my notes and then chucked them all in the bin. Which in itself was quite a nice thing, but not being able to get out of the body bag was not! My therapist at rehab said all I needed was a good man.

My tribunal was a nightmare, in that my solicitor could not make it that day. My consultant psychiatrist, Dr Lutton, had spoken to me for less than 10 seconds before declaring that I was paranoid schizophrenic. I thought that was what M16 wanted me diagnosed as, so that it would get the President off the hook, and provide me with an alibi so that I could work for them. Dr Lutton lied consistently that he had ever said that to me, but I would think that if the security cameras went back to Room 4, in the first week of my stay, they would see the evidence. After our meeting he concluded that I had bipolar.

It really got my back up, and I started arguing with him. He was very defensive, and I got the Care Quality Complaints Commission on the case, sending them emails after every one of our weekly appointments, which he threw me out of all but 2, as I would debate with him my case. He saw that as unruly behavior. I saw his behavior as arrogance. He did not listen to a word that I had to say, and kept calling me mentally ill, before throwing me out of the room. When he met my parents he changed his tune completely, and sucked up to them, and me, something rotten. But his attitude when he was not being observed was completely different and very threatening.

It was like he was deliberately trying to cause a fight, by being so aggressive and stigmatizing to me. He is getting paid a lot of money to do the job he does, and he is not particularly interested in any other explanation rather than pharmaceuticals. It is a self-interested program. A friend told me about her friend who is a GP and is also trained in alternative medicine. He was not handing out enough pharmaceuticals at the surgery and the other doctors told him to leave, telling him that they get more money, the more pharmaceuticals they hand out.

I did not pass my tribunal, as they felt that I did not state strongly enough that I would take my medication on leaving. I think that saying it once was enough, but they would have none of it. Someone, whether they meant it unkindly or not, had told me that if you were put on a Section 3 then you would not be able to become an MP. I was fed up to the back teeth with the medical profession, and told all the nurses this. I had been in their care for 20 years, and only once come off my medication, but had been consistently taking it for all that time. I told the nurses that I had been in their care for 20 years, and they had not once got to the root of the problem. I had been living in hell all that time, and they had never once treated me for rape. The word rape had never even been mentioned. It does get rather annoying, when the hospital cost £600 a day to be there and yet they could not be bothered to give me a counsellor for £40 an hour, after which I would be feeling as right as rain.

They did eventually put me on a section 3, once my 28 days was up on the section 2, for an equally stupid reason that I did not have a cohesive plan on leaving. I did have a plan; they did just not ask me. I was going to stay with my mum for a while, and then find a place to live of my own. Section 3 means that they can legally hold you for 6 months. Section 2 is 28 days.

Dr Lutton was a nightmare. He was not someone I could talk to. I did wonder if the Republican Party were using him deliberately to get at me, he was so bad. He had no qualms in being very aggressive or defensive to me, but absolutely no idea that I was reacting to his authority in a way that suggested I was terrified. He had absolute, total and complete power over the course of my stay. The nurses would all tell me that they could not do anything; it was up to Dr Lutton. In the end, I was being so nice to people on the ward, happy and smiley, that Dr Lutton could not get round the notes that were written up about me and decided that I could go.

Dr Lutton did take away my driving license six months after I had left hospital. He had read this story and was annoyed with me. He claimed that I had had more than four episodes of acute illness in the year before I went to hospital, even though he had previously allowed me to drive. Once I found out that he had said this, I rang the CPN, who rang the DVLA. My license was returned to me in days.

The horse thing terrified me. I had been in an art class in the first ward, and collected lots of HO HO HO stickers. If you looked at them the other way round they said OH. I decided to collect all these pieces together and make an army. The OH's (or hydroxyl group in chemistry) against the HO's (St. Nicholas, or Father Christmas, or spiritual group). This became a theme for me for a few weeks, and I counted each member of the army. I split the group further into colours, as some were red and some were silver. There were many more in the silver group, about 126 to 81. I made the reds, which had less, into the Democrat Party, and I was the silver and the battle that we were going to have was environmental, with both of us leaders in the House of Representatives. I also had a bag of golden swans and a bag of fish, and some medals. I put the animals into the army and gave in the little plastic bags that they were in. They looked like little drug bags, and the member of staff who took them from me (you were not allowed any plastic), did raise an eyebrow to my smile.

I had two red HO's left over, so I gave one to Luke and kept one myself. We were not in the army, and it was important for me to stay out of the army, as well as Luke, as I thought that he was going to kill me, due to the unzipped body bag.

I ended up throwing away the army, as I felt that the battle had already been won.

Anyhow, this horse business, over my tribunal on section 3 was doing my head in. I found a horse in the paper, called Paris, who was a ladies hack, and a very beautiful grey mare. She would have been perfect for me, especially as she was 7 years old. I was desperate to get out of hospital. I did not feel that they were listening to me, or acknowledging what was the real cause of me being ill. This manic depressive diagnosis is really on-going suicidal depression that I push myself out of and then become high, in trying to desperately make the best out of a bad situation, and the root is in rape, and fear of sexual intimacy, which stops me from having any meaningful life and resonates fear round every corner. They try and treat it with pills, but it just makes me sick to think of all the pain that I have been through in the last 15 years, in the work place having panic attacks and the desperation I have felt, not least through resultant poverty and being unable to see my friends, or create a new social life. And yet they don't treat that. There were many others in the hospital who could have benefitted from counselling, and yet none was offered. Even though 6-7 people were re-admitted in the 5 weeks that I was there, even though it was costing the taxpayer £600 a day (much of this in middle management salary). But no help was coming. Hospital did not seem to be working. Hardly surprising in my view when I look at the twenty years in the mental health system I have had. But there seems to be no money, so you are lucky to be balanced on medication and it seems that the emotional side of life has to be worked out in a different arena. They are at last providing CBT, long overdue in my mind, but you do have to wait 6-9 months for that.

I spent about 2 weeks telling everyone this at the top of my voice. They were not particularly impressed, mostly frustrated, as they were doing all that their job specs allowed them to do, but there was a lot of truth in what I was saying. Eventually, after one outburst and pacing of the corridors, I just stood still, and let the situation sink in. I stood by a pillar in the dining room and looked around me.

Then I realized. All that was going on was on-going trauma from Downe House School, the boarding school were I had had a nervous breakdown 20 years previously, and been suicidal ever since. I had been so depressed for 6 months, and although they were in loco parentis, i.e. they had a duty of care to me, and I was still 16 and a minor, not one person inquired into my health in that time. I left the school and have been desperately ill ever since.

But no help was coming in the hospital. Even at £600 a day.

So I had to do something. I was still terribly worried, as Luke would have been an option as someone to go out with, but I did not like the fact that I was scared of him. I decided to try and create different options. I needed to be with someone to get over my problems with intimacy. At the time it seemed paramount and I was being guided to it as a useful diversion from my problems with the police.

The thing is, in my mind, I could not differentiate between the real and the supposed threat that the Republican Party posed me. They had caused me very real problems, and put my life in danger, and that of my mother who had to cope with me when she was seriously ill. I was taking no chances in my life, and did not have the space in hospital to think this all through properly. To me Luke was a very real threat, and yet an opportunity at the same time. I did not know what to do, except create another option or two, and Clive was the perfect stranger.

I might add in my defense that I had had a dream of the President of the USA leading me round several stable yards, trying to find a horse that suited me. It seemed very important to him that I was with someone and he was giving me three options of horses in very different yards.

And I had found a pencil, on which was inscribed the word, 'initiative'. I tried to give it to Clive but I think that it was really meant for me.

I also was told spiritually that it would keep my mind engaged, and off other matters. It was important that I was diverted, especially as now I had access to email.

I tried another tact first, as Clive was also very ill, like me. I asked one of the other men if he would like to share a house with me on leaving. One of my mother's friends had texted to say that I could rent his 3 bedroom farmhouse when I left, but the rent was quite high and I thought it would be nice to share, not only for the company, but to get the rent down. I asked him, and he seemed non-committal, but over the course of the next few weeks I got the distinct impression that he had misread my invitation and was expecting rather more than just renting a room. I was really annoyed, and took the invitation away from him, which pissed him off a bit, but I was not entering into that dynamic.

Clive had very discerning manner about him. He had very wise and beautiful eyes. He was a lot older than me, but I was drawn to him very strongly as he reminded me a lot of my ex-boyfriend, mainly in his independent nature. I did not tell the staff at either hospital about my fears about Luke, as I thought that they would think it illness. All that was on my

208

care plan was for me to build trusting relationships and I was supposed to be on 1:1 enhanced time with the staff, which did not happen, nice though they were, as there were simply never any staff on the ward, they were all ticking boxes in the office.

I liked Clive especially as he did not seem to belong there either. He did not seem to talk to anyone, and he was very independent. He would not be involved with any Government scams, and he would be someone I could trust, namely because he seemed to not trust anyone himself. He was difficult to get to know, but seemed very protective too, if asked. He was a useful diversion.

I did notice however, that if I had chosen to be with him there would have been a strong likelihood that any children would have been taken away from us. One poor girl in the hospital was having to go through exactly that process and it tore her apart. Luckily she was able to keep her elder daughter, on account that her mother was a joint guardian of the child.

It took a long time to build up any sort of relationship with him, and he liked to observe me a lot, a trait which I found very sweet. I would play act for him, reading his mind, and using the others to illustrate a point for him, but he was really hard. I told him one day that he gave me panic attacks, and he seemed absolutely delighted. I had a very big panic attack, and as a result of the anxiety and lack of support did not sleep until 6am, a pattern that is all too familiar to me, and has dominated the last 4 years of my life. I was told by the staff that your body can only panic for 20 minutes and then it runs out of adrenaline, but my body has panicked for hours, several times a day. When I split up with Sid I tried to see several therapists, but none of them would treat me as I was so traumatized, and they all recommended residential therapy.

I tried very hard to make a relationship with Clive. I started studying for RHS horticulture exams, and was doing up to 12 hours a day. I wanted to get back to work, but was interested in the environment, but there do not seem to be any jobs in the environment, or very few, unless you are doing environmental science, so I was thinking of doing a horticulture degree as well as my environmental science degree. Studying for all this time bought me a great sense of peace, as there were at least a few hours in the day when I was in a normal head space. I got the idea off a film I had watched with Sid, where two climbers in the Alps got into trouble, and one had to leave the other with a broken leg, in order to save his own life. The one with the broken leg did not know which way to go, as he had lost his bearings in the ice, and did not know which way was up. He knew that in order to survive he had to take action, and ended up climbing 200m further down into the glacier - the wrong way. In the end however, he managed to make his way, or drag his way, back to base camp and survival. But he said that sometimes you have to take action, even if it is leading to the wrong course.

So I would study, and then observe Clive, and gradually we built up some kind of attraction.

When I left I was wracked with emotion, as I knew that I could not say goodbye to him, as it would hurt too much. I had been having loads of dreams about him, and it gave me the confidence to try and write to him. I was leaving at 11am. I had been out on 4 hour leaves for a good five days, and they had decided to give me a week at home to see how I did.

I just did not know how to say goodbye, and I did not want to.

I ended up doing reiki at 10.30am and then writing out a letter to him, asking him to come and live with me, and enclosing my business card. I posted the letter once my mother had come to pick me up, and having read it to her first. She thought that it was ok.

He emailed, and I emailed back. I shared my life story, and he was kind. I have since asked him to go out with me, saying that I want to get back to work, and I have terrible panic attacks which would be abated if I had a boyfriend, although I was not ready for sexual intimacy. We used to have long lengthy email conversations and began supporting each other in our illness. I found that I had someone to chat to, someone to communicate with, whom it didn't matter if I didn't seem rational. He would just accept it and reply in a similar vein. It was the support that I had been looking for as emotions were kept well out of it. We could have gone on writing until infinity but my email address crashed and I have not been able to get onto it.

I since found out that I had been asked spiritually to ask him to go out with me, as it would push him away as he was not ready for a relationship, and I had more important things to do. He was put there as a distraction from me, to stop me thinking about the Republican Party.

Luke did not work for the M16, and my fear of the Republican Party has dwindled. I went into the local Republican HQ when I left hospital and told them my name and that I was sectioned for being a fixated threat to the Republican Party. I said that I was feeling a whole lot better now, and apologized. I realized that they were not trying to kill me after all, which had been the basis of my fear. I would like to re-iterate that apology to the Republican Party and make it known that I no longer have any interest in being an MP.

A few days after I left I kept dreaming of myself on horseback, riding around a stadium carrying a victory flag. My opponents were defeated.

I would like to say thank you very much to all the staff in both hospitals. I know resources are tight, but they did a really good job with me. Both hospitals were the best institutions that I had ever been in (including Educational Establishments), and I am really appreciative of the care that I received. They certainly blew away the cobwebs from my Downe House School trauma, which is what I needed most, and in doing so allowed me to trust authority and friends once again.

I hope that my comments will be seen in the light that they were intended. I am sorry I have not spent more time on this, but I am hoping to leave it all behind now, and am very much looking forward to moving on with the rest of my life. Thank you to the taxpayers.

What's the betting there will be more persecution (from the media among others) as a result of these stories.

Hospital was the most extremely humbling experience of my life but it taught me manners. My driving license was revoked by my consultant psychiatrist, not because I was unfit to drive, but because he had read my story. It taught me that in Christianity, God's first Law is to love your God with all your might, but his second, is to love your neighbour as yourself. Something I had been completely failing to do, and at last I knew the reason why.

PART 8 - THE BUTTERFLY AND THE CHRYSALIS

Now that I am balanced on the right medication and have returned to normal, and with huge thanks to my father's generosity I got what I always wanted. I am living in a modern house in the town where I always wanted to be. I worked part time (4 days a week) in horticulture for 2 ½ years, and completed an Open University degree in Environmental Studies and Creative Writing, graduating this year, which was one of the proudest days of my life. I even was on the salary that I wanted, which with Disability Living Allowance and Working Tax Credit and money that my father was giving me to see a therapist, made it up to the amount that I wanted to earn per year.

I still suffer from chronic anxiety.


Prayer of St Francis of Assisi

Make me a channel of your peace

Where there is hatred let me bring your love;

Where there is injury, your pardon, Lord

And where there's doubt the true faith in you.


O master, grant that I may never seek

So much to be consoled as to console

To be understood as to understand

To be loved as to love with all my soul.


Make me a channel of your peace

Where there is despair in life let me bring hope,

Where there is darkness only light

And where there's sadness ever joy.


Make me a channel of your peace

It is in pardoning that we are pardoned

In giving to all men that we receive

And in dying that we are born to eternal life

# The End

Thank You For Reading

I have tried to recreate events, locales and conversations from my memories of them. In order to maintain their anonymity in some instances I have changed the names of individuals, I may have changed some identifying characteristics and details such as physical properties, occupations and places of residence.

© Charlotte Day 2016

The contents of this book are not to be altered, copied, re-published or re-distributed without permission from the copyright owner.

Printed in Great Britain
by Amazon